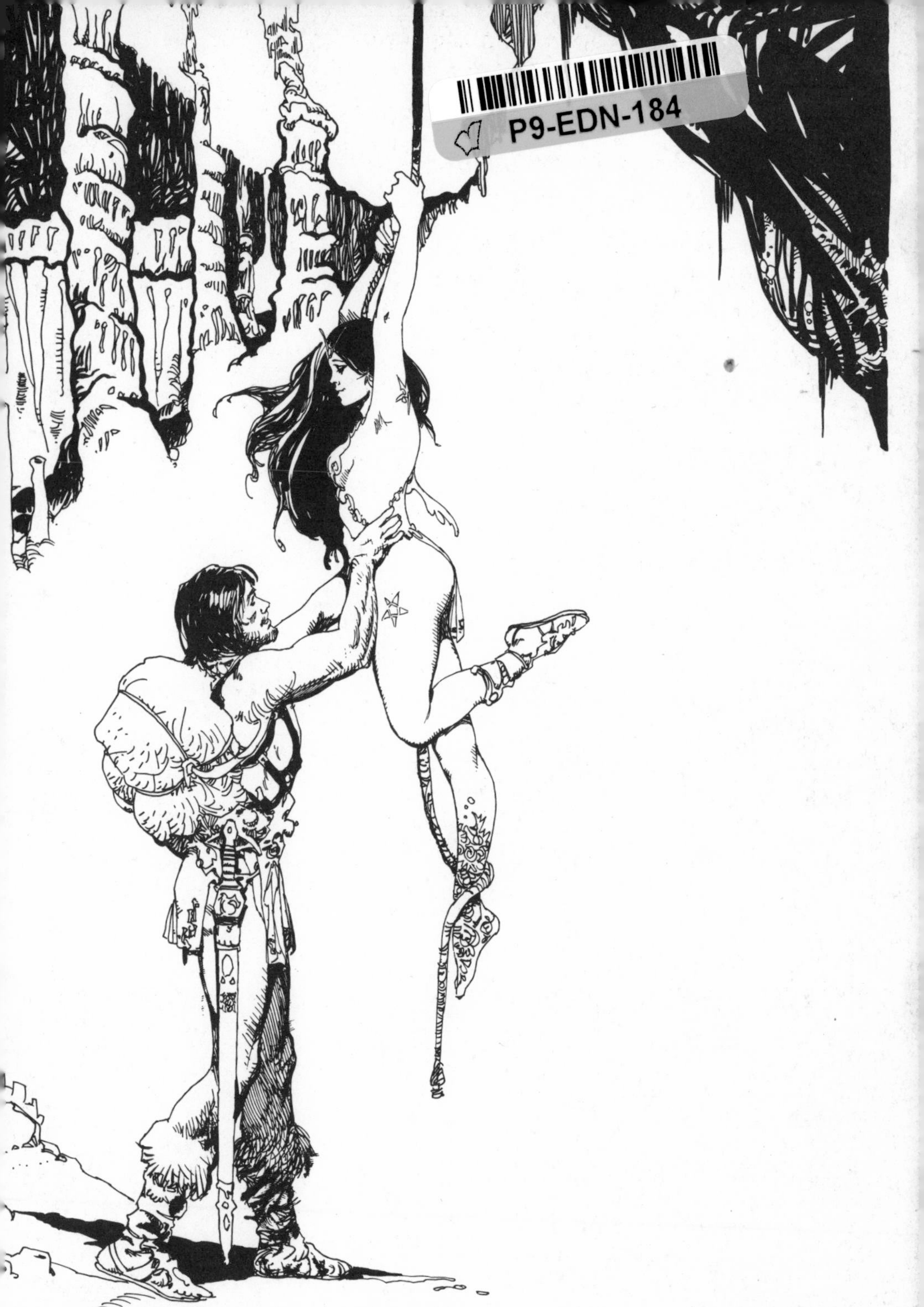

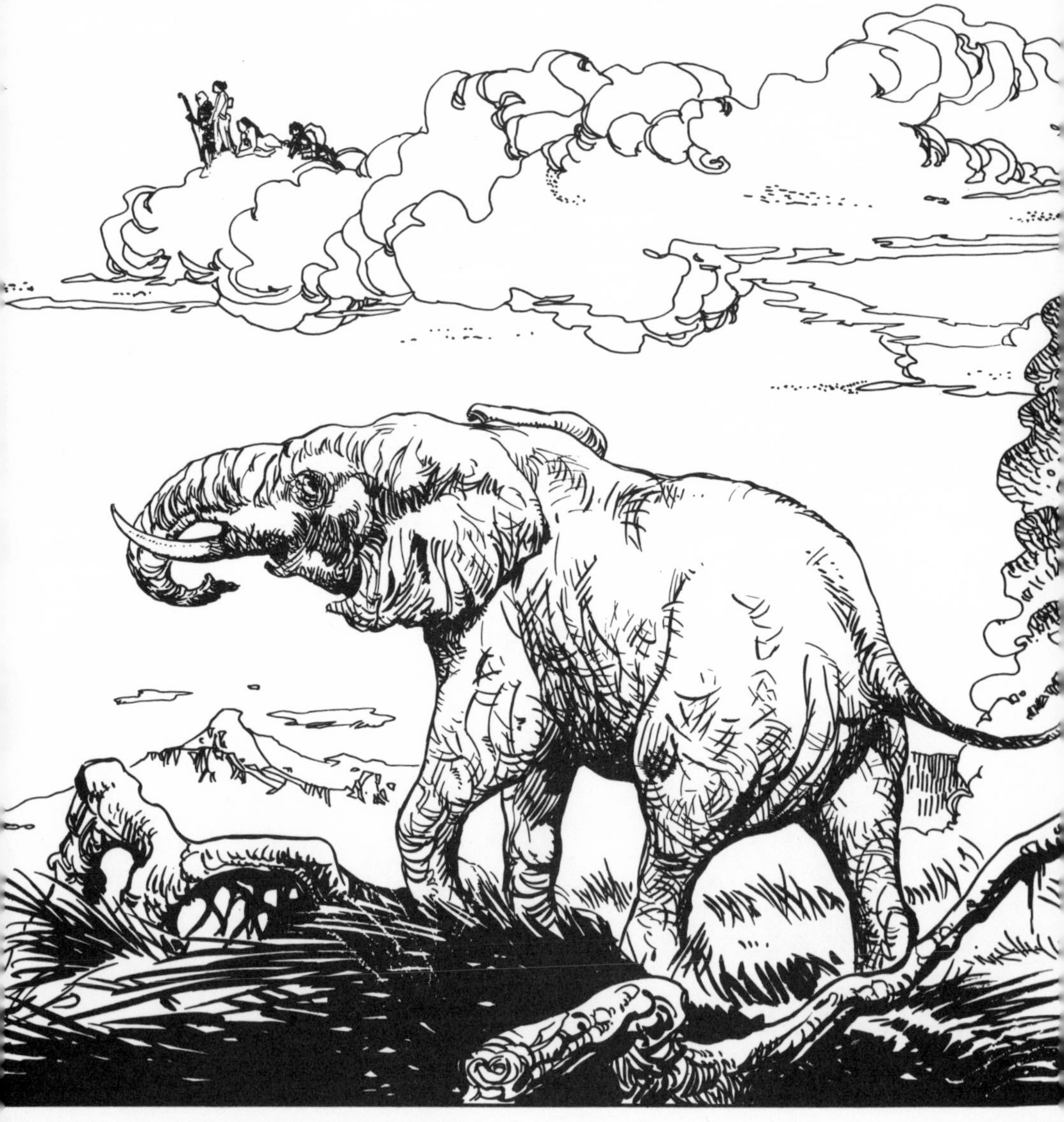

SF

LARRY NIVEN

THE MAGIC GOES AWAY

ace books
A Division of Charter Communications Inc.
A GROSSET & DUNLAP COMPANY
360 Park Avenue South
New York, New York 10010

THE MAGIC GOES AWAY

An ACE Book

Cover art by Boris

First Ace printing: October 1978

Printed in U.S.A.

Table of Contents

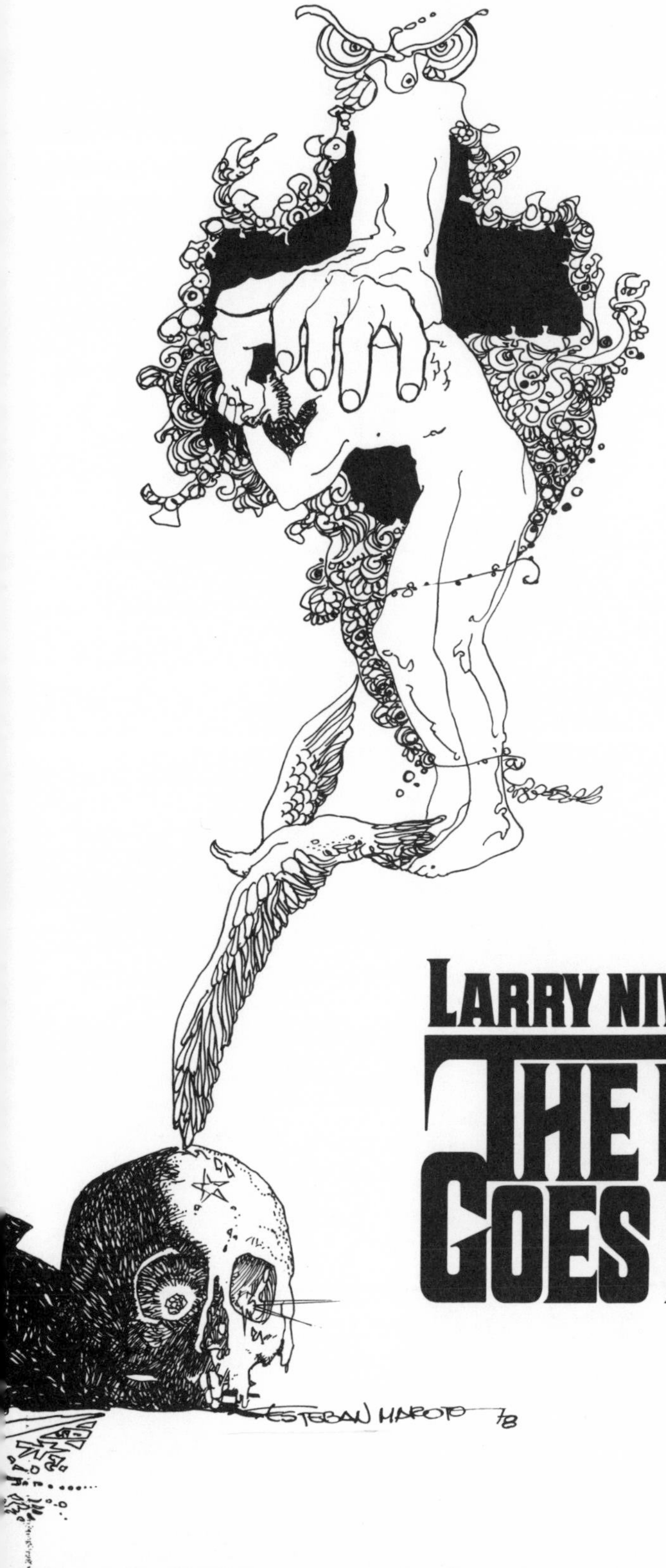
ESTEBAN MAROTO 78

LARRY NIVEN

THE MAGIC GOES AWAY

OROLANDES

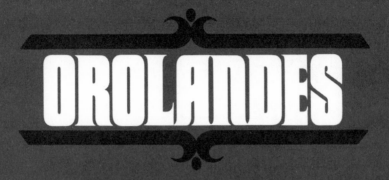

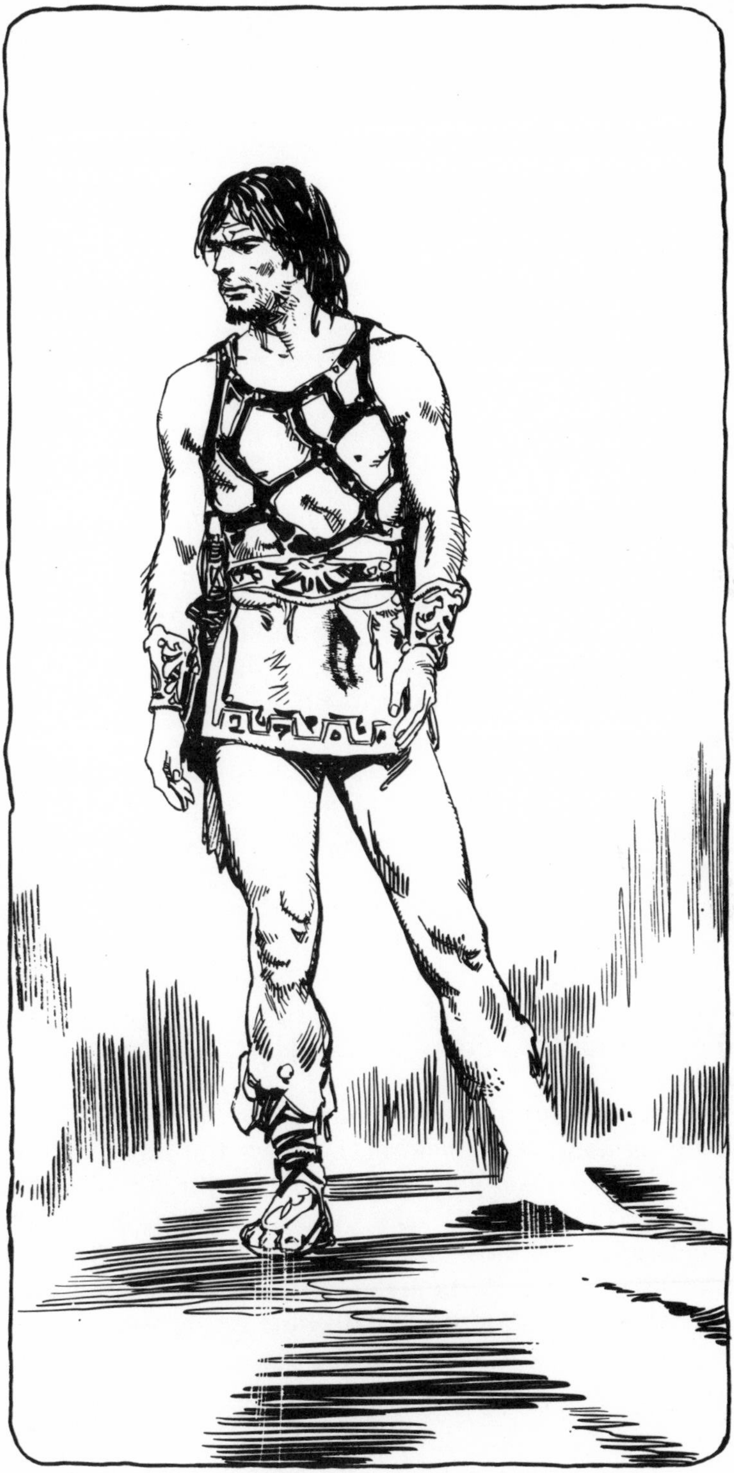

The waves washed him ashore aboard a section of the wooden roof from an Atlantean winery. He was half dead, and mad. There was a corpse on the makeshift raft with him, a centaur girl, three days dead of no obvious cause.

The fisherfolk were awed. They knew the workmanship of the winery roof, and they knew that the stranger must have survived the greatest disaster in human history. Perhaps they considered him a good luck charm.

He *was* lucky. The fisherfolk did not steal the golden arm bands he wore. They fed him by hand until he could feed himself. When he grew strong they put him to work. He could not or would not speak, but he could follow orders. He was a big man. When his weight came back he could lift as much as any two fishermen.

By day he worked like a golem, tirelessly: they had to remember to tell him when to stop. By night he would pull his broken sword from its scabbard — the blade was broken to within two thumbs of the hilt — and turn it in his hands as if studying it.

He stayed in the bachelors' longhouse. Women who approached him found him unresponsive. They attributed it to his sickness.

Four months after his arrival he spoke his first words.

The boy Hatchap was moving down the line of sleeping bachelors, waking them for the day's fishing. He found the stranger staring at the ceiling in grief and anguish. "Like magic. Like magic," he mumbled — in Greek. Suddenly he smiled, for the first time Hatchap could remember. "Magician," he said.

That night, after the boats were in, he went to the oldest man in the village and said, "I have to talk to a magician."

The old man was patient. He explained that a witch lived in the nearest village, but that this Mirandee had departed months ago. By now she would be meeting colleagues in Prissthil. There would be no competent magician nearer than Prissthil, which was many days' journey.

Mad Orolandes nodded as if he understood.

He was gone the next morning. He had left one of his bracelets in the headman's house.

THE WARLOCK

Prissthil and the village called Warlock's Cave were six hundred miles apart. Once the Warlock would have flown the distance in a single night. Even today, they might have taken riding dragons, intelligent allies . . . and in one or another region where too much use of magic had leeched *mana* from the earth, they might have left dragon bones to merge with the rocks. Dragon metabolism was partly magical.

It annoyed the Warlock to be leaving Warlock's Cave on muleback; but he and Clubfoot considered this prudent.

It was worse than they had thought. The *mana*-rich places they expected to cross by magic, were not there. Three of their mules died in the desert when Clubfoot ran out of the ability to make rain.

The situation was just this desperate: Clubfoot and the Warlock, two of the most powerful magicians left in the world, came to the conference at Prissthil on foot, leading a pack mule.

Clubfoot was an American, with red skin and straight black hair and an arched beak of a nose. His ancestors had fled an Asian infestation of vampires, had crossed the sea by magic in the company of a tribe of the wolf people. He limped because of a handicap he might have cured decades ago, except that it would have cost him half his power.

And the Warlock limped because of his age.

Limping, they came to the crest of a hill overlooking Prissthil.

It was late afternoon. Already the tremendous shadow of Mount Valhalla, last home of a quarrelsome pantheon of gods now gone mythical, sprawled eastward across Prissthil. The village had grown since the Warlock had last seen it, one hundred and ten years ago. The newer houses were lower, sturdier . . . held up not by spells spoken over a cornerstone, but by

their own strength.

"Prissthil was founded on magic," the Warlock said half to himself.

Clubfoot heard. "Was it?"

The Warlock pointed to a dish-shaped depression north of the city wall. "That crater is old, but you can still see the shape of it, can't you? That's Fistfall. This village started as a trading center for talismans: fragments of the boulder of starstone that made that crater. The merchants ran out of starstone long ago, but the village keeps growing. Don't you wonder how?"

Clubfoot shrugged. "They must be trading something else."

"Look, Clubfoot, there are *guards* under Llon! Llon used to be all the guard Prissthil needed!"

"What are you talking about? The big stone statue?"

The Warlock looked at him oddly. "Yes. Yes, the big stone statue."

Winds off the desert had etched away the fine details, but the stone statue was still a work of art. Half human, half big gentle guard dog, it squatted on its haunches before the gate, looking endlessly patient. Guards leaned against its forepaws. They straightened and hailed the magicians as they came within shouting distance.

"Ho, travelers! What would you in Prissthil?"

Clubfoot cried, "We intend Prissthil's salvation, and the world's!"

"Oh, magicians! Well, you're welcome." The head guard grinned. He was a burly, earthy man in armor dented by war. "Though I don't trust your salvation. What have you come to do for us? Make more starstone?"

Clubfoot turned huffy. "It was for no trivial purpose that we traveled six hundred miles."

"Your pardon, but my grandfather used to fly half

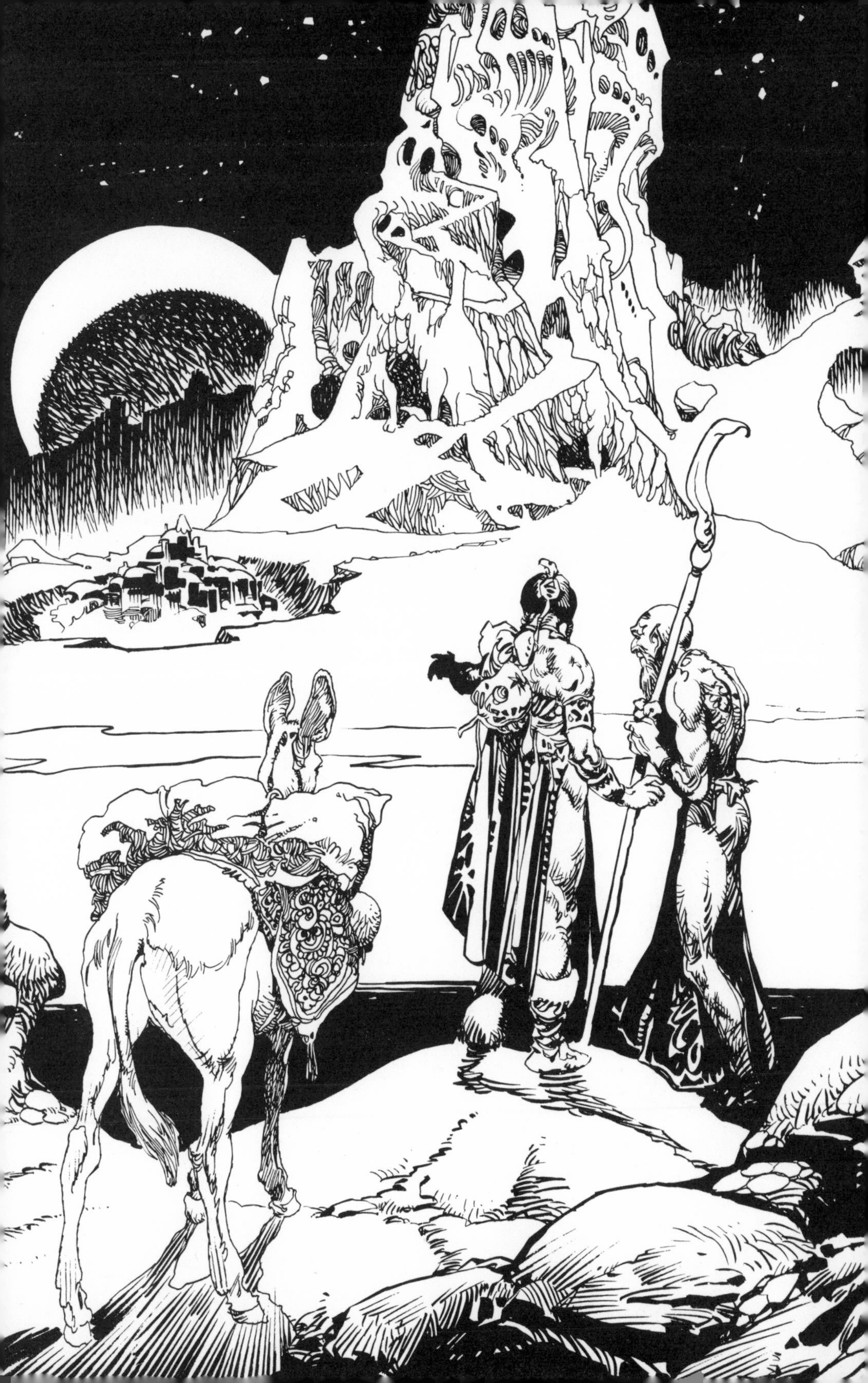

around the world to attend a banquet," said the head guard. "Poor old man. None of his spells worked, there at the end. He kept going over and over the same rejuvenation spell until he died. Wanted to train me for magic too. I had more sense."

A grating voice said, "Waaarrl ... lock."

The blood drained from the head guard's face. Slowly he turned. The other guard was backing toward the gate.

The statue's rough-carved stone face, a dog's face with a scholar's thoughtful look, stared down at the magicians. "I know you," said the rusty, almost subsonic voice. "Waarrllock. You made me."

"Llon!" the Warlock cried joyfully. "I thought you must be dead!"

"Almost. I sleep for years, for tens of years. Sometimes I wake for a few hours. The life goes out of me," said the statue. "I wish it were not so. How can I do my duty? One day an enemy will slip past me, into the city."

"We'll see if we can do something about that."

"I wish you luck."

Clubfoot spoke confidently. "The best brains in the world are gathering here. How can we fail?"

"You're young," said Llon.

They passed on. Behind them the statue froze in place.

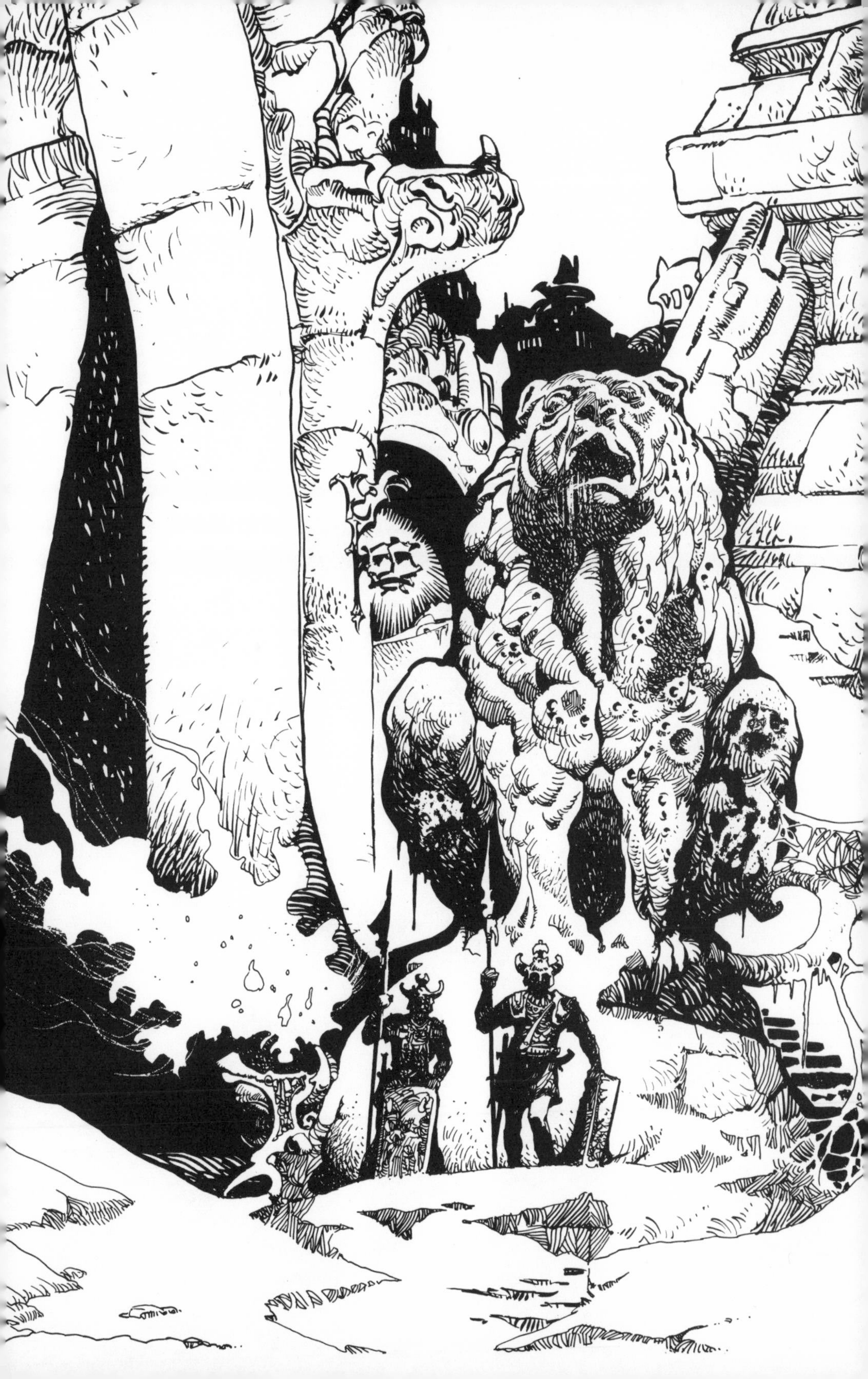

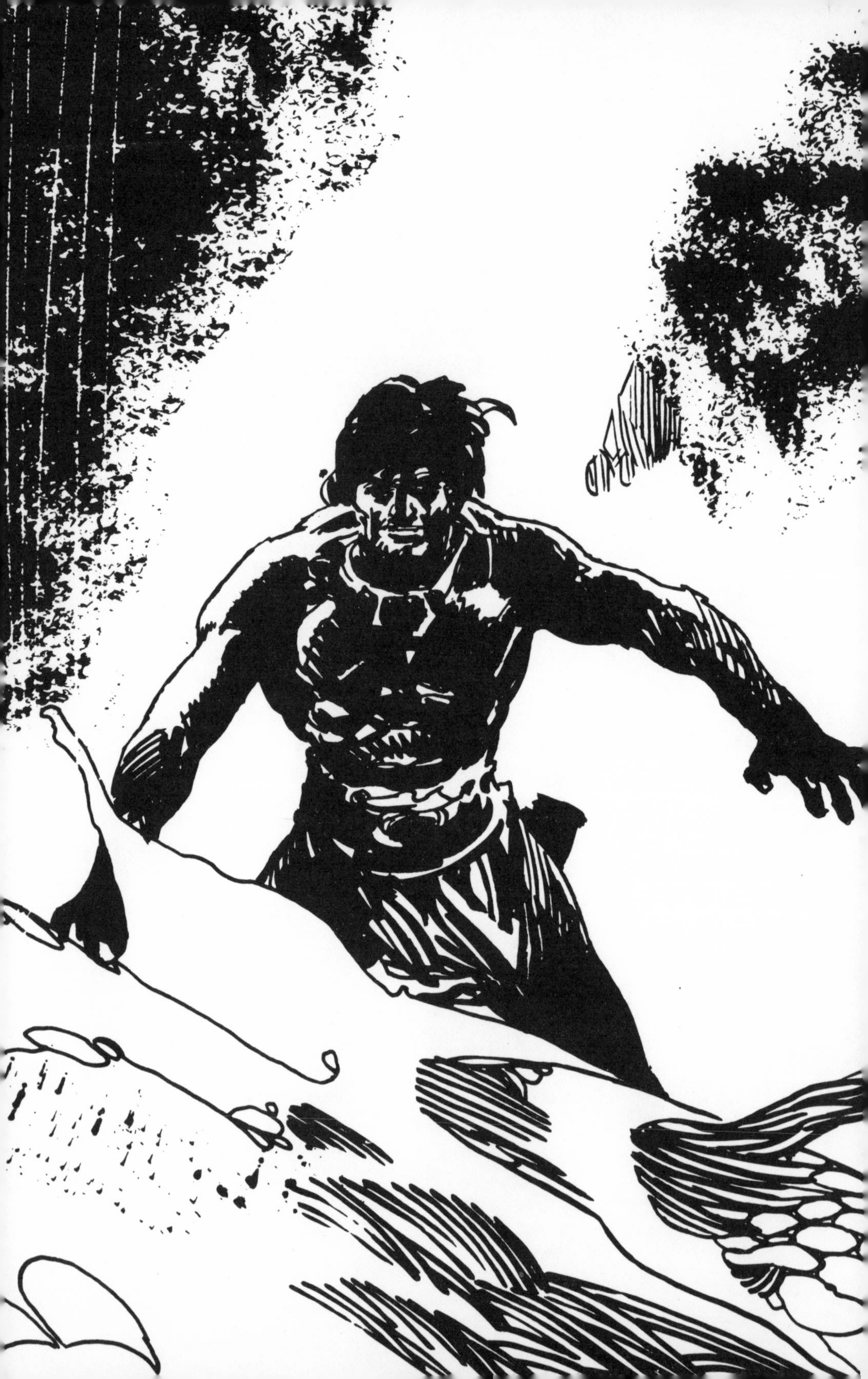

OROLANDES II

It was luck for Orolandes that Prissthil was no farther. Else he would have died on the way. He made for a place he knew only by name, stopping sometimes to ask directions, or to ask for work and food. He was gaunt again by the time he reached Prissthil.

He circled a wide, barren dish-shaped depression. It was too circular, too regular; it smacked uneasily of sorcery. There was a great stone statue before the city gate, and guards who straightened as he came up.

"We have little need for swordsmen here," one greeted him.

"I want to talk to a magician," said Orolandes.

"You're in luck." The guard looked over his shoulder, quickly, nervously; then turned back fast, as if hoping the swordsman wouldn't notice. "Two magicians came today. But what if they don't want to talk to you?"

"I have to talk to a magician," Orolandes said stubbornly. His hand hung near his sword hilt. He was big, and scarred, and armed. Perhaps he was no longer an obvious madman, but the ghost of some recent horror was plain in his face.

The guard forebore to push the matter. The stranger was no pauper; his gold arm band was a form of money. "If you're rude to a magician, you'll get what you deserve. Welcome to Prissthil. Go on in."

THE WARLOCK II

The inn the Warlock loved best was gone, replaced by a leather worker's shop. They sought another.

At the Inn of the Mating Phoenixes they saw their mule stabled, then moved baggage to their rooms. Clubfoot flopped on the feather mattress. The Warlock dug in a saddlebag. He pulled out spare clothing, then a copper disk with markings around the rim. He moved to set it aside; then, still holding it, he seemed to drift off into reverie.

Hundreds of years ago, and far east of Prissthil, there had been a proud and powerful magician. He was barely past his brilliant apprenticeship; but he had the temerity to forbid the waging of war through-out the Fertile Crescent, and the power to make it stick. He consistently hired himself out to battle whichever nation he considered the aggressor.

Oh, his magic had been big and showy in those days! Floating castles, armies destroyed by lightning, phantom cities built and destroyed in a night. In his pride he nicknamed himself Warlock. Had he known that his nickname would become a generic term for magicians, he would not have shown surprise.

But over the decades his spells stopped working. It happened to all magicians. He moved away, and his power returned, to some extent . . . then gradually dwindled, until he moved again.

It happened to nations too. Bound together by its own gods and traditions and laws and trade networks, a nation like Acheron might come to seem as old and stable as the mountains themselves . . . until treaties sealed by oaths and magic lost their power . . . until barbarians with swords come swarming over the bor-ders. All knew that it was so. But the Warlock was the first to learn why, via an experiment he performed with an enchanted copper disk.

If he kept his discovery secret through succeeding decades, his motive was compassion. His terrible truth spelled the end of civilization, yet it was of no earthly use to anyone. Fifty years ago his secret had finally escaped him, for good or evil; it was hard to know which.

"Never mind that," said Clubfoot. "Let's get dinner."

The Warlock shook himself. "Shortly," he said. He set the Wheel aside and reached again into the saddlebag.

Clubfoot snorted. He gathered up spilled clothing and began hanging it.

The Warlock set a wooden box on the table. Inside, within soft fox skins, was a human skull. The Warlock handled it carefully. One hinge of its jaw was broken, and there were tooth marks on the jaw and cheekbones and around both earholes.

Clubfoot said, "I still think we should have contrived to lose that."

"I disagree. *Now* let's get dinner."

The inn was crowded. The dining hall was filled with long wooden tables, too close together, with wooden benches down both sides. The magicians fitted themselves into space on one of the benches. Citizens to either side gradually realised who and what they were and gave them plenty of room.

"Look at this logically," Clubfoot said. "You've carried Wavyhill's skull six hundred miles, when we had to throw away baggage we needed more. It's just a skull. It's not even in good condition. But if there's enough local *mana* to power your spells, and if you work your spells exactly right, you just might be able to bring Wavyhill back to life so he can kill you!"

The Warlock stopped eating long enough to say, "Even if I revive it, it's still just a skull. You'll be all right if you don't stick your fingers in its mouth."

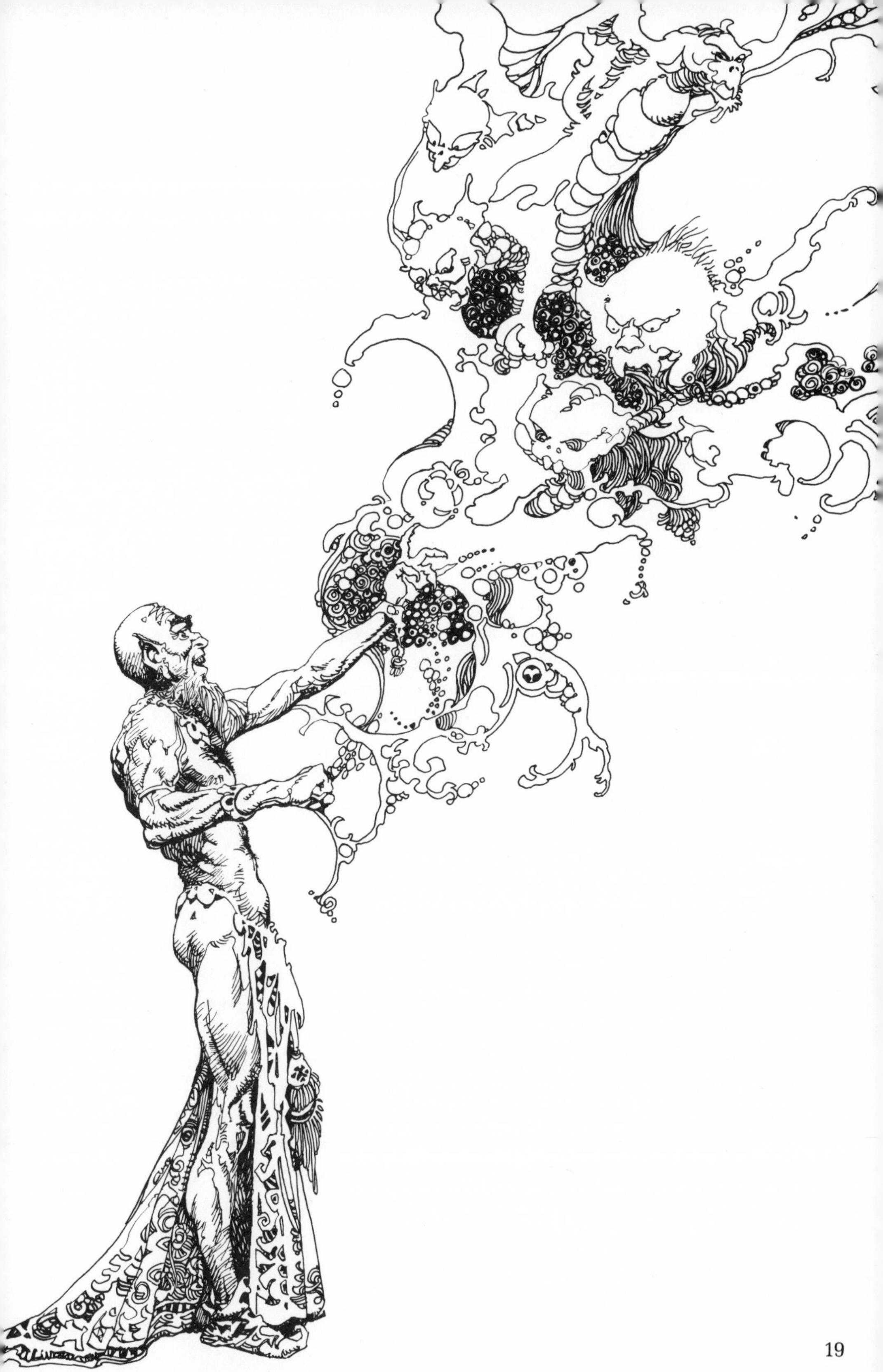

"He's got every reason to want your life! And mine too, because I'm the one who led you to Shiskabil and Hathzoril. If I hadn't found the gutted villages, you'd never have tracked him down."

"He may not have known that."

"I'd rather he did. Hellspawn! He's branded my memory. I'll never forget Shiskabil. Dead empty, and dried blood everywhere, as if it had rained blood. We may never know how many villages he gutted that way."

"I'm going to revive him tonight. Want to help?"

Clubfoot gnawed at the rich dark meat on an antelope's thighbone. Presently he said, "Would I let you try it alone?"

The Warlock smiled. Clubfoot was near fifty; he thought himself experienced in magic. At five times his age the Warlock might have laughed at Clubfoot's solicitude. But the Warlock wasn't stupid. He knew that most of his dangerously won knowledge was obsolete.

The *mana* had been richer, magic had been both easier and more dangerous, when the Warlock was raising his floating castles. Clubfoot was probably more in tune with the real world. So the Warlock only smiled and began moving his fingers in an intricate pattern.

Primary colors streamed up from between the Warlock's fingers, roiled and expanded beneath the beamed roof. Heads turned at the other tables. The clattering of table knives stopped. Then came sounds of delight and appreciative fingersnapping, for a spell the Warlock had last used to blind an enemy army.

Now a lean, scarred swordsman watched the Warlock with haunted eyes. The Warlock did not notice. As he left the dining hall he took with him a bunch of big purple grapes.

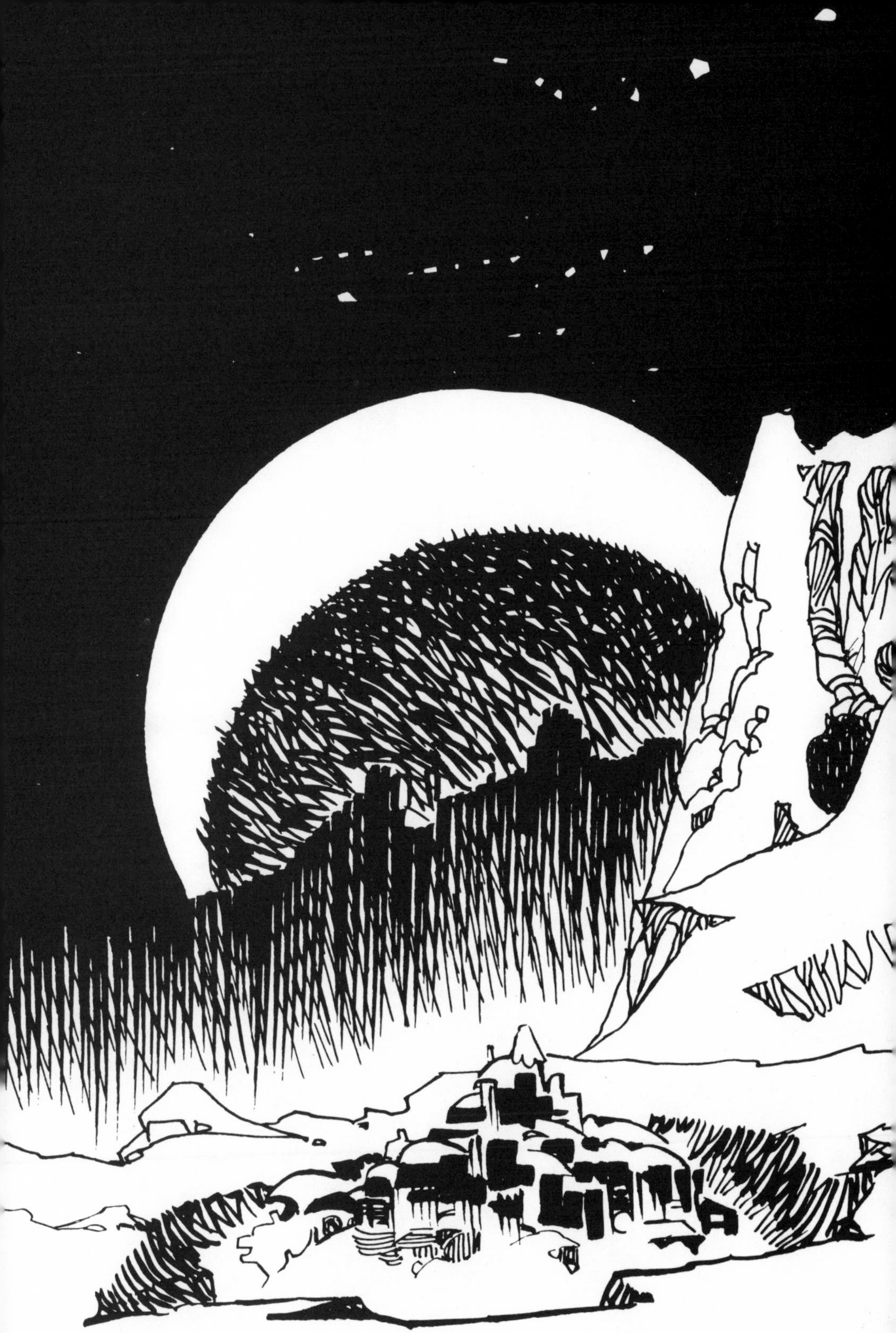

THE SKULL OF WAVYHILL

The Warlock could remember a time when murder was very dangerous; when the mystical backlash from a careless killing could reverberate for generations. But that was long ago.

The magician nicknamed Wavyhill — as all magicians carried nicknames, being wary of having their true names used against them — had learned his trade in an age when all spells were less powerful. There was still strong *mana* in murder, but Wavyhill had learned to control it. He had based a slave industry on the zombies of murder victims, and sold the zombies as servants, then set them to killing their masters to make more zombies . . .

He had also used magic to make himself unkillable. For these past twenty years he must have been regretting that terribly.

Wavyhill's skull sat grinning on the table. Clubfoot regarded it uneasily. "It may be we've had too much wine to try this sort of thing tonight."

"Would you rather try it tomorrow, before dawn, with hangovers? Because I want Wavyhill with me when we meet Mirandee and Piranther."

"*All* right, go ahead." Clubfoot bolted the door, then worked spells against magical intrusion. Reviving a murderous dead man was chancy enough without risk of some outsider interfering — and there were amateur magicians everywhere in Prissthil. Magic was an old tradition here, dating from a time when starstone was plentiful.

The Warlock sang as he worked. He was an old man, tall and lean, his head bald as an egg, his voice thin and reedy. But he could hold a tune. The words he sang belonged to a language no longer used except by members of the Sorcerers' Guild.

He knotted a loop of thin leather thong to mend the broken jaw hinge. Other strips of thong went along the

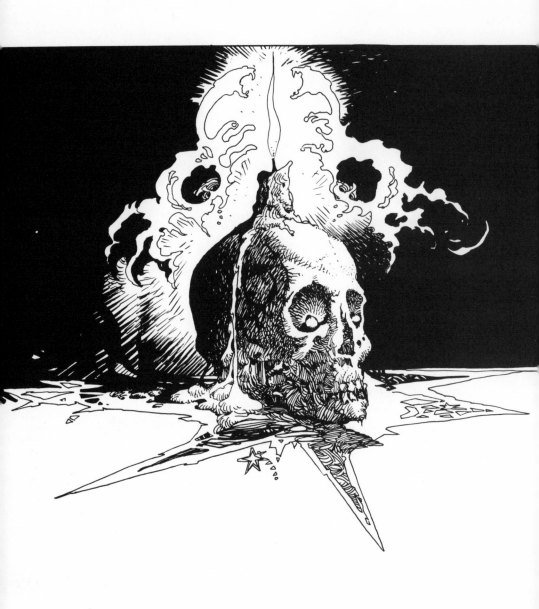

cheekbones, the jaw hinges, the ears. Many overlapped. When he finished they formed a crude diagram of the muscles of a human face.

The Warlock stepped back, considering. He cut up a sheet of felt and glued two round pads behind the ear holes. A longer strip went inside the jaws, the back end glued to the table between the jaw hinges.

He looked at Clubfoot, who had been watching intently. Clubfoot said, "Eyes?"

"Maybe later." The Warlock said in the old language, "Kranthkorpool, speak to me."

The skull opened its jaws wide and screamed.

Clubfoot and the Warlock covered their ears. It didn't help. The skull's voice was not troubling the air, and it did not reach the ears. At least it would not bother the other guests.

"He's insane! Shut him off!" Clubfoot cried.

"Not yet!"

The skull screamed its agony. Minutes passed before it paused as if drawing breath. Into the pause the Warlock shouted, "Kranthkorpool, stop! It's over! It's been over for twenty years!"

The skull gaped. It said, "Twenty years?"

"It took me almost that long to find your true name, Kranthkorpool."

"Call me Wavyhill. Who are you? I can't see."

"Just a minute." The Warlock plucked two of what was left of the grapes. He picked up the skull and inserted them into the eye sockets from inside. He inked in two black dots where they showed through the sockets.

"Ah," said the skull. The black dots moved, focussed. They studied Clubfoot, then moved on. "Warlock?"

The Warlock nodded.

"I thought I'd killed you. You were two hundred

years old when I cancelled your longevity spells."

"I was able to renew them. Partly. I give you a technical victory, Wavyhill. It was my ally who defeated you."

"Technical victory!" There was hysteria in the skull's falsetto laughter. "That werewolf rug merchant kept tearing and tearing at me! It went on forever and ever, and I couldn't die! I couldn't die!"

"It's over."

"I thought it wouldn't ever be over. It went on and on, a piece of me gone every time he got close enough — "

The skull stopped, seemed to consider. Its expression was unreadable, of course. "I don't hurt. In fact, I can't feel much of anything. There was a long time when I couldn't feel or see or hear or smell or . . . Did you say twenty years? Warlock, what do I look like?"

The Warlock detached a mirror from the wall, brought it and held it. Wavyhill's skull studied itself for a time. It said, "You just had to do that, didn't you?"

"I owed you one. Now you have a decision to make. Do you want to die? I can cancel the spell of immortality you put on yourself."

"I don't know. Let me think about it. What do you want of me, Warlock?"

"Some technical help."

The skull laughed. "From me?"

"You were the world's first necromancer. You were powerful enough to defeat *me*," said the Warlock. "I'd be dead if I hadn't brought help. You used your power for evil, but nobody doubts your skill. Tomorrow I meet two powerful magicians. We'll want your advice."

"Do I know of them?"

"Piranther. Mirandee."

"Piranther!" The skull chuckled. "I'd like to see that meeting. Piranther walked out on your conference,

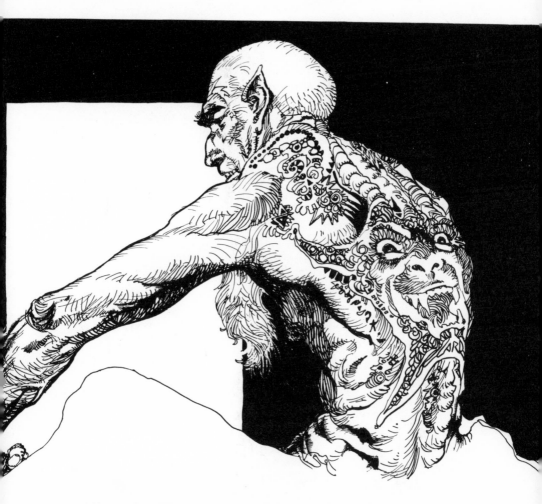

didn't he? After you called him a shortsighted fool. I heard that he took a whole colony of his people to the South Land Mass and swore never to come back."

"You heard right. And he never did come back, but he's coming now."

The skull was silent for a time. Then it said, "You've roused my interest. I don't care to die just now. Under the circumstances that may be silly, but I can't help it. Can you make me a whole man again?"

"Look at me."

The Warlock's back was festive with colored inks: a five-sided tattoo, hypnotic in its complexity. The famous demon trap, once a housing for the Warlock's guardian demon, was empty now; but he still preferred to wear nothing above the waist. Its purpose had been lost, but the habit remained.

It showed him to disadvantage. The Warlock's ribs protruded. His small pot belly protruded. Pouchy, wrinkled, unflexible skin masked the strong lines of his face and showed the shrinkage of his musculature. Vertebrae marched like a tiny mountain range across the fading inks of the empty demon trap.

The skull sighed mournfully.

"Look at me! I'd wish my youth back, if wishing were all it took," the Warlock said. "I was young for two hundred years. Now the spells are failing. All spells are failing."

"So you need a necromancer." The dots on the grapes turned to the red man. "Are you involved in this madness too?"

"Of course."

The Warlock said, "This is Clubfoot, our ally."

"A pleasure. I'd take hands, but you see how it is," said Wavyhill.

Clubfoot was not amused. "One day you may have hands again, but you will never take my hand. I've seen the villages you gutted. I helped kill you, Wavyhill."

The dots on the grapes turned back to the Warlock. "And this tactless boor is to be our ally? Well, what is your project?"

"We're going to discuss means of restoring the world's *mana*."

The skull's laugh was high and shrill. The Warlock waited it out. Presently he said, "Are you finished?"

"Possibly. Will it take all five of us?"

"I tried to call a full meeting of the Guild. Only ten answered the call. Of the ten, three felt able to travel."

"Has it occurred to you that magic can only use up *mana?* Never restore it?"

"We're not fools. What about an outside source?"

"Such as?"

"The Moon."

The Warlock expected more laughter. It did not come. "*Mana* from the Moon? I never would have thought of that in a thousand years. Still . . . why not? Starstones are rich in *mana*. Why not the Moon?"

"With enough *mana*, and the right spells, you could be human again."

The skull laughed. "And so could you, Warlock. But where would we find magic powerful enough to reach the Moon?"

The door rocked to thunderous knocking.

The magicians froze. Then Clubfoot stripped a bracelet from his upper arm. He looked through it at the door. "No magic involved," he said. "A mundane."

"What would a mundane want with us?"

"Maybe the building's on fire." Clubfoot raised his voice. "You, there — "

Neither the old spells, nor the old bar across the door, were strong enough. The door exploded inward behind a tremendous kick. An armed man stepped into the room and looked about him.

"I have to talk to a magician," he told them.

"You are interrupting magicians engaged in private business," said the Warlock. No sane man would have needed more warning.

The intruder was raggedly shaved, his long black hair raggedly chopped at shoulder length. His dark eyes studied two men and a skull decorated with macabre humor. "You *are* magicians," he said won-

deringly. In the next instant he almost died; for he drew his sword, and Clubfoot raised his arms.

The Warlock shook Clubfoot's shoulder. "Stop! It's broken!"

"Yes. I broke it," said the intruder. He looked at the bladeless hilt, then suddenly threw it into a corner of the room. He took two steps forward and closed hands like bronze clamps on the Warlock's thin shoulders. He looked searchingly into the Warlock's face. He said, "Why did it happen?"

Clubfoot's arms were raised again.

Human beings are fragile, watery things. Death spells are the easiest magic there is.

"Back up and start over," said the Warlock. "I don't know what you're talking about. Who are you?"

"Orolandes. Greek soldier."

"Why did you break your sword?"

"I hated it. I thought maybe it happened because of the people I killed. Not the other soldiers. The priests."

Clubfoot exclaimed, "You were in the Atlantis invasion!"

"Yes. We finally invaded Atlantis. First time Greeks ever got that far." Orolandes released the Warlock. He looked like a sleepwalker; he wasn't seeing anything here in the room. "We came for slaves and treasure. That's all."

"And trade advantage," said the Warlock.

"Uh? Maybe. Nobody told me anything like that. Anyway, we won. The armies of Atlantis must have gotten soft. We went through them like they were nothing. But the priests were something else. They stood in a long line on the steps of the big temple and waved their arms. We got sick. Some of us died. But we kept coming, crawling — I was crawling, anyway — and we got to them and killed them. And then Atlantis was ours."

He looked with haunted eyes at the magicians. "Ours. At last. Hundreds of years we'd dreamed of conquering Atlantis. We'd take their treasure. We'd take away their weapons. We'd make them pay tribute. But we never, we never wanted to kill them all. Old men, women, children, everyone. Nobody ever thought of that."

"You son of a troll. I had friends in Atlantis," said Clubfoot. "How did you live through it? Why didn't you die with the rest?"

"Uh? There was a big gold Tau symbol at the top of the steps. We were laughing and bragging and binding up our wounds when the land started to shake. Everybody fell over. The Tau thing cracked at the base and fell on the steps. Then someone pointed west, and the horizon was going up.It didn't look like water. It was too misty, too big. It looked like the horizon was getting higher and higher.

"I crawled under the Tau thing with my back against the step. Captain Iason was shouting that it wasn't real, it was just an illusion, we must have missed some of the priests. The water came down like the end of the world. I guess the Tau thing saved my life — even the water couldn't move it, it was so heavy — but it almost killed me too. I had to get out from under it and try to swim up.

"I grabbed something that was floating up with me. It turned out to be part of a wooden roof. I got on it. A centaur girl came swimming by and I hauled her up on the roof. I thought, well, at least I saved one of them. And then she just fell over."

Clubfoot said, "There's magic in centaur metabolism. Without *mana* she died."

"But what happened? Did we do it?"

"You did it," said Clubfoot.

"I thought ... maybe ... you'd say ..."

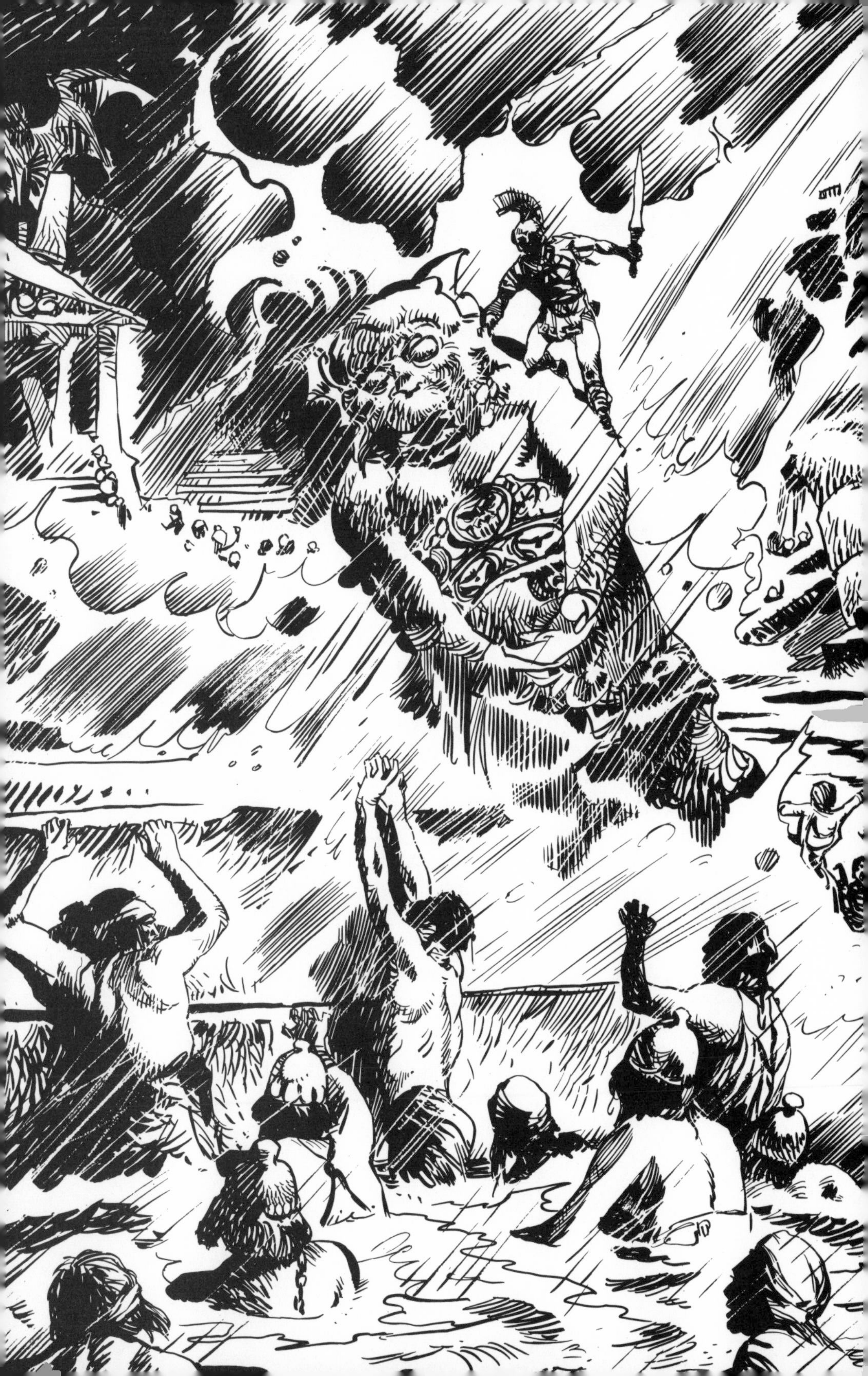

"You did it. You killed them all."

The Warlock said, "Atlantis should have been under the ocean hundreds of years ago. Only the spells of the priest-kings kept that land above the waves."

Orolandes nodded dumbly. He turned to the door.

"Stop him," said Wavyhill. As Orolandes turned to the new voice, the skull snapped, "You. Swordsman. How would you like a chance to make amends?"

Orolandes gaped at the talking skull.

"Well? You wiped out a whole continent, people and centaurs and merpeople and all. You broke your sword, you were so disgusted at yourself. How would you like to do something good for a change? Keep it from happening to others."

"Yes."

Clubfoot asked, "What *is* this?"

"We may need him. I may know of a source of very powerful *mana*."

'Where?"

"I'll reserve that. Do the words 'god within a god' mean anything to you?"

"No."

"Good." The skull chuckled. "We'll see what develops tomorrow. See to it that this ... Orolandes is with us when we meet your friends. You, Orolandes, have you got a room here?"

"I can get one."

"Meet us at dawn, for breakfast."

Orolandes nodded and walked out. There was no spring in his walk. His sword hilt he left lying in a corner.

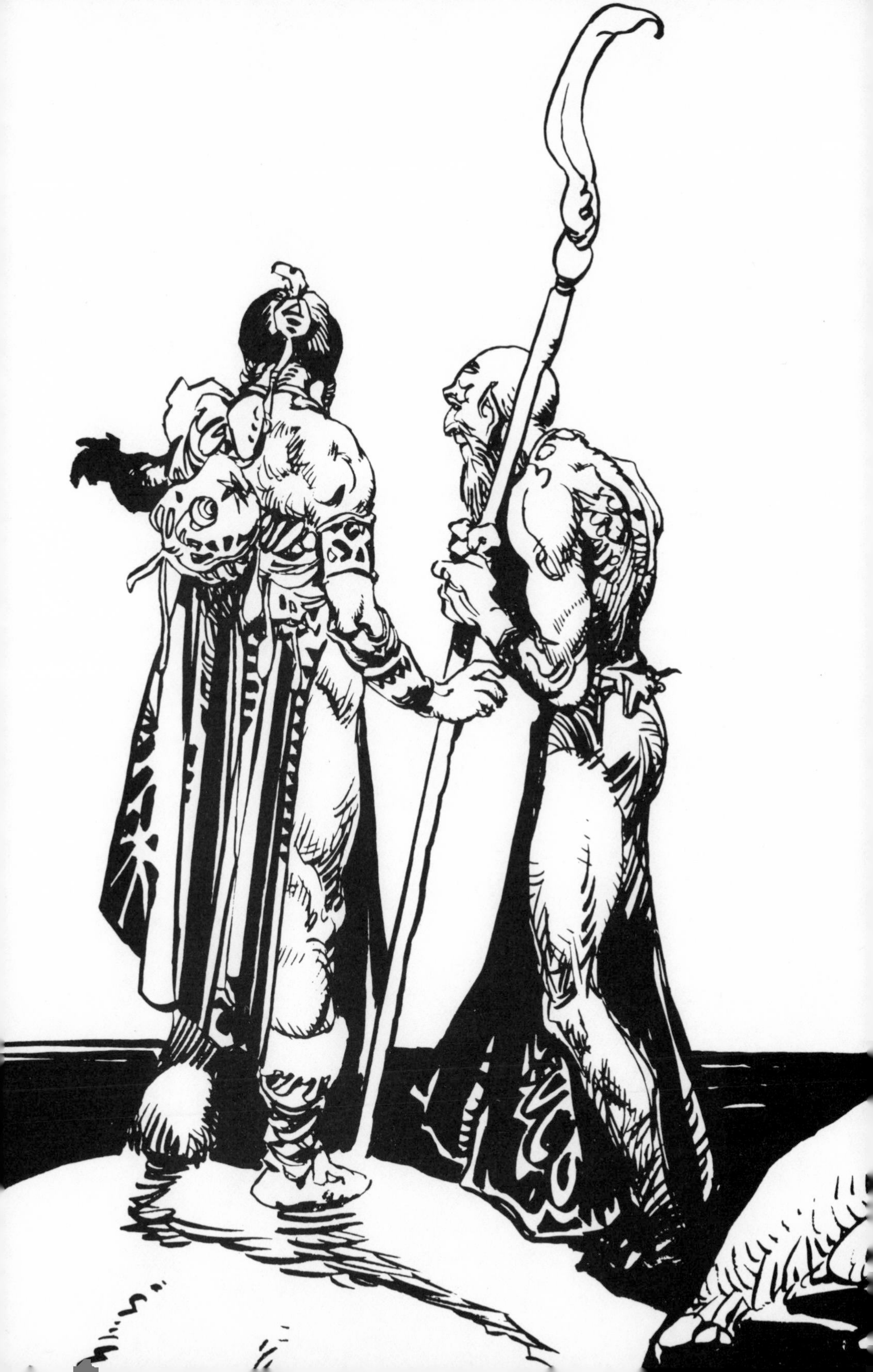

FISTFALL

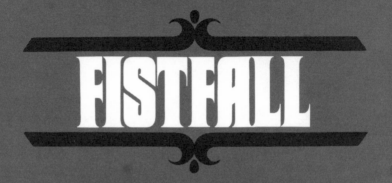

From Prissthil's gate one could make out an elliptical depression, oddly regular, in the background of low green hills. Time had eroded Fistfall's borders; they disappeared as one came near. Greenery had covered the pits and dirt piles where earlier men had dug for starstone. From what must be the rim, Orolandes could see only that the land sloped gradually down, then gradually up again.

It was just past sunrise; there was still shadow in the hollow. Orolandes shivered in the morning chill.

The old man did not shiver, though he walked naked to the waist. A talking skull sat on his shoulder, fastened by straps over the lower jaw. He and the skull and the younger man chatted as they walked: trivia mixed with incomprehensible shop talk mixed with reminiscence from many lifetimes.

Orolandes shivered. He had fallen among magicians, willingly and by design, and he was not sure of his sanity. Before that terrible day in Atlantis he would never have considered a magician to be anything but an enemy.

In the village of the fisherfolk Orolandes had waited for the images to go away. Don't speak of it, don't think of it; the vivid memories would fade.

But in the dark of sleep the sea would rise up and up and over to swallow the world, with his spoils and his men and the people he'd conquered. He would snap awake then, to stare into the dark until it turned light.

Or on a bright afternoon he would heave at the awkward weight of a net filled with fish ... and he would remember pulling at the limp, awkwardly right-angled centaur girl, trying to get her up on the broken roof. She'd *had* to lie on her side; he'd felt unspeakably clumsy trying to give her artificial respiration. But he'd seen her breath at last! He'd seen her eyelids flicker open, seen her head lift and look at him . . . seen the life go out of her then, draining away to somewhere else.

What had happened that day? If he knew *why*, then the horror would leave him, and the guilt . . . He had clung to that notion until last night. Now he knew. What the magicians had told him was worse than he had imagined.

The notion he clung to now might be the silliest of all. Orolandes could read nothing in the white bone face of the dead magician. Even to its friends it was a tolerated evil. But nobody else had offered Orolandes any breath of comfort.

On the strength of a skull's vague promise, he was here. He would wait and see.

The Warlock felt uncommonly alive. As they moved into Fistfall his vision and his hearing sharpened, his normal dyspepsia eased. Over the centuries the townspeople had removed every tiniest fragment of the boulder that had come flaming down from the skies; but vaporised rock had condensed and sifted down all over this region, and there was no removing it. Old spells took new strength.

Down there in the shadow, two walked uphill toward them.

"I recognise Mirandee," said Clubfoot. "Would that be Piranther?"

"I think so. I only met him once."

Clubfoot laughed. "Once was enough?"

"I'm surprised he came. We didn't part as friends. I was so sure I was right, I got a little carried away. Well, but that was fifty years ago." The Warlock turned to the swordsman. "Orolandes, I should have said it before. You can still turn back."

The big man's hand kept brushing his empty scabbard. He looked at the Warlock with too-wide eyes and said, "No."

"You are about to learn the secrets of magicians. It isn't likely you'll learn too much, but if you do, we may have to tamper with your memory."

It was the first time the Warlock had seen him smile. The swordsman said, "There are parts you can cut out while you're about it."

"Do you mean that?"

"I'm not sure. What kind of man is that? Or is it the woman's familiar?"

The man approaching them was small and dark-skinned and naked in the autumn chill. His hair was white and puffy as a ripe dandelion. A skin bag hung on a thong around his neck.

"His people come from the South Land Mass," said Clubfoot. "They're powerful and touchy. Be polite."

Piranther's companion was a head taller than he was, a slender woman in a vivid blue robe. Snow-white hair fell to her waist and bobbed with her walk. Mirandee and the Warlock had dwelt together in a year long past, sharing knowledge and other things, experimenting with sex magic in a way that was only partly professional.

But now her eyes only brushed the Warlock and moved on. "Clubfoot, a pleasure to see you again! And your friends." Visibly she wondered what the scarred, brawny, bewildered man was doing here. Then she turned back to the Warlock, and the blood drained from her face.

What was this? Was she reacting to the bizarre decorated skull on his shoulder? No. She took a half-step forward and said, "Oh my gods! Warlock!"

So that was it. "The magic goes away," he told her gently. "I wish I'd thought to send you some warning. I see that your own youth spells have held better."

"Well, but I'm younger. But you are all right?"

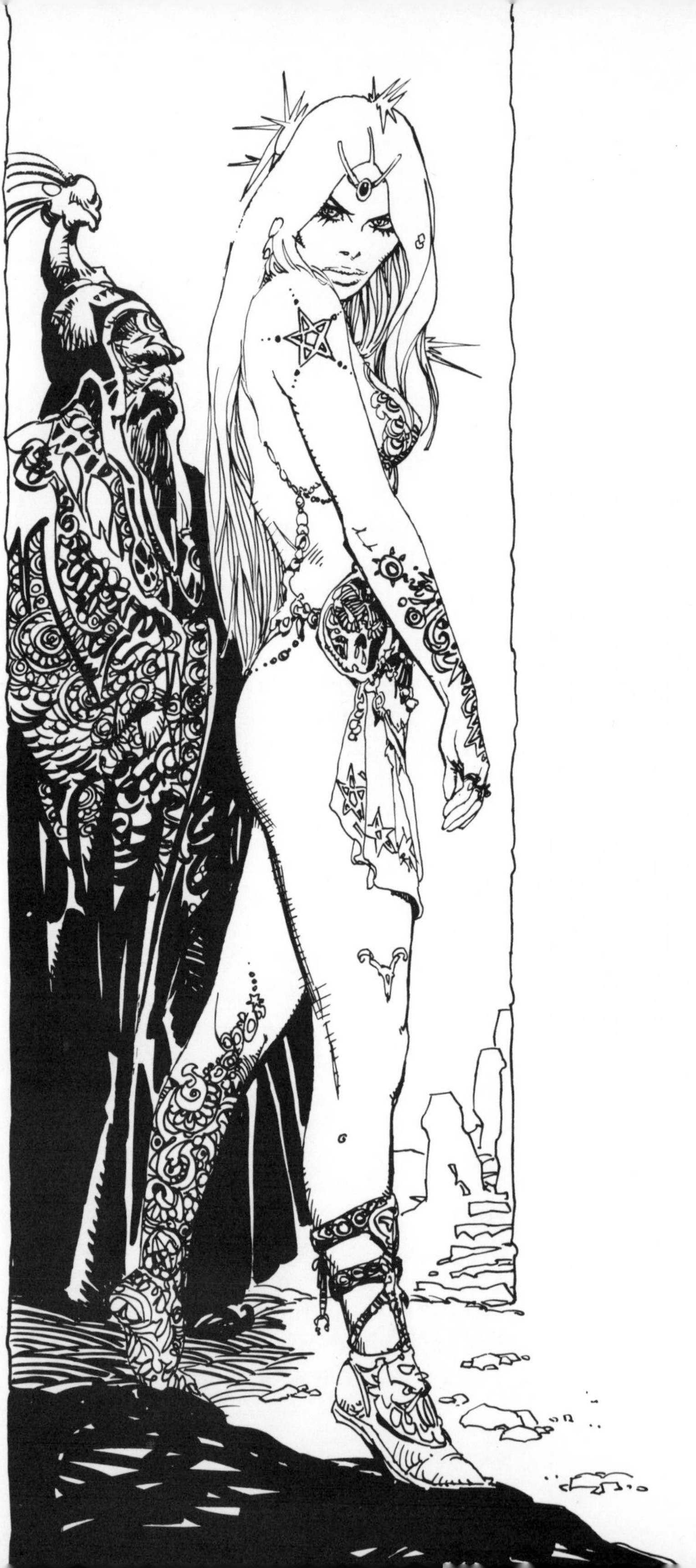

"I live. I walk. My mind is intact. I'm two hundred and forty years old, Mirandee."

Wavyhill spoke from the Warlock's shoulder. "He's in better shape than I am."

The woman's eyes shifted, her brow lifted in enquiry.

"I am Wavyhill. Mirandee, I know you by reputation."

"And I you." Her voice turned winter-cold. "Warlock, is it proper that we deal with this . . . murderer?"

"For his skill and his knowledge, I think so."

The skull cackled. "I know too much to be absent, my dear. Trust me, Mirandee, and forgive me the lives of a few dozens of mundanes. We're here to restore the magic that once infused the world. I want that more than you do. Obviously."

But Mirandee was looking at the Warlock when she answered Wavyhill. "No. You don't."

The age-withered black man spoke for the first time. "Skull, I sense the ambition in you. Otherwise you conceal your thoughts. What is it you hide?"

"I would bow if I could. Piranther, I am honored to meet you," said Wavyhill. "Do you know of the god within a god?"

Piranther's brow wrinkled. "These words mean nothing to me."

"Then I have knowledge you need. A point for bargaining. Please notice that I am more helpless than any infant. On that basis, will you let me stay? I won't ask you to trust me."

Piranther's eyes shifted. His face was as blank as his mind, and his mind was as dark and hidden as the floor of the ocean. "Warlock, I should be gratified that you still live. And you must be Clubfoot; I know you by reputation. But who are you, sir?"

"Orolandes. I, I was asked to come."

Wavyhill said, "I asked him. His motives are good. Let him stay."

Piranther half-smiled. "On trust?"

Wavyhill snorted. "You're a magician, they say. Read his mind. He hasn't the defenses of a turtle."

That, and Piranther's slow impassive nod . . . "No!" cried Orolandes, and his hand spasmed above the empty scabbard. He backed away.

The skull said, "Stop it, Greek. What have you to hide?"

Orolandes moaned. His guilt was agony; he wanted to burrow in the ground. One flash of hate he felt for these who would judge him: for the Warlock's sympathy, the woman's cool curiosity, the black demon's indifference, the red magician's irritation at time-wasting preliminaries. But Orolandes had already judged himself. He stood fast.

Corpses floated in shoals around his raft. They covered the sea as far as the horizon. Sharks and killer whales leapt among them . . .

Piranther made a grimace of distaste. "You might have warned me. Oh, very well, Wavyhill, he's certainly harmless. But he trusts you no more than I do."

"And why should he?"

Piranther shrugged. He settled gracefully onto a small grassy hillock. "I had hoped to be addressing thirty or forty trained magicians. It bodes ill for us that no more than five could come. But here we are. Who speaks?"

There was an awkward pause. Clubfoot said, "If nobody else wants to . . ."

"Proceed."

Mirandee and the Warlock settled cross-legged on the ground.

Clubfoot looked toward Mount Valhalla, collecting

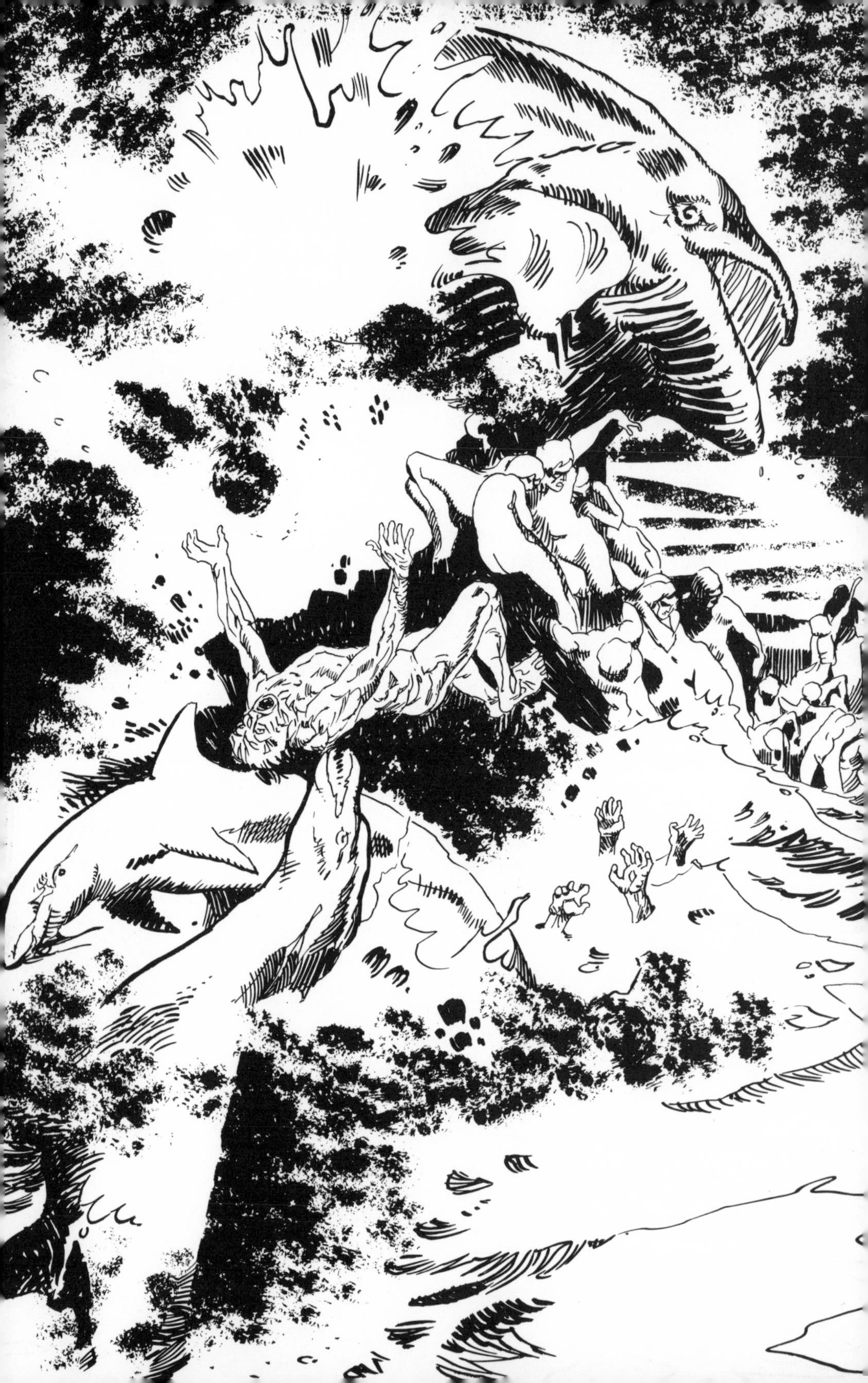

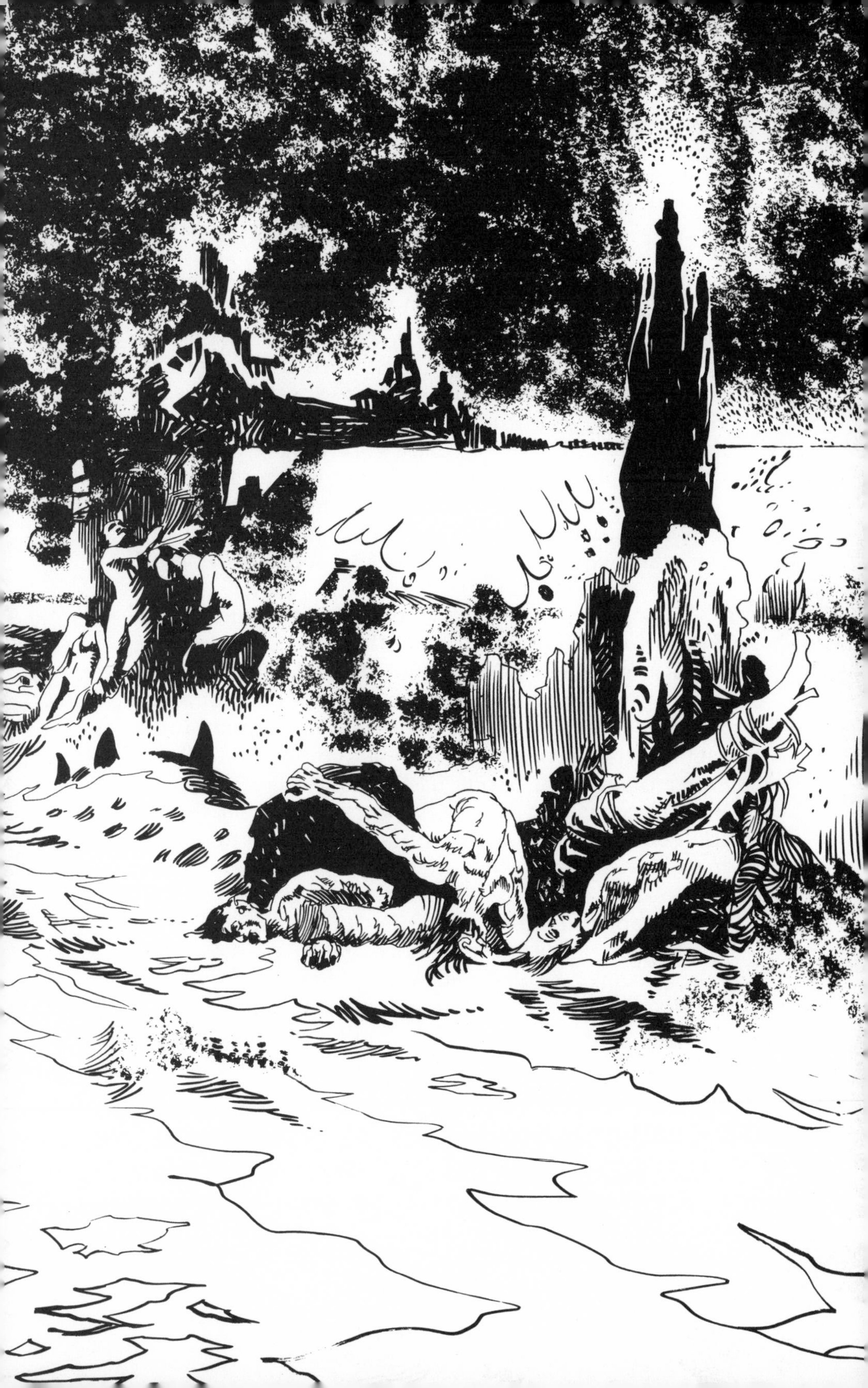

his thoughts. He may have been regretting his temerity. After all, he was the youngest of the magicians present. Well ——

"First there were the gods," he said. "Earth sparkled with magic in those days, and nothing was impossible. The first god almost certainly created himself. Later gods may not have been *that* powerful, but there are tales of mountains piled one on another to reach sky-dwelling gods and overthrow them, of a god torn to pieces and the fragments forming whole pantheons, of the sun being stopped in its track for trivial purposes. The gods' lives were fueled by magic, not fire. Eventually the *mana* level dropped too low, and the gods went mythical . . . as I suppose we'd die if fires stopped burning.

"We still have the habit of thanking the gods, mundanes and sorcerers alike. With reason. Before they died, some of the gods played at making other forms of life. Their creations were their survivors. Some live by what seems to be slow-burning fire . . . men, foxes, rabbits . . . and most plants use fire from the sun. Other plants and beasts use fire and *mana* both. We find unicorns surviving in *mana*-poor regions, though the colts are born with stunted horns, or none. But many *mana*-dependent peoples are going mythical: mer-people, dragons, centaurs, elves. Hey —"

Clubfoot did a strange thing for a man making a speech. He darted over to a boulder, heaved at it and turned it over. Underneath was a blob of grayish jelly two feet across.

In his youth the Warlock had killed carnivorous *goo* the size of houses. To a mere warrior they were more dangerous than dragons: a sword was generally too short to reach the beast's nucleus. By contrast this *goo* was tiny. It was formless and translucent, with darker organs and vacuoles of food showing within its body. It arched itself in the morning sunlight and tried to

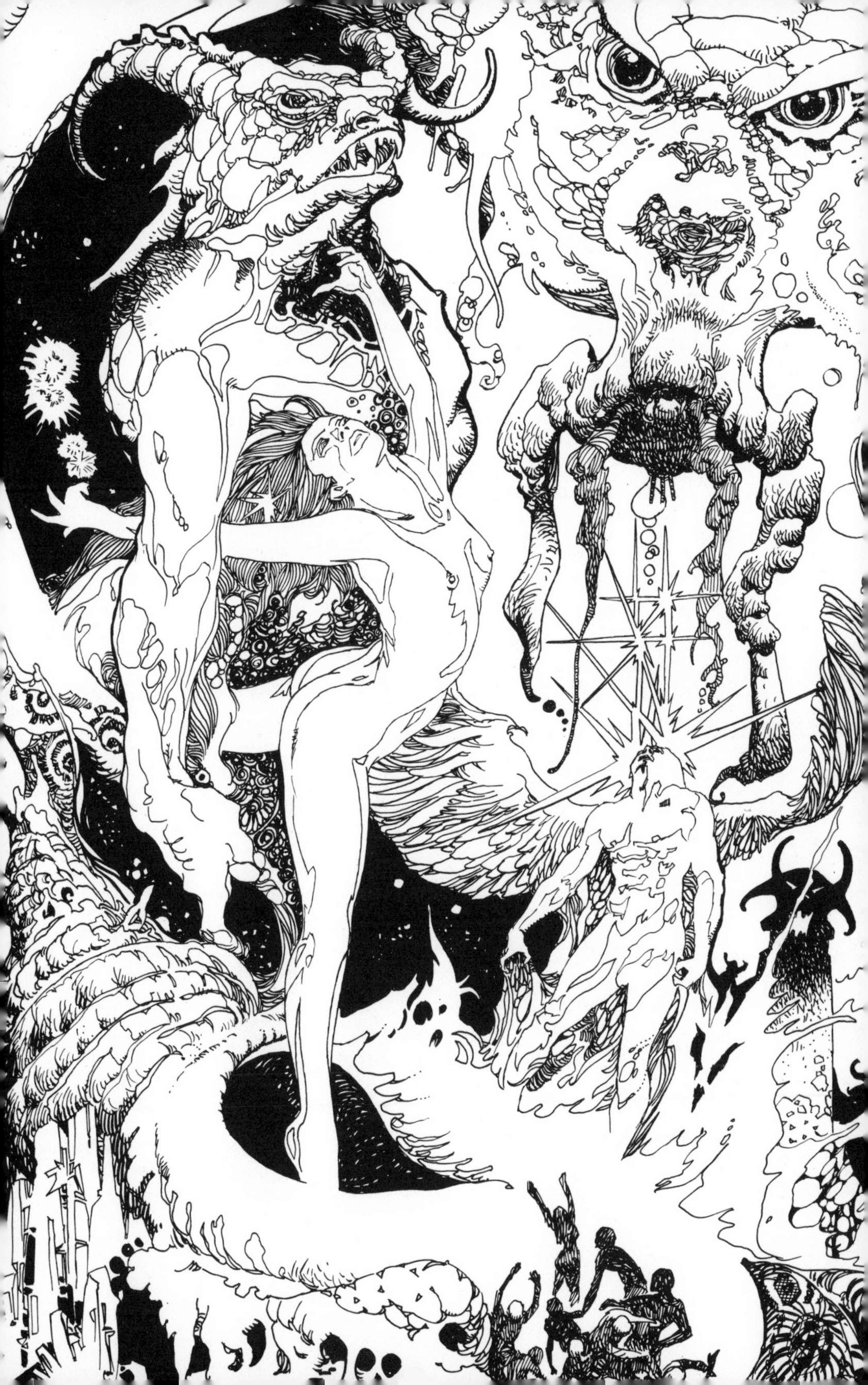

flow into Clubfoot's shadow.

"There! That's what I'm talking about!" Clubfoot cried. "The *goo* are surviving, but *look* at it. *Goo* are named for the first word spoken by a baby. They're said to be children of the first god: formless, adaptable, created in the image of the Crawling Chaos. We saw them smaller than a man's fist in the desert, where the *mana* is poor. Do you see how small it's gotten? *Goo* live by fire and magic, but they can use fire alone. When the world is barren of magic the *goo* will remain, but they'll probably be too small to see.

"And we'll survive, because we live by fire alone. But we'll be farmers or merchants or entertainers, and the swordsmen will rule the world. That's why we're here. Not to save the centaurs or the dragons or the *goo*. To

save ourselves."

"Thank you. You're very eloquent," said Piranther. He seemed to have taken charge, with little challenge from anyone. He looked about at the rest. "Suggestions?"

Mirandee said, "What about your project, Piranther? Fifty years ago you were going to map the *mana*-rich regions of the world."

"And I said that was self-limiting," said the Warlock.

"And you called me a short-sighted fool," Piranther said without heat. "But we carried through in spite of you. As you know, there are places human magicians never reached or settled, where the *mana* remains strong. I need hardly point out that they are the least desirable living places in the world. The land beneath the ice of the South Pole. In the north, the ice itself. The clouds. Any fool who watches clouds can tell you they're magic. I know spells to render cloud-stuff solid and to shape it into castles and the like."

"So do I," said the Warlock.

"So did Sheefyre," Mirandee said dryly. "The witch Sheefyre will not be joining us. She took a fall. Where are you on a cloudscape when the *mana* runs out?"

"Precisely. It was our major problem," Piranther said. "There are places one can practice magic, but when the spells stop working, where are you? A desert, or an inaccessible mountaintop, or the terrible cold of the South Pole. But our search turned up one place of refuge, an unknown body of land in the southern hemisphere.

"Australia was probably infested with demons until recently. They're gone now. All we have of them is the myth of a Hell under the world. But why else should the fifth largest land mass in the world have been uninhabited until we came? You know that when we finished our mapping project," said Piranther, "I took my people there, all who would go. The *mana* is rich. There are new fruits and roots and meat animals. On a nearby island we found a giant bird, the moa, the finest meat animal in the world —"

The Warlock grinned. "Do I hear an invitation to emigrate?"

For a moment Piranther looked like a trapped thing. Then the bland, expressionless mask was back. He said, "I'm afraid we have no room for you."

"What, in the world's fifth largest land mass?"

"At the conference fifty years ago you said . . . what was it you said? You said that mapping *mana*-rich places only brings magicians to use up the *mana*. So —" Piranther shrugged delicately. "I take you at your word."

They looked at him. He was hiding something . . . and he knew they knew . . . "I must," he said. "The castles we raised by magic along the coast are falling down. The ambrosia is dying. We must migrate inland. I fear the results if my students can't learn to use less powerful spells."

"They'll go further and further inland," Mirandee said in a dreamy voice, "using the *mana* as they go." Her face was blank, her eyes blind. Sometimes the gift of prophecy came on her thus, without warning. "Thousands of years from now the swordsmen will come, to find small black people in the barren center of the continent, starving and powerless, making magic with pointing-bones that no longer work."

"There is no need to be so vivid," Piranther said coldly.

Mirandee started. Her eyes focussed. "Was I talking? What did I say?"

But nobody thought it tactful to tell her. Clubfoot cleared his throat and said, "Undersea?"

The Warlock shook his head. "No good. There's

nothing to breath in the water, and the *mana* is in the sea floor. When the spells fail, where are you?" He looked around him. "Shall we face facts? There's no place to hide. If we can't bring the magic back to the world, we might as well give it to the swordsmen."

Piranther asked, "Do you have something in mind?"

"An outside source. The Moon."

Nobody laughed. Even the Greek swordsman only gaped at him. Piranther's wrinkled face remained immobile as he said, "You must have been thinking this through for hundreds of years. Is this really your best suggestion?"

"Yes. Silly as it sounds. May I expound?"

"Of course."

"I don't have to say anything that isn't obvious. Stones and iron fall from the sky every night. They burn out before they touch earth. Their power for magic is low; it has to be used fast, while they still burn.

"Some starstones do reach earth. The bigger they are, the more power they carry. Correct?" The Warlock did not wait for an answer. "The Moon is huge. Watch it at moonrise and you'll know. It should carry enormous power — far more than the Fist carried, for instance. In fact, it must. What else but magic could hold it up? I suggest that the Moon carries more *mana* than the world has seen since the gods died.

"But you don't need me to tell you that, do you? — Orolandes, is there magic in the Moon?"

The ex-soldier started. "Why ask me? I know no magic." He shrugged uncomfortably. "All right, yes, there's magic in the Moon. Anyone can feel it."

"We all know that," said Piranther. "How do you propose to use it?"

"I don't know. If our spells could reach the Moon at all, its own *mana* would let us land it."

"This all seems very . . . hypothetical," Mirandee said delicately. "I don't know what holds the Moon up. Do you? Does anyone?"

There were blank looks. Wavyhill's skull cackled. "We could pull the Moon down and find we'd used up all the *mana* doing it."

Mirandee was exasperated. "Well, then, does anyone know how *big* the Moon is? Because the bigger it is, the higher it must be, and the harder it's going to hit! It could be thousands of miles up!"

"It must be tremendous," Piranther said. "From Iceland and from Australia, it looks exactly the same. Nothing remotely as large has ever struck earth. Otherwise we'd find old records of it in the sky, records of a time when there were two moons."

"We'll have to give it plenty of room, if we solve the other problems." The Warlock hesitated. "I'd thought of the Gobi Desert."

Wavyhill said, "There's even more room in the Pacific."

Clubfoot made a rude noise. "Tidal waves. And we couldn't get to it after it sank." He tugged thoughtfully at a single braid of straight black hair. "Why not the South Pole? No, forget I said that. The Moon never gets over the Poles."

Piranther wore an irritating half-smile. "Basics, brothers, basics. We don't know how big the Moon is. We don't know what it weighs, or what holds it up. We don't have magic powerful enough to reach it. You're all thinking like novices, trying to do it all in one crackling powerful ceremony of enchantment, whereas in fact we need spells and power to *reach* the Moon, and *study* it, and *learn* enough to tell us what to do next, and finally to *use* that magic to tap the Moon's power." His smile deepened. "There is nothing in the world today that is sufficiently sacred to do all that. Warlock,

you once called me a short-sighted fool. I will not call you short-sighted. Your daydream would be work for generations, if it could be done at all."

The Warlock was not pleased.

"What exactly are you gloating about? We had the big conference fifty years ago. The power existed, *then*.

But you and your group wanted to make maps."

Piranther's half-smile disappeared. His small black hand stroked the skin bag at his chest — and forces could be felt gathering.

"I know of a *mana* source," said the skull on the Warlock's shoulder.

Wavyhill saw that he had everyone's attention. "I thought I had better interrupt while we still had a conference. I wish I could give guarantees, but I can't. I may know of a living god, the last in the world. I'll lead you to it."

"I find this hard to believe," Piranther said slowly. "A remaining god? When even the dragons are nearly gone? When half the world's fishing industries are run by men, from boats, because the merpeople have died off?"

"It seems more believable when you know the details. I'll tell you the details, and I'll lead you to it," said Wavyhill. "But I want oaths sworn. To the best of your abilities, when we have gained sufficient *mana* for the spells to work, will each of you do your best to return me to my human form?"

Nobody hurried to answer.

"Remember, your oaths will be binding. A *geas* is more powerful than any natural law, in a high-*mana* environment. Well?"

"I had other projects in mind," Piranther said easily. "Your oath would claim too much of my time. Also, you have a much greater interest in the Warlock's project than any of us."

"Your interest isn't slight," said Wavyhill. "We who pull down the power of the Moon will rule the world."

"True enough. But why should you have a head start on the rest of us while we fulfill your *geas*? Swear us the same oath, Wavyhill. Then we can *all* scurry about for ways to put you back together again. Otherwise we'll wake to find you ruling us."

"Willingly," said Wavyhill, and he swore.

Piranther listened with his half-smile showing, while Mirandee and the Warlock and, reluctantly, Clubfoot swore Wavyhill's oath.

Then, "I will not swear," said Piranther. "Thus I presume you will not guide me?" He stood, lithely, and walked away. If he expected voices calling him back, there were none, and he walked away toward Prissthil.

"That means trouble," said Wavyhill.

"We can do it without him," said Clubfoot.

"You don't follow me," said Wavyhill. "I meant what I said. If we fail, there is no world. If we draw the power of the Moon, we rule the world. If Piranther follows us and learns what we learn, and if Piranther is there when we pull down the Moon or whatever, he's the only one of us who can concentrate purely on controlling it."

Clubfoot saw it now. "You and your stupid oath."

"He'll have serious trouble following us," said the Warlock.

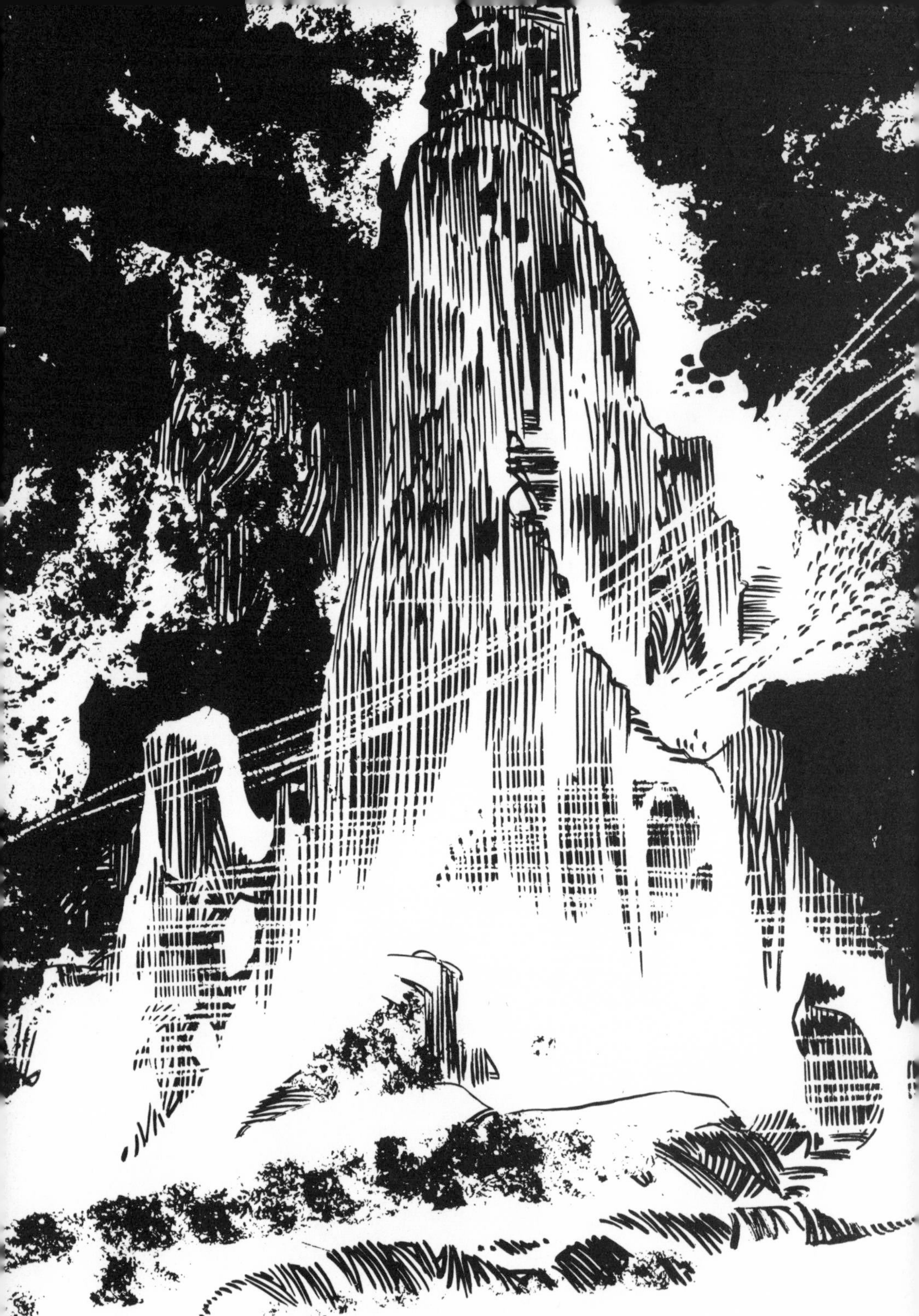

THE MOUNTAIN

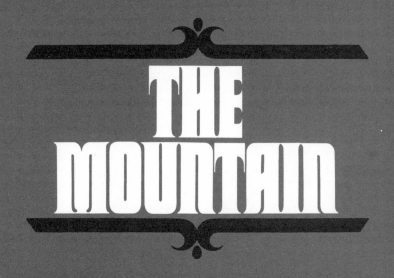

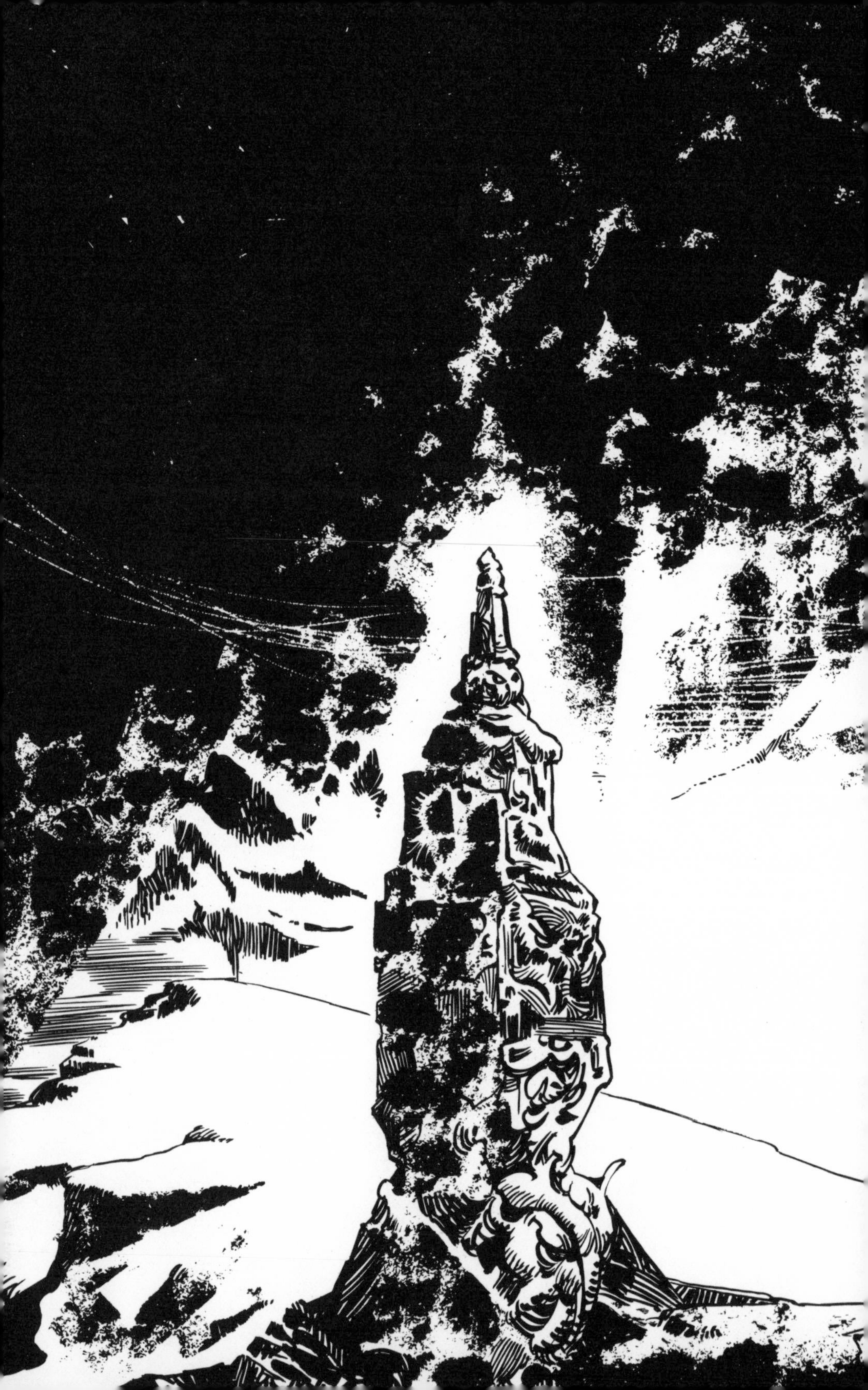

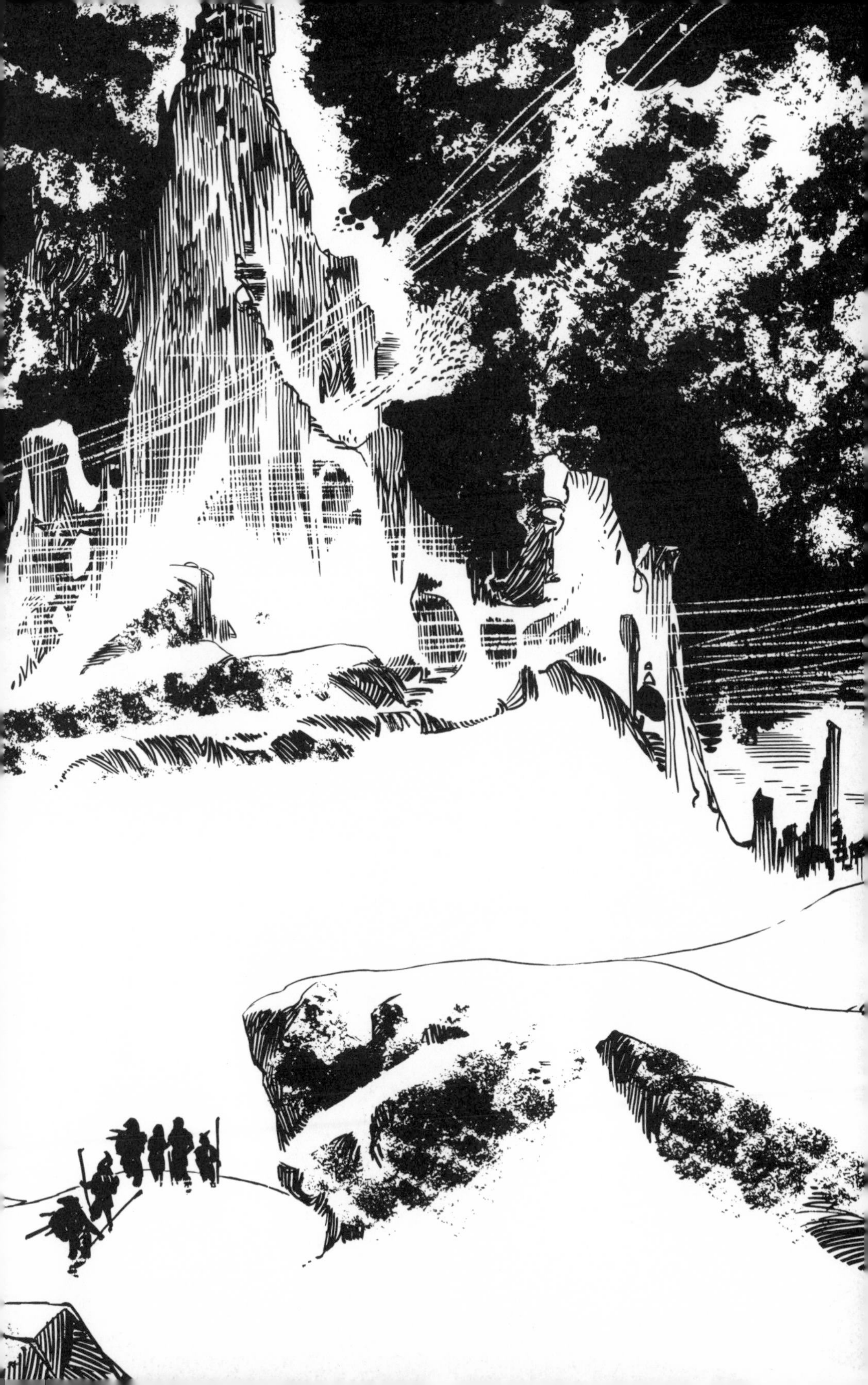

They climbed Mount Valhalla on foot: three magicians, two porters hired in Prissthil, Orolandes carrying a porter's load, and the skull of Wavyhill still moored to the Warlock's shoulder. Wavyhill's eyes had been replaced with rubies.

He had hired the porters, he had chosen their equipment, but Orolandes had no idea why he was going up a mountain. He had asked Wavyhill, "Is the last god at the peak, then?"

"Gear us for the peak," Wavyhill had told him, "and don't think too much. Piranther can read your mind. He'll be getting your surface thoughts until we can break you loose."

The porters were small, agile, cheerful men. They did better than Orolandes at teaching the magicians elementary climbing techniques. They showed neither awe of the magicians' power nor scorn for their clumsiness. To natives of Prissthil a magician was a fellow-professional, worthy of respect.

Clubfoot was a careful climber, little hampered by his twisted foot. But they were all aging, even Mirandee of the smooth pale skin and the white hair. On the first night they hurt everywhere. They couldn't eat. They moaned in their sleep. In the morning they were too tired and stiff to move, until hunger and the smell of breakfast brought them groaning from their blankets.

It was good for Orolandes' self-confidence, to see these powerful beings so far out of their element. He became marginally less afraid of them. But he wondered if they had the stamina to continue.

As the ascent grew steeper the packs grew lighter. Food was eaten. Heavy cloaks were taken from the packs and worn. But the air grew lean, and Orolandes and the porters panted as they climbed.

Not so the magicians. With altitude they seemed to

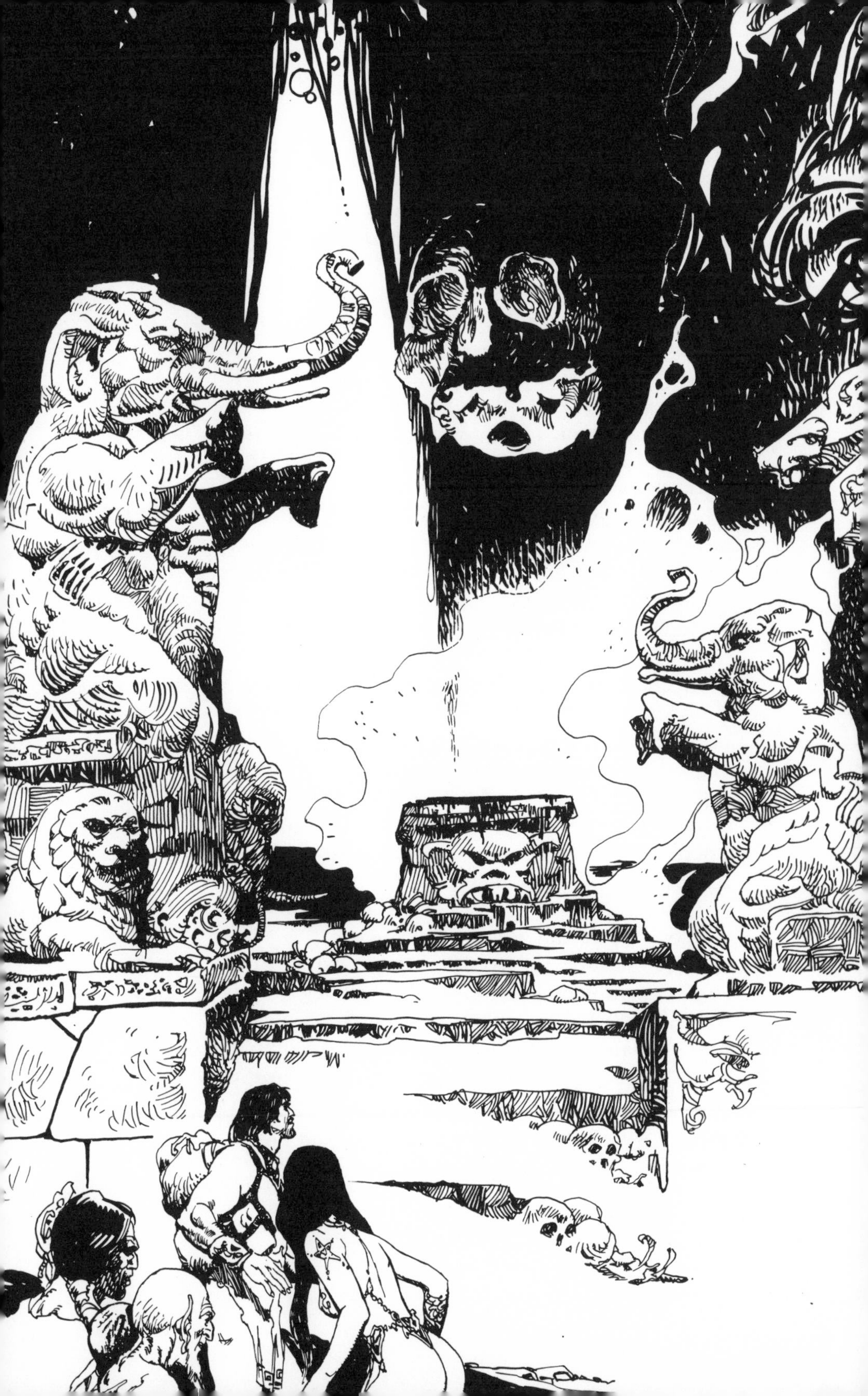

gain strength. Here above the frost line there were even times when the rich creamy fall of Mirandee's hair would darken momentarily, then grow white again.

It usually happened when they were passing one of the old fallen structures.

They had passed the first of these on the third day. No question about what it was. It was an altar, a broad slab of cut rock richly stained with old blood. "This was why the gods survived so long here," the Warlock told Orolandes. "Sacrifice in return for miracles. But when the gods' power waned in the lands below the mountain, the miracles weren't always granted. The natives didn't know why, of course. Eventually they stopped sacrificing."

Higher structures were stranger, and not built by men. They passed a cluster of polished spheres of assorted sizes, fallen in a heap in a patch of snow. They glowed by their own light: four big spheres banded in orange and white, one with a broad ring around it; three much smaller, one mottled ochre and one mottled blue-and-white and one shining white; and two, the smallest, the yellow-white of old bone. Further on was a peaked circular structure sitting on the ground. It looked like a discarded roof.

Though Orolandes was still the master climber, this was evidently magicians' territory.

There was no firewood on the third night. It was not needed. After they made camp the magicians — tired but cheerful, no longer bothered by strained muscles — sang songs in a ring around a sizeable boulder, until the boulder caught fire. Another song brought a unicorn to be slaughtered and butchered by the porters. Orolandes could only admire the porters' aplomb. They roasted the meat and boiled water for herb tea on a burning rock, as if they had been doing it all their lives.

After dinner, as they were basking around the fire, Clubfoot said to Mirandee, "You know that I've admired you for a long time. Will you be my wife while our mission lasts?"

Orolandes was jolted. Never would he have asked a woman such a question except in privacy. But Clubfoot did not expect to be turned down . . . and it showed in his face when Mirandee smiled and shook her head. "I gave up such things long ago," she said. "Being in love ruins my judgement. It takes my mind off what I'm doing, and I ruin spells. But I thank you."

On the morning of the fourth day they came on a flight of stairs leading up from the lip of a sheer cliff. Aided by climbing ropes, they crawled sideways along an icy slope to reach the stairs: broad slabs of unflawed marble that narrowed as they rose, but that rose out of sight into the clouds.

Placed on random steps were statues, human, half-human, not at all human. Orolandes tried to forget, and could not, a half-melted thing equipped with tentacles and broad clawed flippers and a single eye. But there was a hardwood statue of a handsome, smiling man that Orolandes found equally disturbing, and for no reason at all. Magic. Here where men could not live because they could not grow food, magic still lived.

Snow and ice covered the rocks to either side, but no ice had formed on the marble. The stairway rose past strange things. Here was something shattered, a hollow flowing shape that must have looked like a teardrop flowing upward before it broke at the base and toppled. There, a single tree bore a dozen kinds of ripe fruit; but it withered as the magicians came near, until nothing was left but a dry stick.

And there, a section seemed to have been bitten out

of the mountainside to leave a broad flat place. An arena, it was, where two sets of metal-and-leather armor stood facing each other in attack position, weapons raised, each piece of armor suspended in air. As the little party climbed past, the armor dropped in two heaps.

The Warlock stopped. "Orolandes, climb down there and get one of those swords."

"I gave up swords," said Orolandes.

"Maybe you won't use it, but you should have it.

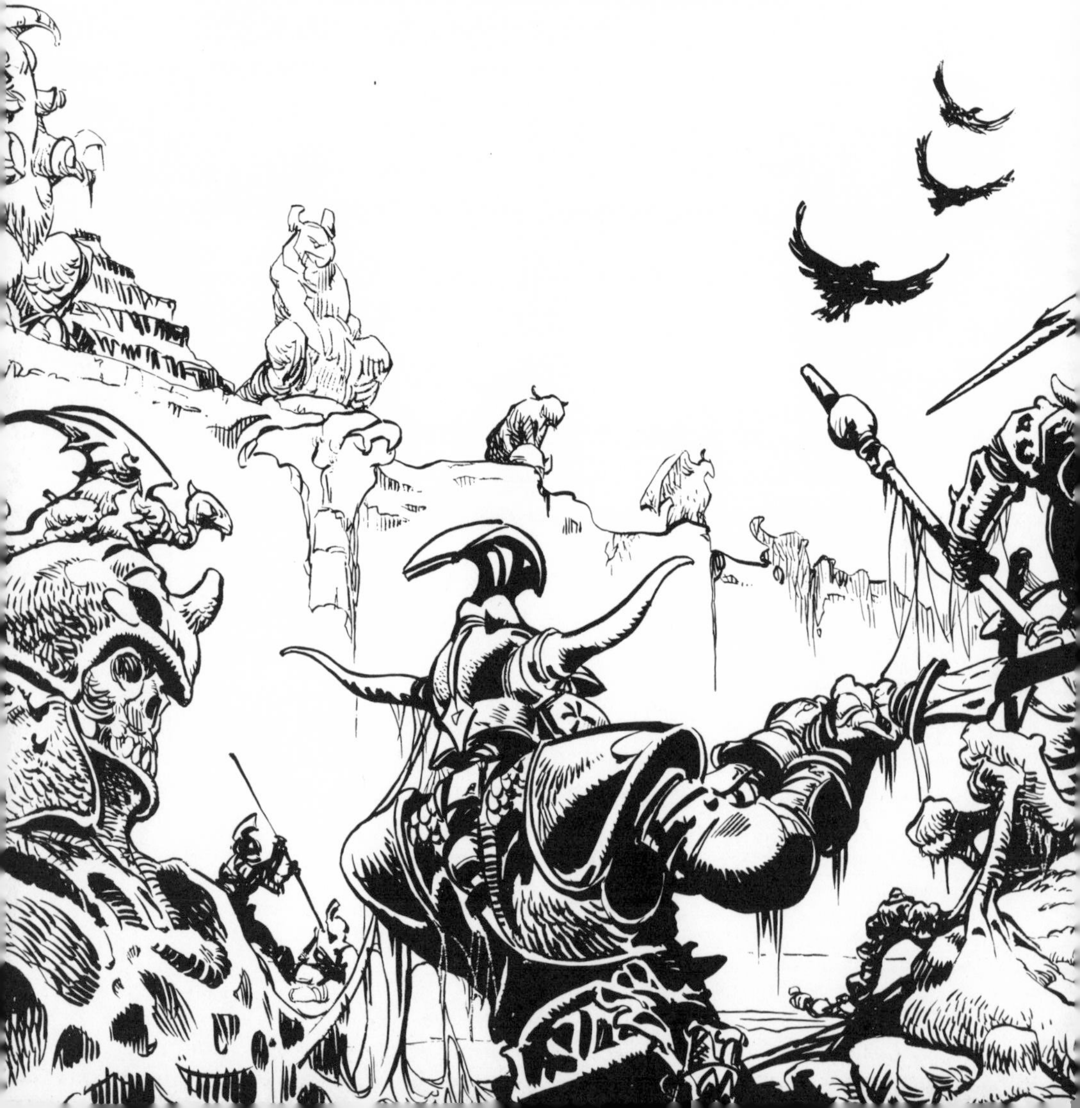

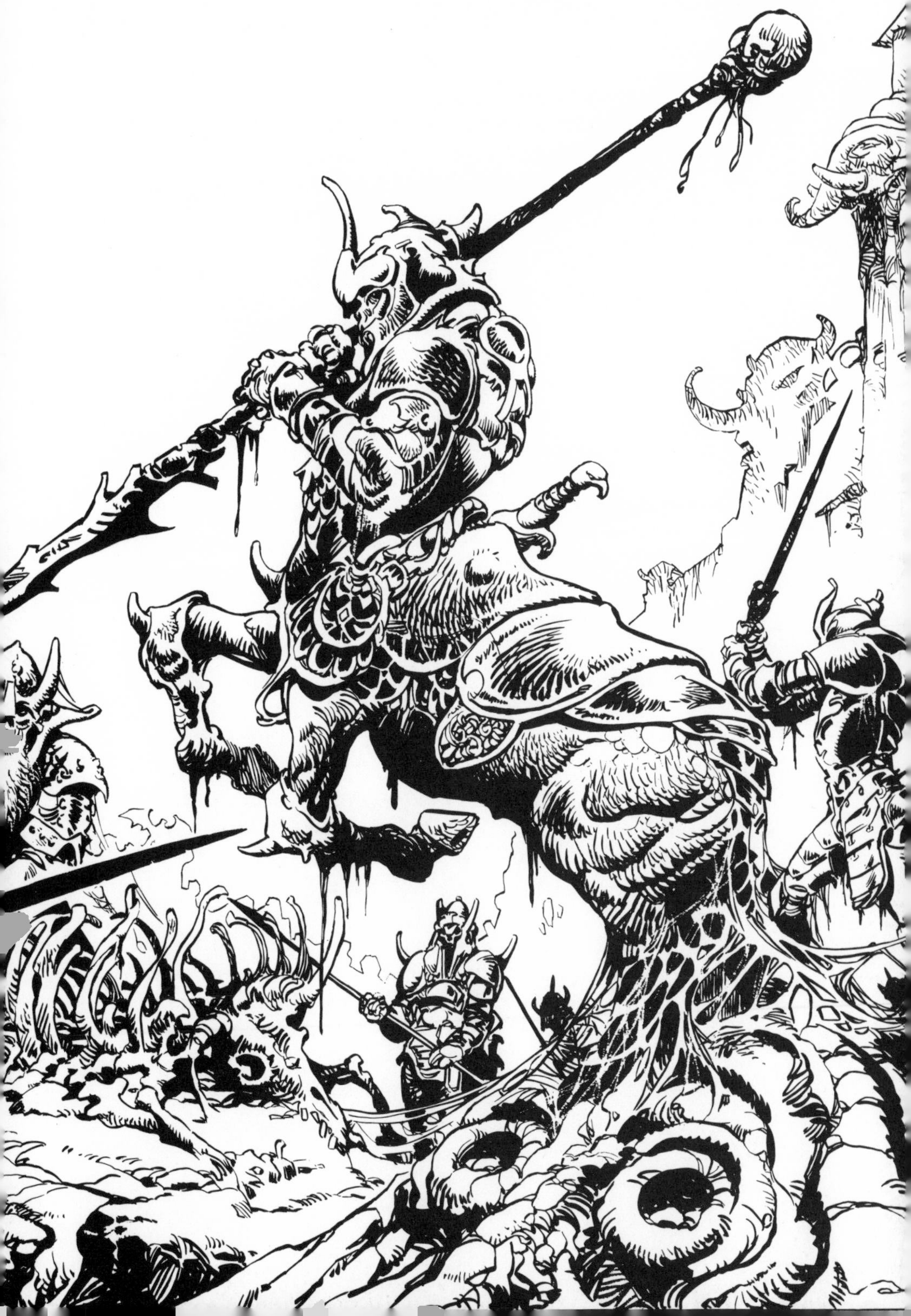

Magic can't do everything. None of us has ever used a sword . . . except Wavyhill."

The skull laughed on his shoulder. "Much good it did me, then and now. Get the sword, Greek."

Orolandes shucked his pack and clambered down and across the icy slope. At his approach the fallen armor stirred, then slumped. He chose the straight-bladed sword over the scimitar. It would fit his scabbard. It felt natural in his hand, but it roused unpleasant memories.

He was turning to go when he saw what had been hidden from the stair by a shoulder of rock.

Rows of thrones carved into the slanted rock face. Stands for the battle's audience. On each of the scores of thrones a wisp of fog shifted restlessly.

Orolandes retreated behind his sword. Nothing followed.

Now the marble stairs above them were hidden by cloud, the banner of cloud that always streamed from the mountain's peak.

The Warlock dismissed the porters, paying them in gold. Orolandes piled what was left in the packs into one pack, and they went on, up into the cloud.

The cold became wet cold. Ice crystals blew around them. The magicians below were half-hidden. Orolandes climbed with one hand on the rock wall. The other side was empty space.

The snow-fog thinned. They were climbing out of the cloud.

They emerged, and it was glorious. The cloud bank stretched away like a clean white landscape, under a brilliant sun and dark blue sky. The Warlock rubbed his hands in satisfaction. "We're here! Orolandes, let me get into that pack."

The others watched as he chose his tools. If the

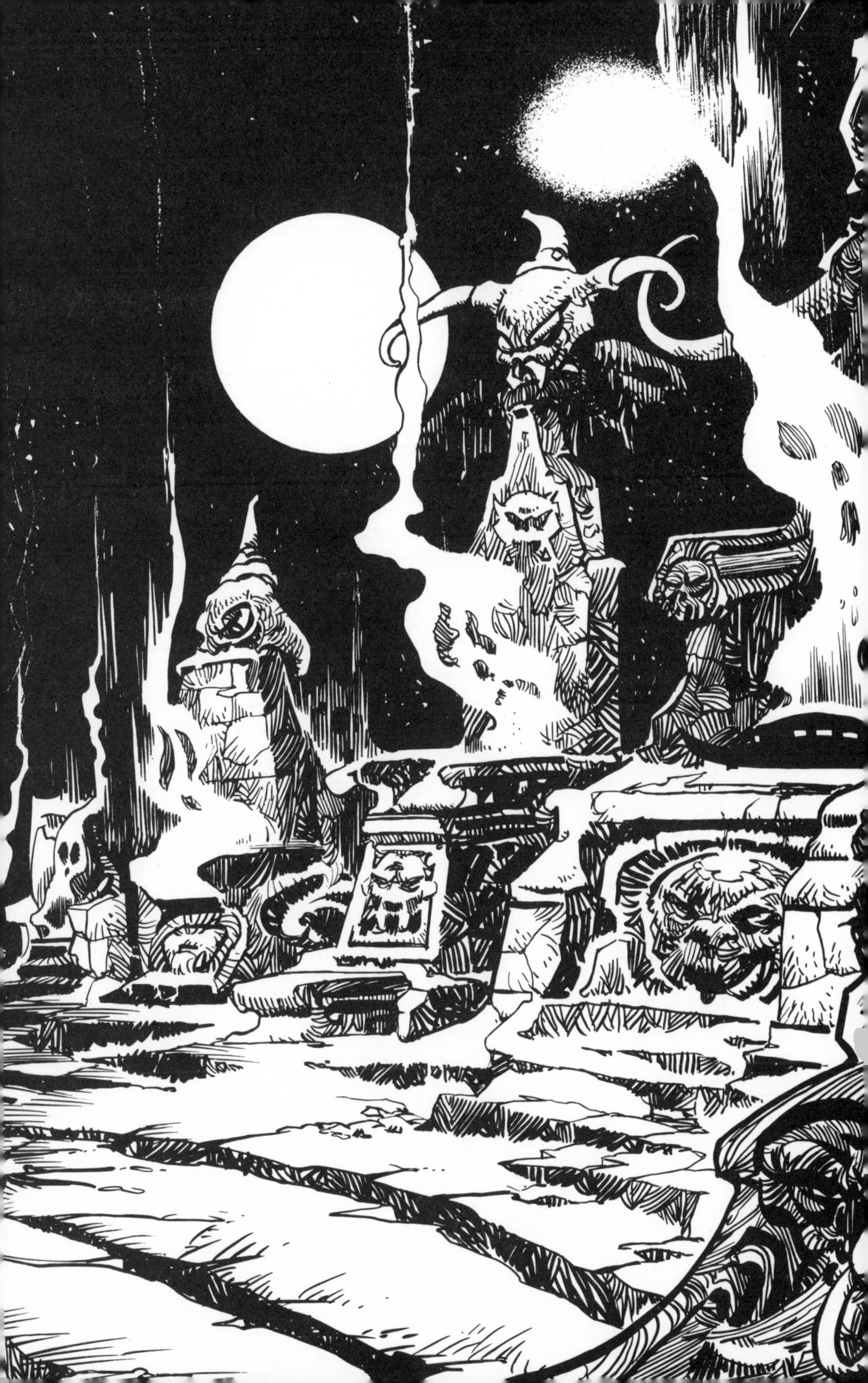

Warlock had told them what he was about, Orolandes hadn't heard it. He did not speculate. He waited to know what was expected of him.

The attitude came easily to him. He had risen through the ranks of the Greek army; he could follow orders. He had given orders, too, before Atlantis sank beneath him. Since then Orolandes had given over control of his own fate.

"Good," muttered the Warlock. He opened a wax-stoppered phial and poured dust into his hand and scattered it like seeds into the cloudscape. He sang words unfamiliar to Orolandes.

Mirandee and Clubfoot joined in, clear soprano and awkward bass, at chorus points that were not obvious. The song trailed off in harmony, and the Warlock scattered another handful of dust.

"All right. Better let me go first," he said. He stepped off the stairs into feathery emptiness.

He bounced gently. The cloud held him.

Clubfoot followed, in a ludicrous bouncing stride that sank him calves-deep into the fog. Mirandee walked out after him. They turned to look back at Orolandes.

Clubfoot started to choke. He sat down in the shifting white mist and bellowed with a laughter that threatened to strangle him. Mirandee fought it, then joined in in a silvery giggle. There was the not-quite-sound of Wavyhill's chortling.

The laughter seemed to fade, and the world went dim and blurry. Orolandes felt his knees turn to water. His jaw was sagging. He had climbed up through this cloud. It was cold and wet and without substance. It would not hold a feather from falling, let alone a man.

The witch's silver laughter burned him like acid. For the lack of the Warlock's laughter, for the Warlock's exasperated frown, Orolandes was grateful. When the

Warlock swept his arm in an impatient beckoning half-circle, Orolandes stepped out into space in a soldier's march.

His foot sank deep into what felt like feather bedding, and bounced. He was off balance at the second step, and the recoil threw him further off. He kicked out frantically. His leg sank deep and recoiled and threw him high. He landed on his side and bounced.

Mirandee watched with her hands covering her mouth. Clubfoot's laugh was a choking whimper now.

Orolandes got up slowly, damp all over. He waded rather than walked toward the magicians.

"Good enough. We don't have a lot of time," said the Warlock. "Take a little practice — we all need that — then go back for the pack."

CLOUDSCAPES

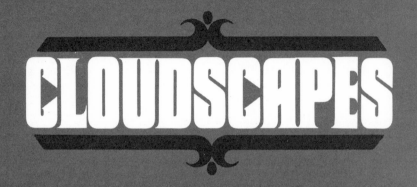

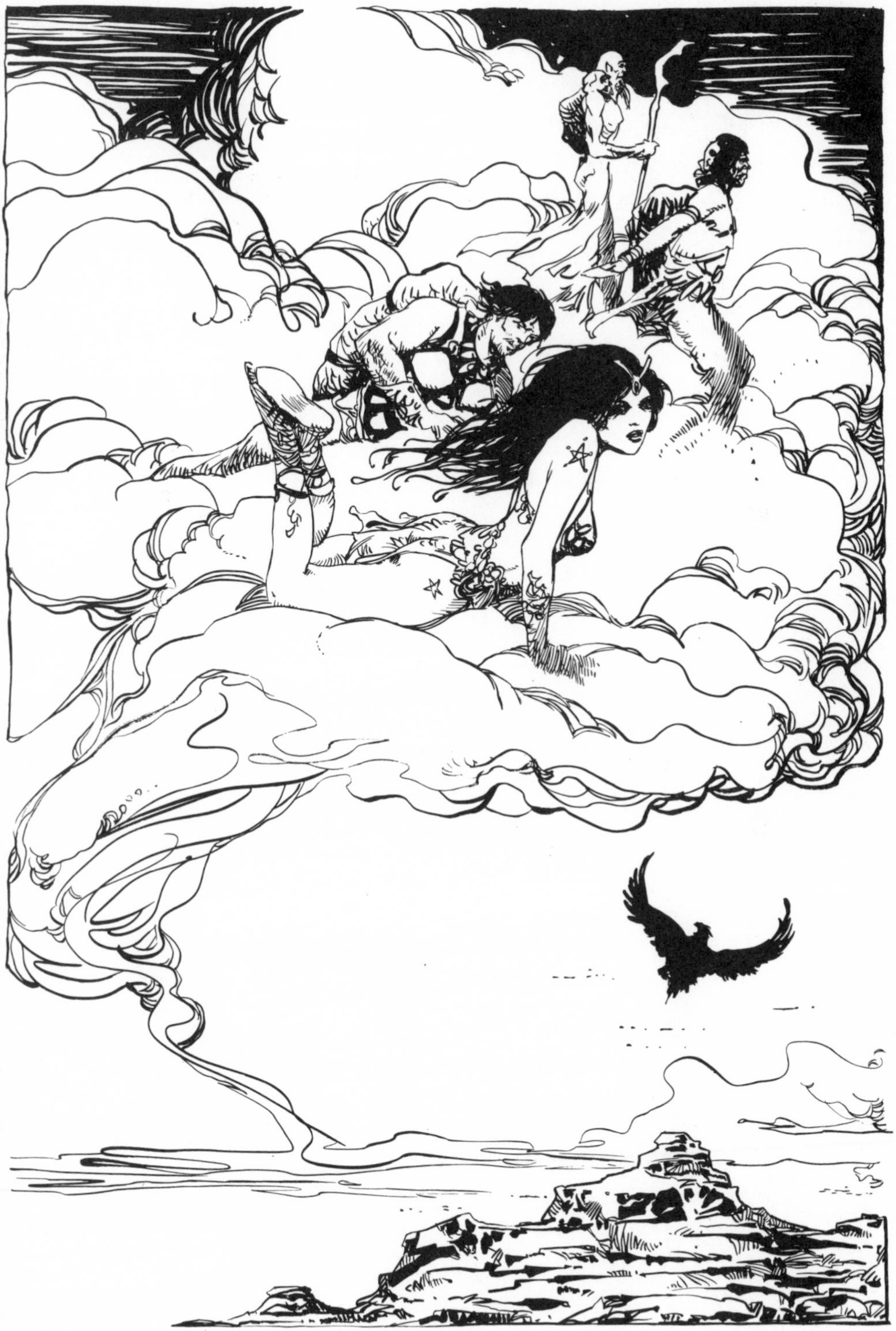

The layer of cloud stirred uneasily around them. It was not flat. There were knolls of billowing white that they had to circle round. It was like walking through a storehouse full of damp goose down. The cloud-stuff gave underfoot, and pulled as the foot came forward.

Orolandes found a stride that let him walk with the top-heavy pack, but it was hard on the legs. Half-exhausted and growing careless, he nearly walked into a hidden rift. He stared straight down through a feathery canyon at small drifting patches of farm. A tiny plume of dust led his eye to a moving speck, a barely visible horse and rider.

He turned left along the rift, while his heart thundered irregularly in his ears.

Clubfoot looked back. Mount Valhalla rose behind them, a mile or so higher than they'd climbed, blazing snow-white in the sunlight. "Far enough, I guess. Now, the crucial thing is to keep moving," he said, "because if the magic fails where we're standing it's all over. Luckily we don't have to do our own moving."

He helped Orolandes doff the pack. He rummaged through it and removed a pair of water-tumbled pebbles, a handful of clean snow, and a small pouch of grey powder. "Now, Kranthkorpool, would you be so kind as to tell us where we're going?"

"No need to coerce me," said Wavyhill. "We go east and north. To the northernmost point of the Alps."

"And we've got food for four days. Well, I guess we're in a hurry." Clubfoot began to make magic.

The Warlock did not take part. He knew that Clubfoot was a past master at weather magic. Instead he watched Mirandee's hair.

Yes, her youth had held well. She had the clear skin and unwrinkled brow of a serene thirty-year-old noblewoman. Her wealth of hair was now raven black, with a streak of pure white that ran from her brow all

the way back. As she helped Clubfoot sing the choruses, the white band thickened and thinned and thickened.

The Warlock spoke low to Orolandes. "If you see her hair turn sheer white, run like hell. You're overloaded with that pack. Just get to safety and let me get the others out." The Greek nodded.

Now the clouds stirred about them. The fitful breeze increased slightly, but not enough to account for the way the mountain was receding. Now the clouds to either side churned, fading or thickening at the edges. Through a sudden rift they watched the farmlands drift away.

"Down there they'll call this a hurricane. What they'll call us doesn't bear mentioning," Clubfoot chuckled. He walked back to where Orolandes was standing and settled himself in the luxurious softness of a cloud billow. In a lowered voice he said, "I've been wrestling with my conscience. May I tell you a story?"

Orolandes said, "All right." He saw that the others were beyond earshot.

"I'm a plainsman," said Clubfoot. "My master was a lean old man a lot like the Warlock, but darker, of course. He taught half a dozen kids at a time, and of course he was the tribe's medicine man. One day when I was about twelve, old White Eagle took us on a hike up the only mountain anywhere around.

"He took us up the easy side. There were clouds streaming away from the top. White Eagle did some singing and dancing, and then he had us walk out on the cloud. I ran out ahead of the rest. It looked like so much fun."

"Fun," Orolandes said without expression.

"Well, yes. I'd never been on a cloud. How was a plains kid to know clouds aren't solid?"

"You mean you never ... realised ..." Orolandes started laughing.

Clubfoot was laughing too. "I'd seen clouds, but way up in the sky. They looked solid enough. *I* didn't know why White Eagle was doing all that howling and stamping."

"And the next time you went for a stroll on a cloud — "

"*Oh*, no. White Eagle explained that. But it must have been a fine way to get rid of slow learners."

Mirandee was saying, "Do you really think Piranther can't follow us?"

"There's no way he can travel this fast on the ground," said the Warlock. "If he's in the clouds, we'll know it. Just as our weather pattern must be fairly obvious to him. Do you see any stable spots in this cloud canopy?"

"No . . . but there used to be other ways to fly."

The Warlock snorted. "Used to be, yes."

Mirandee seemed really worried. "I wonder if you aren't underestimating Piranther. Warlock, I had occasion to visit Australia not long ago."

"Mending fences for me?"

"If you like. I thought he might be ready to forget heated words long cooled. He wasn't." She gestured nervously. "Never mind that. I saw *power*. There are roc chicks in that place, baby birds eight feet tall, that breed as chicks and never grow up. Piranther's people raise them for the eggs! and let children ride on their backs! I watched apprentice magicians duel for sport, with adepts standing by to throw ward-spells. It was like stepping two hundred years into the past. I watched a castle shape itself out of solid rock — "

"And now all the castles are falling down, or so says Piranther. The *mana* can't be *that* high, not if the rocs have turned neotenous. Piranther can't be as powerful as all of us put together."

"He's their leader. The most powerful of them all."

The Warlock settled his back against a soft billow of cloud. "This place is paradise for a lazy man. Orolandes!" he called.

Orolandes and Clubfoot came chuckling about something. The swordsman let the Warlock put his hands on his head and mutter an ancient spell.

"That should break the link between you and Piranther. Now, Wavyhill, tell us about the last god."

Orolandes settled himself cross-legged. He felt no different . . . and he was never going to relax here, despite the infinity of feather bed. But he would not show it either.

"Roze-Kattee was male and female," said the skull on the Warlock's shoulder, "and his attributes were

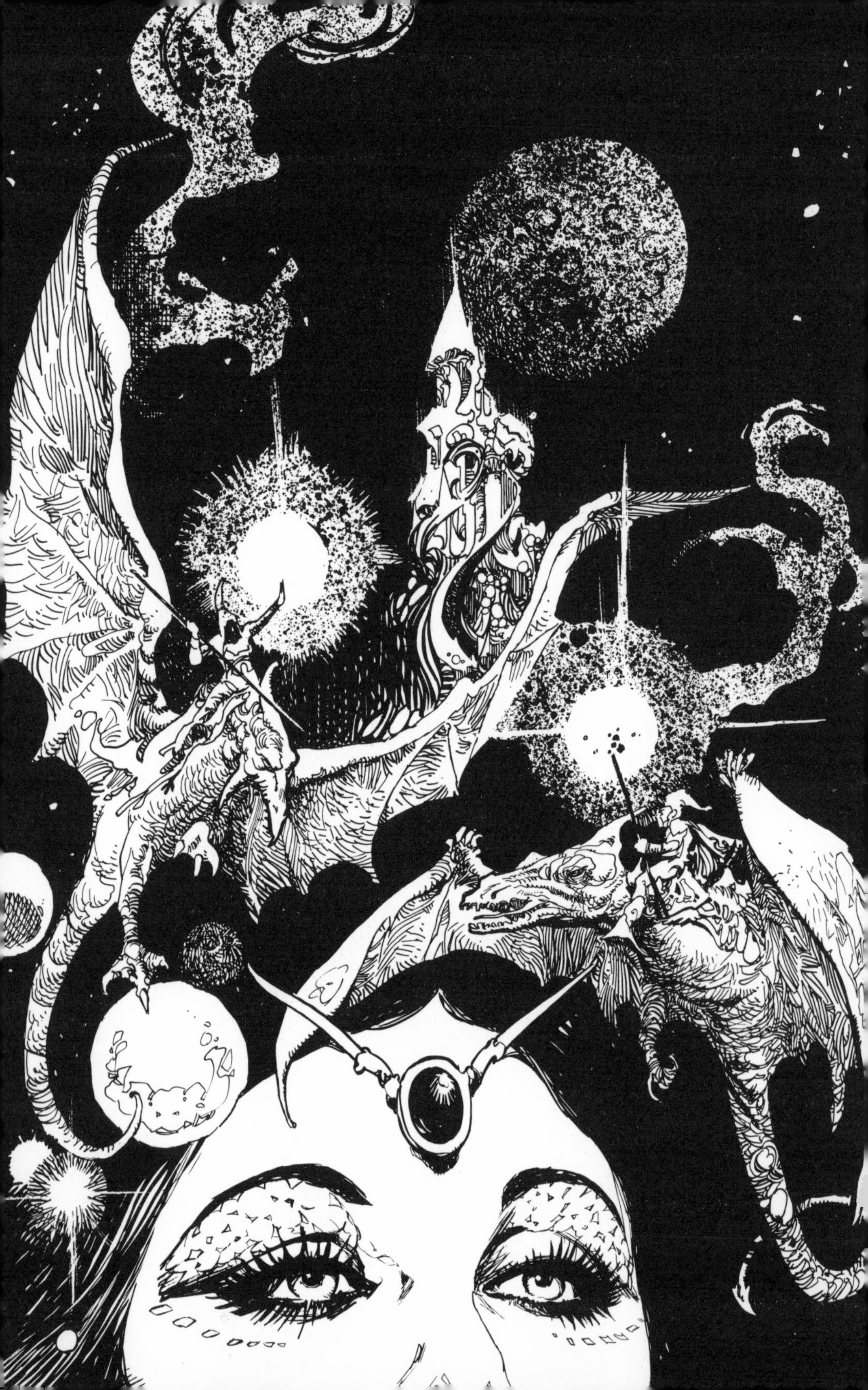

love and madness. He was god to the Frost Giants, way north of here, where we're going. He hasn't been heard of in half a thousand years, not since the Nordiks conquered the Frost Giants. But he's said to be dormant, not dead."

"Said by whom?" Mirandee asked. "The Frost Giants are nearly mythical."

"Oh, the Nordiks still have a few Frost Giant slaves. But the Frost Giants never talked about Roze-Kattee. All I've got is the old Nordik epic, the Hometaking Wars Cycle, which is certainly slanted and possibly garbled."

Mirandee was shaking her head. "I've heard other tales of sleeping gods."

"This one's different. Mirandee, when I was still an apprentice, my master Harper was interested in the Hometaking Wars. He didn't see how the Nordik gods beat the Frost Giant gods on their home ground. In fact they won every war except the last one."

"But we know that," the Warlock said. "The Nordik gods were destroyed when the Nordiks were driven out of the Fertile Crescent. They had no gods. So they fought with swords, and the Frost Giants used magic, and over three generations they used up the magic."

"Right, and the Nordiks came swarming in before the Frost Giants could learn swordsmanship. But Harper never learned about *mana* depletion. That was left to you, Warlock. You and your damned Wheel. Harper and I spent some time trying to learn why Roze-Kattee failed his and her people."

"Well?"

"It's an unusual story," said Wavyhill's skull. "According to the Hometaking War Cycle, the Frost Giants took it on themselves to protect their god, instead of the other way around. When the Nordiks beat their army, three of the Frost Giant hero-priests were taking

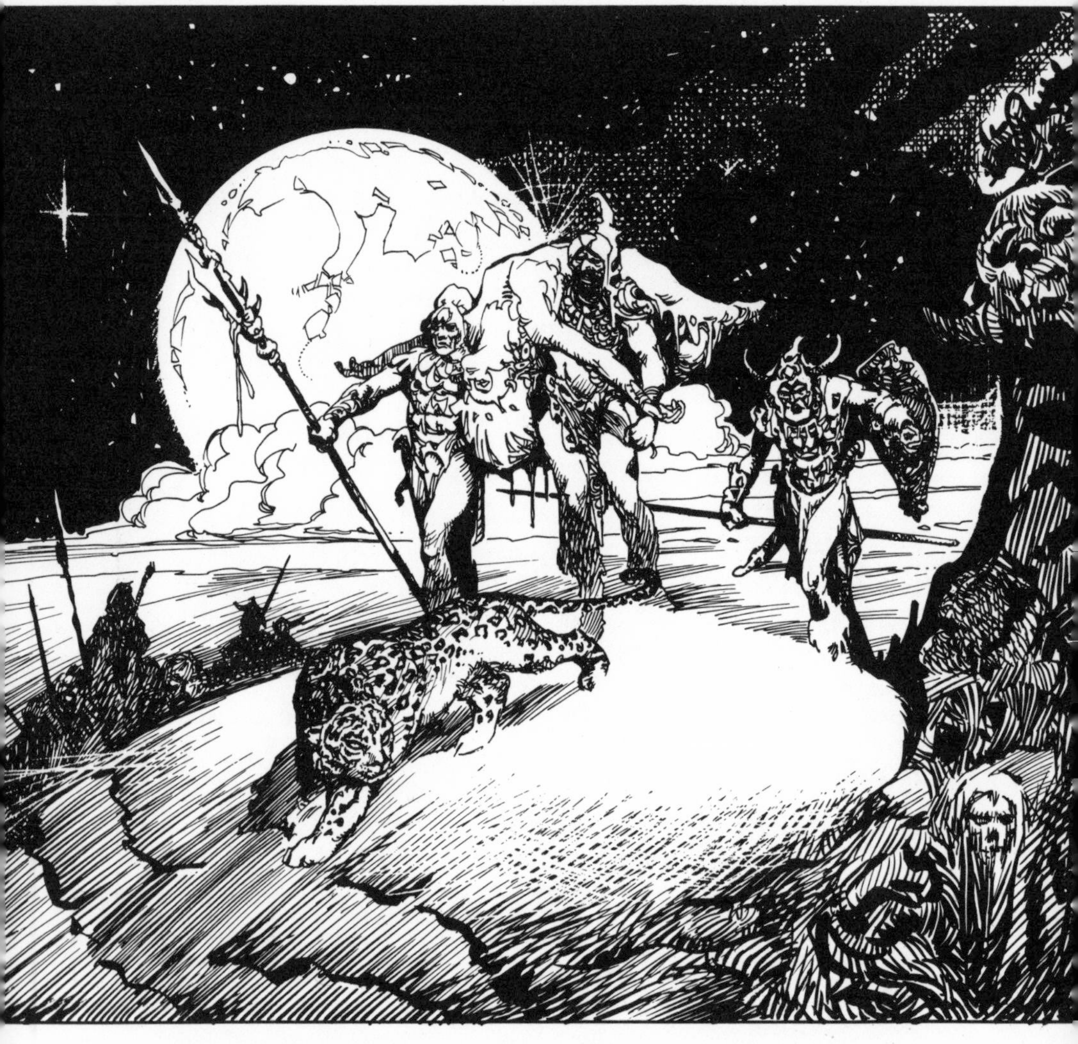

Roze-Kattee to safety. The god had lost all his power. He could barely move."

Clubfoot said, "That's not the kind of tale someone makes up about his enemies. But, look: why didn't the Nordiks just find out where the god was and dig him up?"

"Oh, they probably tortured a few Frost Giants. Maybe they got the wrong ones. Maybe the hero-priests migrated afterward, or cut their own throats. But maybe the Nordiks didn't try too hard. Why should they? Roze-Kattee did *not* save the Frost Giants. He went peacefully to sleep, somewhere. The poor time-weakened thing might be barely capable of killing any Nordik who found him."

The setting sun was still brilliant, under a higher cloud canopy that thickened as night came on. Mount Valhalla was a mere point of splendor far to the south-east. The clouds were soft against Orolandes' back. He was relaxing in spite of himself. It was all so unreal. Could one die in a dream?

"The magic went away and the gods died," the War-lock said. "What makes you think Roze-Kattee didn't? What would a Frost Giant consider a place of safety?"

"The cycle speaks of a 'god within a god'."

"You've already said Roze-Kattee had a dual na-ture."

"Harper and I found another interpretation. We have to stretch the definition a little, but . . . if we're right, then Roze-Kattee could still be alive. And the Nordiks had plenty of reason not to go looking for him."

"And we don't?"

"Time has passed. We know more than those bar-barians did. We have more to gain. And less to lose," said Wavyhill.

An upper cloud layer covered the stars. It had not been cold during the day, when sunlight was bounc-ing back at them from all of the reflecting white land-scape; but it was cold now. Orolandes lay in the dark, afraid to move, hoping that a rift would not form where he was lying. When the silence had become unbearable he said, "I wish I could see your hair."

Mirandee was nearby. She said, "Why, swordsman! Is that a compliment?" as if she didn't much care for it.

"If your hair turns white, we're about to fall."

After a time she said, "Magicians and swordsmen go together like foxes and rabbits. What are you doing among us?"

"Ask Wavyhill."

"But you didn't have to come."

"I did a terrible thing. I don't want to talk about it."

She laughed, invisible silver. "Tell me now, or I'll read your mind. Wavyhill said you had no defenses."

Out of the need to confess; out of his sure knowledge that the words would block his throat, rendering him mute, as he had been mute among the fishermen; out of some obscure need to be punished ... Orolandes said, "Go ahead. Piranther did."

There was a long dark silence. Then the witch woman said, "Oh, Orolandes!" in a voice filled with tears.

"I'm sorry."

"I know. I can see it. All charged up with the need to prove you were a man. Running into death waving that big damned sword. Crawling to kill the priests because they were killing your friends."

"Yes."

"I shouldn't have looked. That's usually the way of it. I find out I shouldn't have looked."

"I can't do anything about the people that drowned. Maybe I can help put the magic back in the world. What does Wavyhill have in mind for me? Do you know?"

"No. His mind's locked tight. I trust the Warlock, though. He'll control Wavyhill. Go to sleep, swordsman."

Little chance of that, Orolandes thought. He looked

toward where her voice had been. Was there a pale spot in the enveloping darkness? Long hair turning white?

"There's circulation in the clouds around and beneath us. The *mana* circulates. We won't fall. Go to sleep," she said.

Something touched his sword arm and he woke and rolled hard to the left and came up on his feet, sword in hand. It was black as the inside of a mole's belly. The footing was unfamiliar, treacherous. A woman's voice cried, "Don't!"

And he remembered.

"Mirandee? Did you wake me up?"

"You were having nightmares."

"Sorry. Was I screaming or something?"

"No. Just the nightmares. I wish I'd stayed out of your mind. I've never met anyone so unhappy."

"Can you blame me?" He sank down in unseen softness.

"Yes. You've killed a dozen men at least with your sword. Why be so upset about Atlantis? You killed more people, but it's the same thing, isn't it?"

"When I kill a man with a sword, it's because he's a soldier. He's trying to kill me."

"If you weren't on his territory — "

"Then he'd be on mine! If Greece didn't have an experienced army she'd be meat for the first wolf that came at the head of an experienced army. Magic didn't help the Frost Giants, and that was a long time ago. These days magic doesn't even slow down an army. So everyone needs armies."

"Wars of magic aren't much prettier. Get the Warlock to tell you about his duel with Wavyhill. Or get Wavyhill to tell you."

"All right." Orolandes was sliding back into sleep.

But the nightmare waited for him ...

The touch of her hand on his arm startled him. "You're still unhappy."

"I can't do anything about it."

"I can." Her hand moved up into his sleeve, caressingly.

He laughed. "Does the fox bed with the rabbit?"

"We are two human beings. How long has it been since you were with a woman?"

"A long time. I — " He hadn't wanted one. He would have thought: she is sharing love, all unknowing, with a man who murdered thousands. When the women of the fishing village came, he had turned them away without speaking, as if his voice alone would tell them what he was.

This Mirandee: he had never seen her as a woman. A figure of power she had been, a dangerous being who tolerated him, whose presence was necessary to his goal. Her mockery had hurt —

"Well, but you were so frightened! You should have seen yourself. I was frightened myself," she confessed.

"I've never been on a cloud before."

Her hand felt good on his arm. It was so cold and so lonely here. He found her face with his fingers. He traced the contours gently; he stroked her temples, and scratched her behind the ears, as he would with a Greek woman. They lay against each other now, but he felt only a double thickness of fur, and the cold of a mountain night on his face ... and then her cheek against his, barely warmer.

This was better than going back to the nightmare. And she knew; he was hiding nothing from her. She knew, yet she was willing to touch him. He was grateful.

He was half asleep when the lust rose up in him, burning. She sensed it. They began opening each other's robes, leaving them on to protect their backs against the cold. Even now his urgency was tempered by that uncharacteristic gratitude. He wanted to make her feel good.

He succeeded. In climax she was wildcat and python combined: her arms and legs clasped him

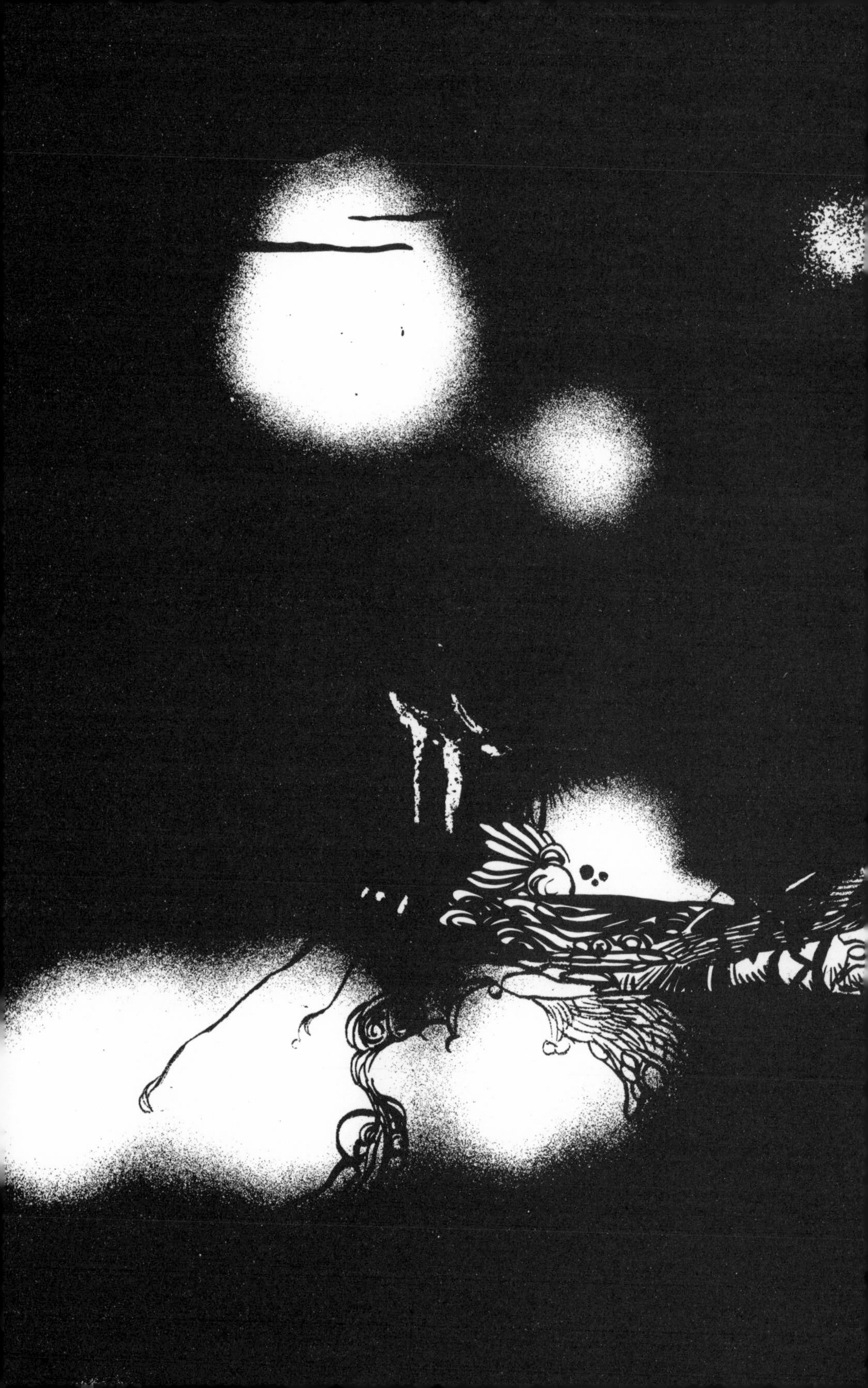

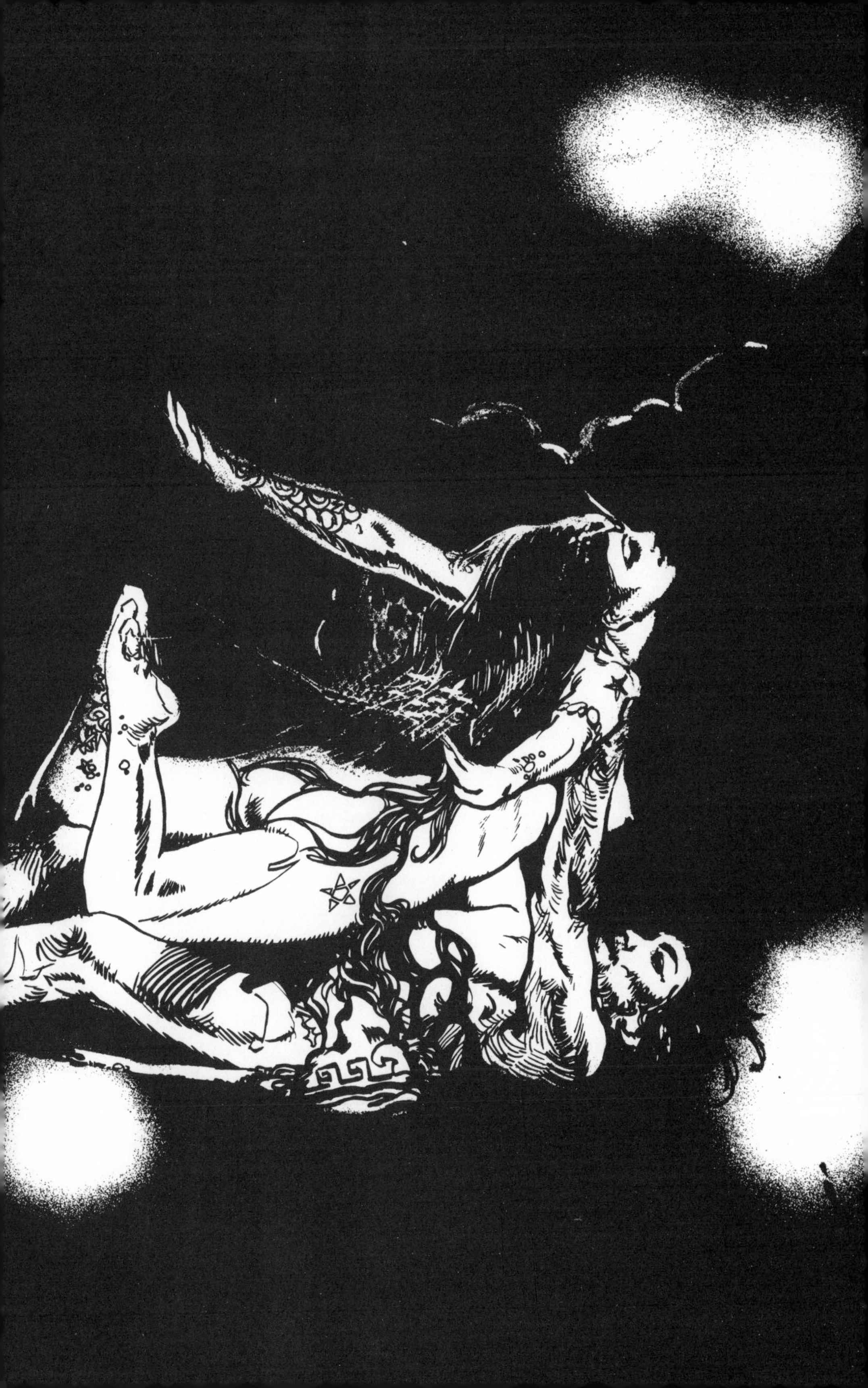

hard, pulling him into her.

They lay against each other with their robes over-lapping. Orolandes was pleased and proud.

A thought crossed his mind . . . and she laughed softly in his ear. "No, I did not falsify my pleasure to give you confidence. And no, you have not become a lover fit for a queen's harem. Your mind is in mine. I feel what you feel. It's . . . exciting."

Ruefully, but not very, he said, "What joy you would have had of another mind reader!"

She laughed more loudly. "If I were ready to die, yes, that would be a fine way to leave the world!"

"Oh."

"You've found your voice. When we shared love you didn't speak at all."

His mind flashed back to the fishing village.

"Never mind," she said quickly. "Shall we sleep like this?"

He nestled against her and slept without dreams.

The Warlock woke blinking in the sudden dawn. He was hungry. His face was sharply cold where it poked through the robes. The rest of him was warm and comfortable in the robes and the cloud-stuff.

Clubfoot was on his back, sprawled out like a starfish in the clouds, looking indecently comfortable. Wavyhill's skull was where the Warlock had mounted it last night, on a billowing knoll of cloud.

The Warlock called up to Wavyhill. "Anything?"

"Nothing attacked. The *mana* level stayed high. It's still high; all my senses, such as they are, are razor sharp. I think I heard something that wasn't just the wind, around midnight. I couldn't tell what. It might have been wings, big wings."

"Something big enough to carry Piranther?"

"I don't know. That's the trouble: you think some

beast has gone mythical, and then you get into a place of high magic and it swoops down at you. There might be all kinds of survivals, here in the sky ... Warlock, had you thought of probing the Moon from here?"

"No raw materials. No food sources either." The Warlock grinned. "That might not bother you, but you can't work alone."

"Right. Someone has to make the gestures."

During the night much of the cloudscape had melted away. The mass they still occupied was pushing upward in the center. For some hours it must have blocked Wavyhill's view forward.

Wavyhill asked, "Are you sure we've lost Piranther?"

"I ... no."

"All right. Neither am I."

"I don't see how he could be following us. But that's no guarantee at all. Piranther and his people have had most of fifty years to explore the South Land Mass. What could he have found in the way of talismans?"

"Another Fistfall?"

"Or more than one. He could be pacing us on dragonback." The sky burned deep blue, nearly cloudless, but the Warlock said, "Behind that one cloud, maybe, watching us. I was overconfident."

"Did you have a choice? Relax. This is a fun way to travel. By the way, there has been another development. Tiptoe around this knob of cloud and you'll see."

Tiptoe? The clumsiest giant would not make an audible footfall here. The Warlock waded around, and saw Mirandee and Orolandes wrapped in each other's arms in the cloud-shadow.

Perhaps he lied, to Wavyhill or to himself. "Good. I was afraid they would't get along."

The air mass rushed steadily north and east. The

center continued to push upward. By noon they were high on the slope of a billowing mountain, a storm thunderhead.

Clubfoot trekked up to the peak. "It's steeper on the forward face," he reported when he came back. "I don't like the footing much, but the view is terrific. Wavyhill, let's set you up there as lookout."

"Lookout and figurehead. Why not?"

In the end they stayed up there, Clubfoot and Wavyhill and the Warlock. Orolandes and Mirandee declined to join them.

It was a heady view. The crackle of lightning sounded constantly from underneath them. Flights of birds passed far away, flying south. Once an eagle came screaming down to challenge their invasion of its territory. That was worrying. They had nothing to throw at the bird, and any magic might melt the cloud beneath them. Fortunately the eagle saw the size of them and reconsidered.

Wavyhill said, "We might be the last human beings ever to see this, for thousands of years, maybe forever."

They were passing over an endless forest. To their right the cloud-shadow brushed the treetops; on the left a behemoth waded through crackling tree trunks, stopped, looked up at them with intelligent eyes. The cloudscape sloped steeply down from here, dazzling white, with shadowed valleys and rifts in it.

"We couldn't ask for a better vantage point," said the Warlock. "Or more comfortable seating." And he glanced at Clubfoot. "What's wrong with you? You look like your last friend just died."

"Orolandes is a fine young man," Clubfoot stated. "He is brave and loyal, and unlike many swordsmen, he has a conscience. Bearing all that in mind, would you tell me what the hell Mirandee sees in that bloody-handed mundane?"

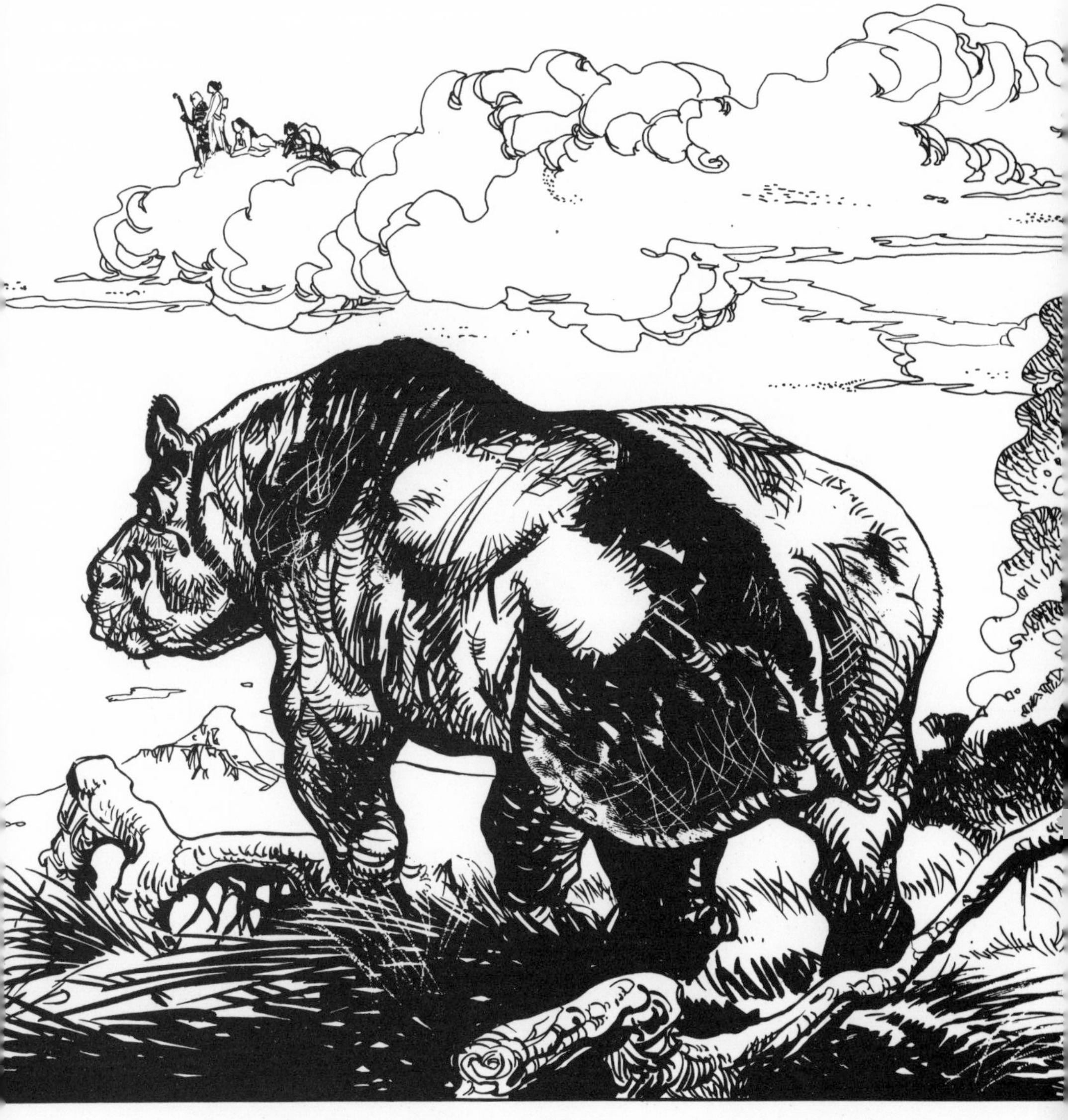

"You could ask Mirandee."

"I'd rather not."

"Would it help if I told you why Mirandee turned down your offer? I think she was being polite. To me.

We shared a bed once. She didn't want to remind me of what I've lost."

"All right. That was nice of her. But *why* — "

"Nobody can tell you." The Warlock looked at him. "I'd have thought you were too old for this kind of acidic jealousy."

"So would I," said Clubfoot.

At sunset the winds around the peak turned chilly. The two magicians climbed down the back slope of the thunderhead. The cloud surface was uneasy, in constant slow-flowing motion. They ate their cold rations and went to sleep.

But Wavyhill remained on the peak, on duty.

The third day was very like the second. Orolandes and Mirandee kept their own company, finding privacy in one of the shadowed valleys well aft of the thunderhead peak. Clubfoot and the Warlock lolled on the peak.

Clubfoot seemed to have come to terms with himself. He had been stiffly polite to Mirandee at breakfast, but here he could relax. "This is the way to travel. We should have gone to Prissthil this way, Warlock."

The Warlock chuckled. "That would have been nice, wouldn't it? We couldn't. No mountains to climb near Warlock's Cave. And the only place to get off would have been high on Mount Valhalla. Without porters. Come to that, we'll have a problem when we get to where we're going. Just where are we going, Wavyhill?"

"It'll be part of a mountain range, and our weather magic should work," said Wavyhill, "unless I'm wrong from the start. At this speed we'll get there late tomorrow. We will have to do some climbing."

Clubfoot shifted in the cloud-stuff. "So we'll rest up for it."

Wavyhill studied him. "Comfortable, isn't it? You complacent troll, you. You've all been sleeping like the dead. And Mirandee and the swordsman, I guess they earned it, mating like mad minks all day. I wish I could *sleep!*"

Clubfoot's anger left him as suddenly as it had come. "We could block your senses."

"It's not the same. It's not the same as sleeping, or blinking, or — or crying. I want *eyelids.*"

"Let's try something," said Clubfoot.

They tied a line to his jawbone, for a marker, and pushed Wavyhill a foot deep into cloud. They pulled him up a minute later, and then half an hour later. He said he was comfortable. It was not like sleeping, Wavyhill said, but it was like resting with his eyes closed.

They left him there until sunset.

In a shadowed valley, enclosed in cottony wisps of fog that resisted motion, Orolandes lay with his cheek on Mirandee's belly. The sunlight filtered through the cloud walls to bathe them in pearly light.

"Love and madness," he mused. "They go together, don't they?"

"You feel your sanity returning?"

"Why, no, not at all."

"Good." She chuckled. The flat abdominal muscles jumped pleasantly under his ear.

"I wonder," he said. "What makes this Roze-Kattee a god of love and madness? The gods came before men, didn't they? Did gods fall in love? and go mad?"

Troubled, she shifted position. "Good question. We'll have to know the answers before we do anything drastic. I'd guess that one day an anonymous god looked around itself and decided it would die without worship. There were men around. What did they need that Roze-Kattee could supply? Some gods were more versatile than others. Roze-Kattee probably wasn't."

"What would a god of love and madness *do?*"

"Oh . . . bestow madness on enemies. Ward it from friends. Love? Hmmm."

"The same thing? Make the Frost Giants' enemies love them?"

"Why not? And arrange good political alliances by fiddling with the emotions of the king or queen. Priests learn to be practical, if their gods don't."

"Do you think this god will fight us?"

She shifted again. "It needs us as much as we need it. We'll know better when we see this dormant god." Her long fingernails tickled his chest hairs. "Don't think about it now. Think about sharing love on a cloud. Few mundanes have that chance."

"It does take practice."

"We've had practice."

"I'm the only fighter among you. Magicians wouldn't break their backs to protect a swordsman."

"But I would."

In the night something woke the Warlock. He stirred in seductive comfort while his eyes searched the vivid starscape. Nothing, only stars . . . He was dropping off to sleep when it came again: a surging beneath him, like a cloud-muffled *bump.*

Clubfoot's sleepy voice said, "What?"

"Don't know."

There was a more emphatic *bump.*

Orolandes felt it too: a surging beneath him. He stirred and felt momentary panic.

"Cloud. You're on a cloud," Mirandee said reassuringly. Her eyes were inches away; her breath tickled his growing beard.

"All right. But what was that — "

The cloud surged again.

Orolandes ran his fingers through her hair — it was raven black by starlight — rolled away and stood up. The others would be around the side of the puffy thunderhead peak. He walked that way, aware that Mirandee was following him.

Clubfoot and the Warlock were on their feet. Clubfoot called, "Did you see anything?"

"No, but I felt — "

Beyond the two sorcerers, beyond the edge of the cloudscape, a shadow rose up and blotted the stars. Starlight reflected faintly from huge wide-set eyes.

Mirandee was behind him, her hand on his hip.

"Don't make magic," the Warlock called. "Not yet. It's a roc."

The great bird was treading air, holding itself in position with an occasional flap of its wings. It cocked first one eye, then the other, to study the people on the cloud. Then it spoke to them in a basso profundo thunderclap.

"CAW!"

"Caw yourself!" Orolandes snarled, and he stamped toward it. His sword was longer than the bird's beak, he thought. It would reach an eye. This would be a wild way to die. But Mirandee would be safe, if he could put out an eye.

"CAW!" bellowed the bird. Its wings rose and snapped down.

A hurricane gust threw Orolandes backward. He curled protectively around the sword blade, somersaulted twice and came up crouched. Another blast beat straight down on his head and shoulders.

The bird was overhead, stooping down on Mirandee.

Orolandes tried to run toward her. The cloud-stuff

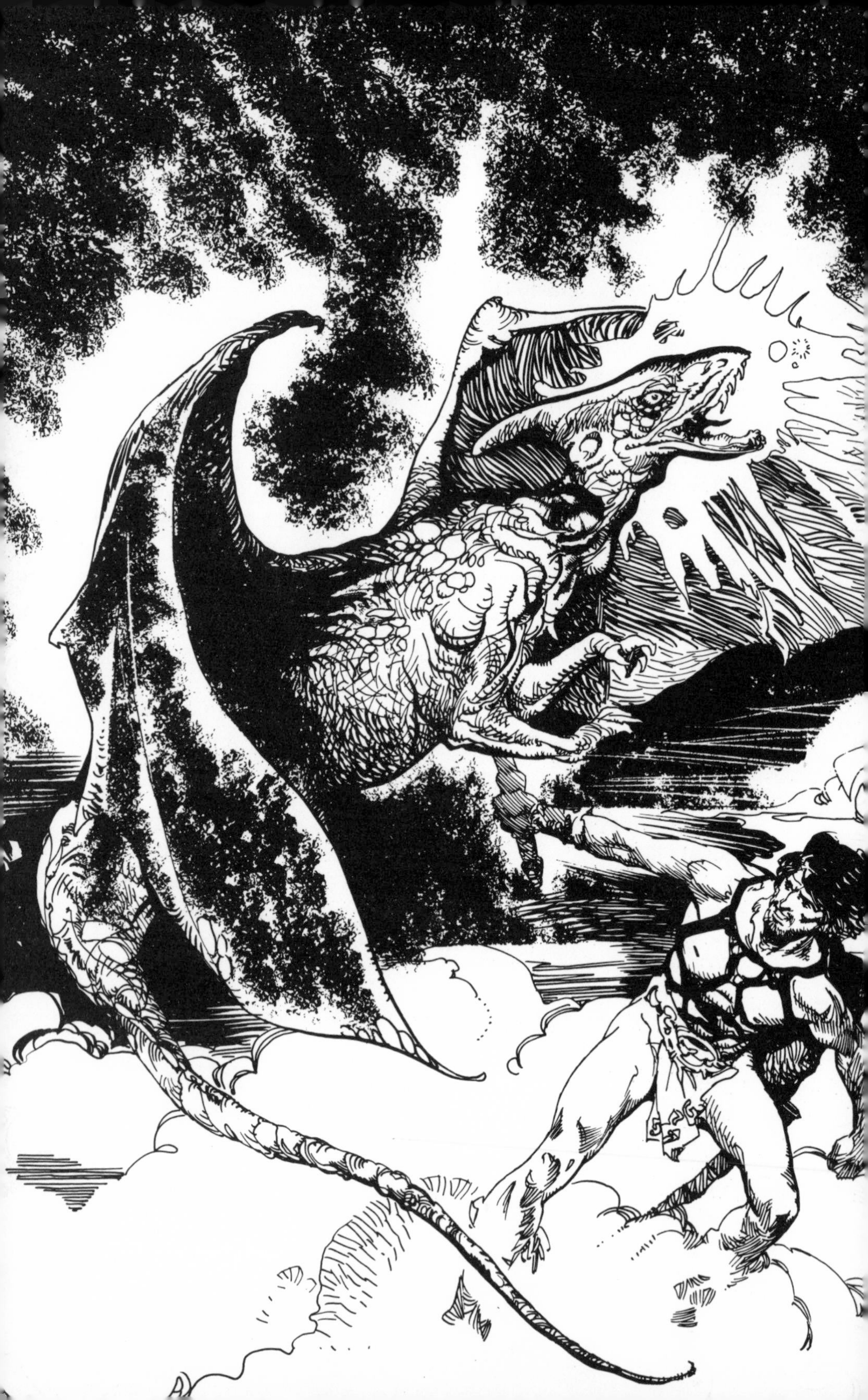

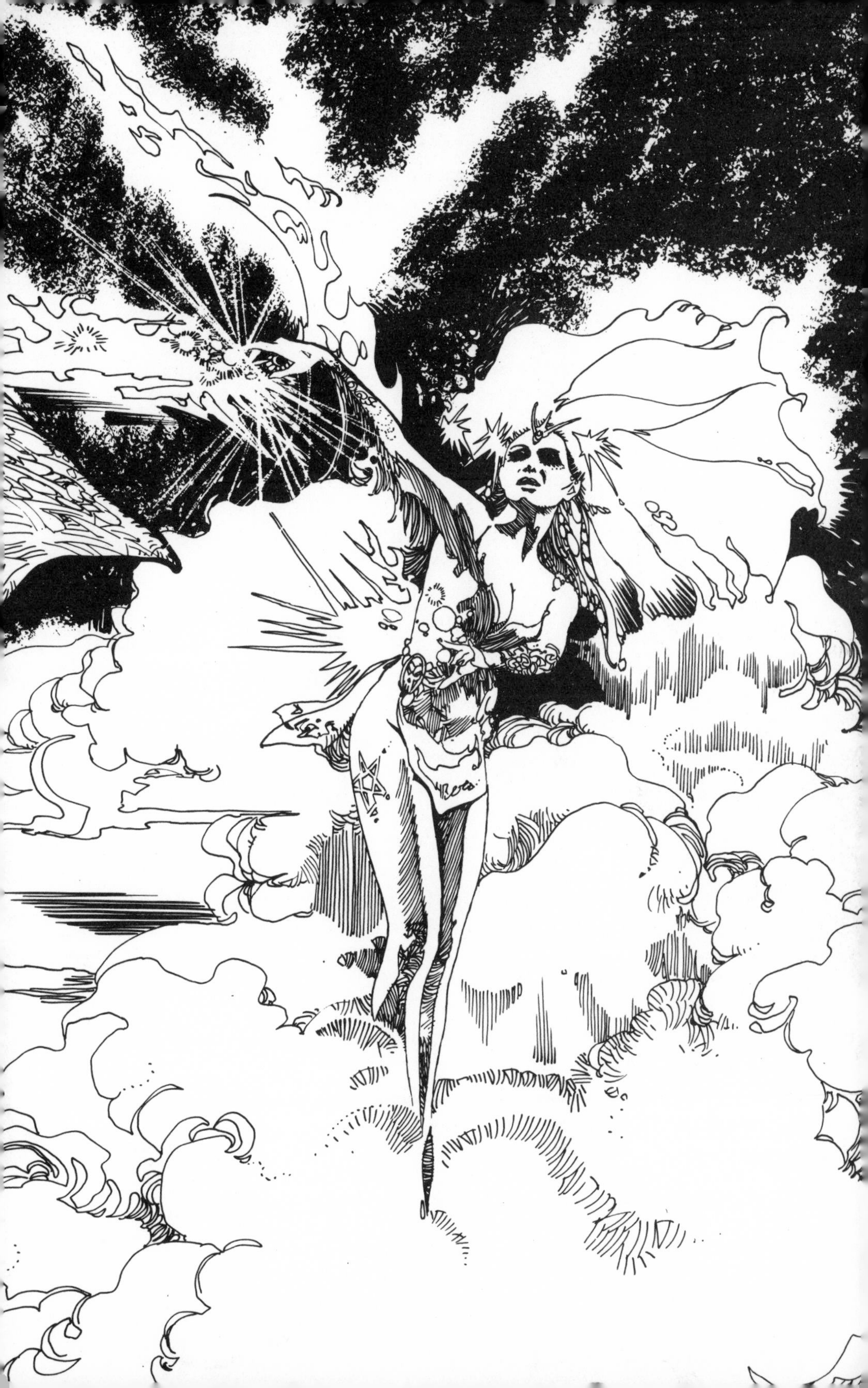

tangled his feet, slowing him.

Mirandee shouted something complex in nonsense syllables.

Soft blue radiance jumped between her outspread arms and the bird's descending beak. Her hair flashed white, and she dropped.

Orolandes howled.

The bird fluttered ineffectually and fell into the cloudscape in a disorganized tangle.

Orolandes attacked. His blade's edge buried itself in feathers. He set his feet, yelled and slashed again at the neck. He cut only feathers.

The bird's wings stirred feebly. It lifted its head with great effort, said, "CAW?" and died.

Mirandee cried, "Help!"

Her hair was a black cloud spilled across white. She was buried to the armpits. "I stole its power. Gods, I feel all charged up! Lucky I remembered that vampire spell or I'd be trying to fly myself." She was babbling in the shock of her brush with death. "Clubfoot, can you get me out of here?"

Orolandes went to her, treading carefully, knee-deep in viscous cloud. He lifted her by the elbows, pulled her out of the pit and set her down.

"Oh! Thank you. That vampire spell, old Santer taught it to me a hundred years ago, and I just knew I'd never use it. I thought I'd forgotten it. It wouldn't even work anymore, most places. Oh, 'Landes, I was so *scared*."

Clubfoot said, "You sucked that bird dry, all right. Look."

The bird was deep in cloud and sinking deeper. As they watched it vanished under the surface.

"We can't stay here," said Clubfoot. "We don't want anyone walking into that patch. It wouldn't hold a feather, and you can't tell it from the rest of the cloud."

They moved far around the steeper northern face of the travelling storm.

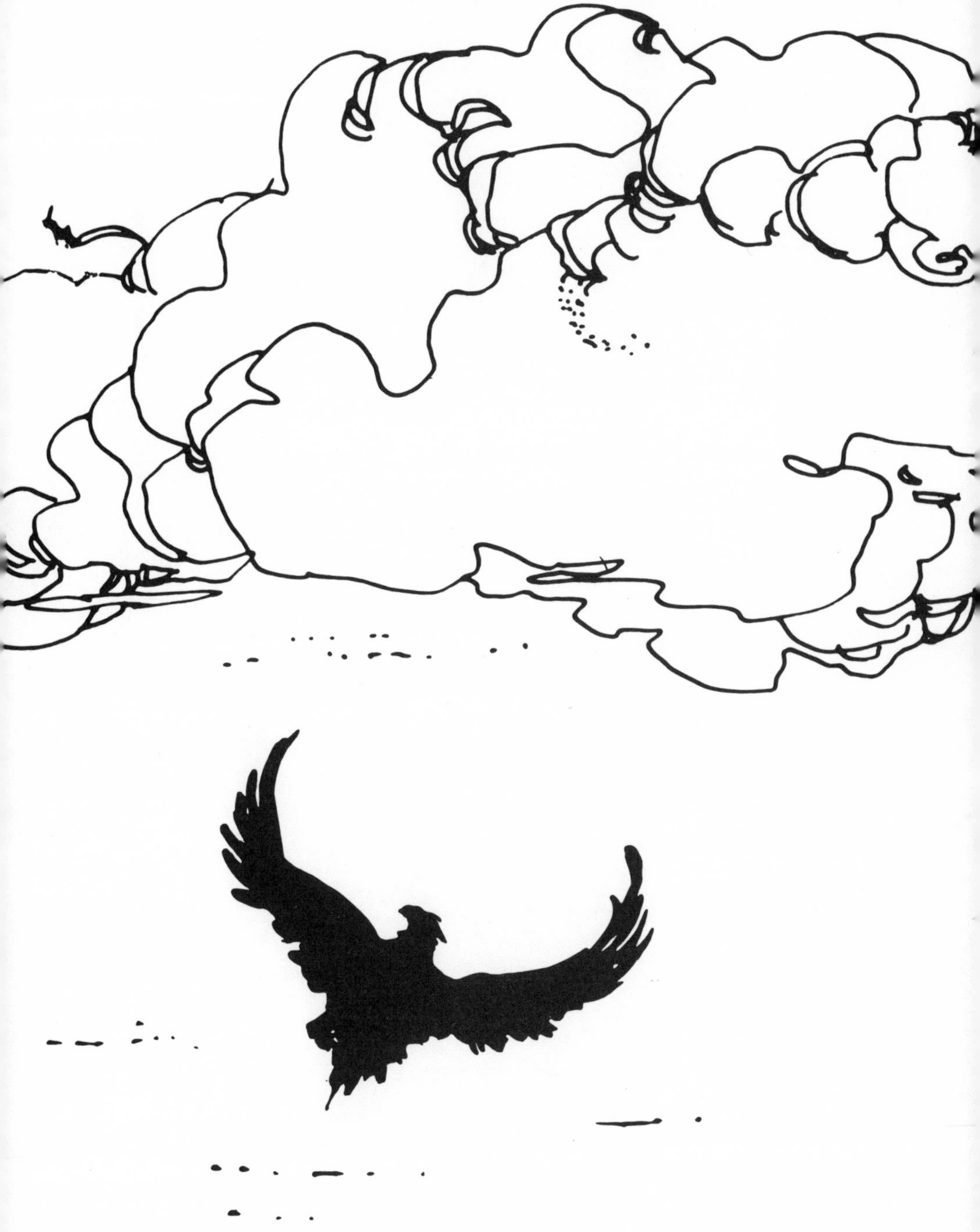

THE NORDIKS

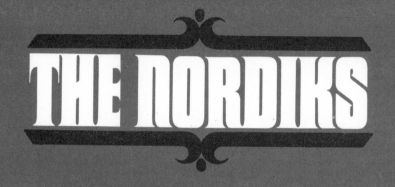

On the third morning black-and-white mountains reared their tremendous peaks to east and north. "Aim for the northernmost peak in the range," Wavyhill ordered.

Clubfoot began his weather magic. The Warlock pulled a band of silver from his upper arm and peered through it for a time. One distant rounded peak glowed a faint blue-white. "That's it. There's magic in that mountain," he said. "Wavyhill ..."

"Well?"

Slowly the Warlock said, "I'm only just starting to grasp the *audacity* of what we're doing. I never tried anything this big, even when I was young."

"What have we got to lose?" Wavyhill chuckled.

"I wish you'd stop saying that. Clubfoot, how are you doing?"

"Having some trouble."

The cloudscape drifted east. Clubfoot continued to try to swing them north. By noon the clouds were sweeping across the foothills, and surging like a sluggish sea. It was no use trying to stand. Even Clubfoot gave up the effort.

At first it wasn't bad, riding a continual earthquake on an infinity of damp featherbed. Then Orolandes grew seasick. Twice in his life he had ridden out a storm aboard a warship; but in a way this was worse. They were trying to steer the storm itself. Clubfoot wore a grim look Orolandes didn't like at all. Sections of cloudscape roiled into sudden ridges and hills; others tore away and drifted off in white puffs. Once the limping magician tried to stand and gesture, and a hill of cloud-stuff surged up under him and sent him spinning downslope. After that he stayed down.

The spell-hardened cloud deformed like taffy as it surged against the dark mountain slopes. Orolandes clenched his teeth against the tumbling of his belly.

Ships didn't do that! He was flat on the cloud now, like all the others, with his arms and legs spread wide.

The cloudscape slid up the mountain face; slowed; and finally, balked from crossing the range, the mass slid north instead. The ride became less chaotic. Orolandes began to relax.

"At least we're going in the right direction," Clubfoot muttered. He stood up. "Now let's see if I can — " And he stopped, astonished. He was hip deep in cloud.

And Orolandes was sinking deeper, deeper in cloud. He couldn't see the others.

Clubfoot bellowed, "Stay down! Flatten out!" He began to sing in the Guild tongue, unfamiliar words in a tone of desperation. He was chest deep and sinking, like a captain going down with his ship, as the clouds converged over Orolandes' head.

He sank through white blindness. He held his breath and readied himself — he thought he was ready — for the moment when he would drop out of the cloud.

Too long. He gasped for breath, and found he could breath cloud-stuff.

Somewhere above his head Clubfoot was still singing. If Orolandes yelled for Mirandee he might interrupt that spell; but it was very lonely to die like this. The white had turned light gray. The seconds stretched excruciatingly . . . then rough ground brushed against him and spun him head over heels.

He was on his back on solid, solid ground, with dirt and small stones beneath him and gray cloud all around. He stayed there and shouted. "Mirandee!"

Nothing.

"Clubfoot! Warlock!" He was afraid to move. To find solid ground in a cloud was too much of sorcery with too little warning. And he was still blinded by cloud!

Then a shape formed in the cloud, and resolved. He

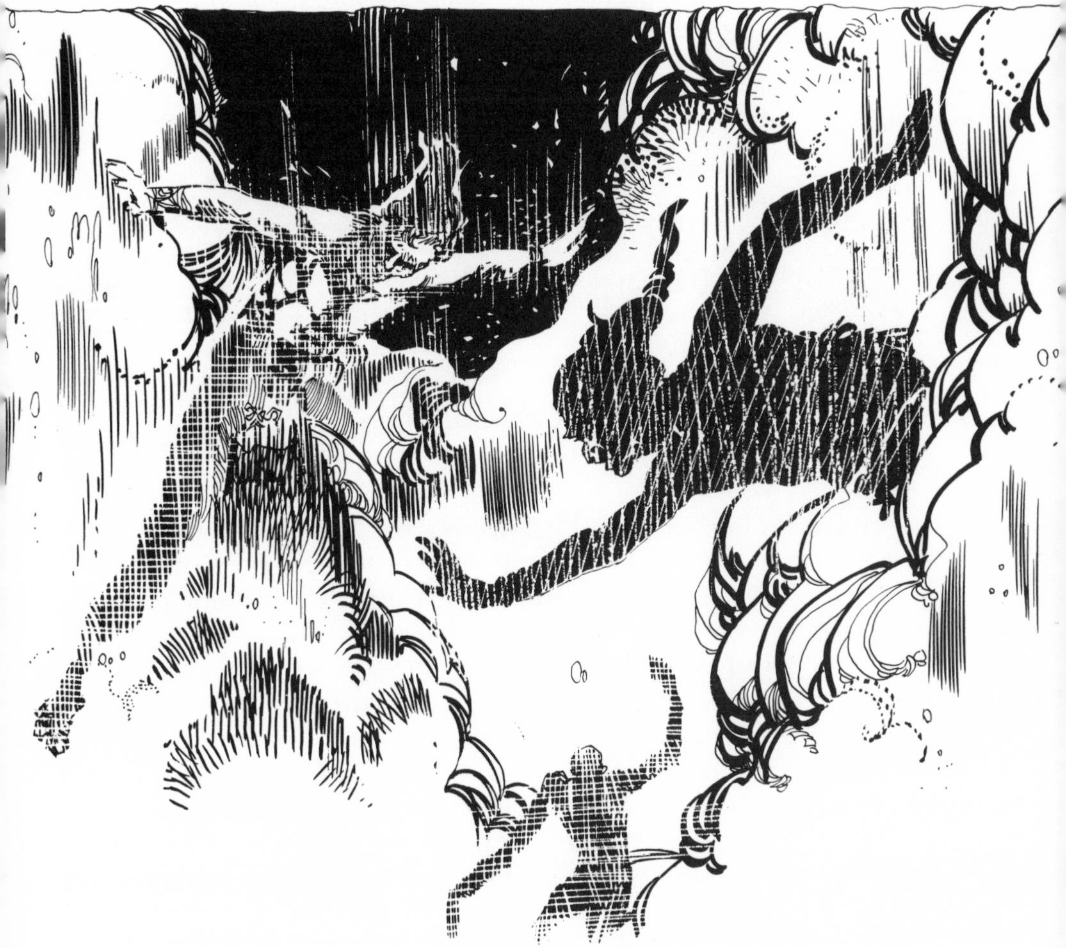

saw a pale, blond, very hairy warrior. The armored man walked in a furtive, silent crouch, his eyes shifting nervously, trying to see in all directions at once. His spear was poised to kill. But he didn't look down.

This, at least, was in Orolandes' field of experience.

The stranger's first glimpse of Orolandes showed him much too close, in the air, with sword drawn. The

stranger's jaw dropped; then he tried to scream and
thrust at the same time. Orolandes batted the
spearhead aside and stabbed him through the open
mouth.

He waited. No more blond warriors came. Presently
Orolandes allowed himself to look down.

The dead man was armored in leather reinforced by
brass strips. He carried sword and dirk in addition to
the spear. He looked to be just past twenty, and well
fed; and none of that was good. A well fed populace
could support many soldiers, and a young man
wouldn't be wearing the best of the armor. A good-
size, well-equipped band could be moving out there in
the . . . fog.

Of course, fog! Orolandes grinned at himself. A
cloud on the ground must be fog! Clubfoot must have
managed to land the cloud while it was still viscous
enough to hold them. That must have shaken the soldiers: sticky fog, and a hillside seeded with magicians.

Orolandes walked into the fog. He was painfully
alert. In this white blindness you could kill friend as

easily as foe. He spent some time stalking a small tree. Later two man-shaped shadows formed faintly in the mist, standing motionless above ... a seated man? Orolandes charged in silence, and killed one of them before they knew they were threatened. The other fended Orolandes off long enough to scream for help. He fought badly ... and lost.

The Warlock did not get up. He looked bad; as if he had collapsed in upon himself. He blinked and spoke in a feeble whisper. "Orolandes?"

"Yes. They'll be coming, we've got to move. Are you hurt?"

"Youth spells worn off. No *mana* here. Take — "

"Where are the others?"

"Don't know. You can't find them. Take Wavyhill. Go up."

"But — "

"Uphill till Wavyhill talks. Go." The Warlock slumped back. His breathing was an ugly sound.

Orolandes bent quickly and detached the skull and its harness from the Warlock's bony shoulder. The decorated skull seemed a pathetic toy; there was no life in it. He tucked it under his arm and moved into the fog in a crouched and silent run. Nordik warriors would be answering that scream.

He had to find Mirandee.

The Warlock rested with his eyes closed. There were bruises and a wrenched shoulder, but it was years that crippled him now. Cold seeped into his bones.

Metal clinked. He opened his eyes.

Large magics had deserted him in this dead place, but at least one small magic remained. The gift of tongues was no big, showy sorcery. Some could learn languages with no magic at all. But the gift could be useful.

The Warlock spoke in Nordik. "Don't kill me."

The man in beaten bronze armor said, "I make no such promise. Are you such a weakling as you seem? How did you slay these my men?"

"The swordsman we hired to guide us slew them, then fled."

"Describe him."

If Orolandes was caught he would be killed anyway, the Warlock told himself. He described Orolandes accurately, and added, "He was the only one of us who knew how to find the treasure."

"What treasure was that?"

"The god within a god," the Warlock said. If they wanted the treasure they would capture Orolandes alive . . . maybe. It was worth a try. "Such a thing would be immensely valuable to us. We were all magicians save him."

"How many are you?"

"Me, and a cripple named Clubfoot, and a woman named Mirandee." And a skull. Pitiful, thought the Warlock. "We can't harm you here."

"I know. Stand up or I'll cut your throat."

It was a long and painful process, but the Warlock got to his feet. The man in bronze watched in disgust. "You'll never walk alone," he said.

He called, and two soldiers came out of the fog with Clubfoot between them. Clubfoot had a nosebleed. It seemed his only injury, save that he shambled like a man who had lost all hope.

"You may carry each other," the man in bronze instructed them. "Do not delay me. You still live because you've not become a nuisance. Your swordsman is a thorough nuisance, and he will die."

The white mist enclosed them still as they made their way downslope. The Nordiks seemed unsure of

their path. Perhaps they were lost. It slowed them, and
that was good, for the magicians were nearly killing
themselves keeping up. Clubfoot was carrying half the
Warlock's weight. He limped heavily on his birth-man-
gled foot.

The first time the Warlock tried to speak to him, a
spear shaft rapped his funnybone. It hurt like hell. The
man in bronze armor said, "You must speak only in
our tongue. We have no wish to be cursed."

"Curses won't work here," Clubfoot said.

"We know that. We're so certain that we won't even
bother to test it. Right?"

Clubfoot nodded. He was morose, tired, defeated.

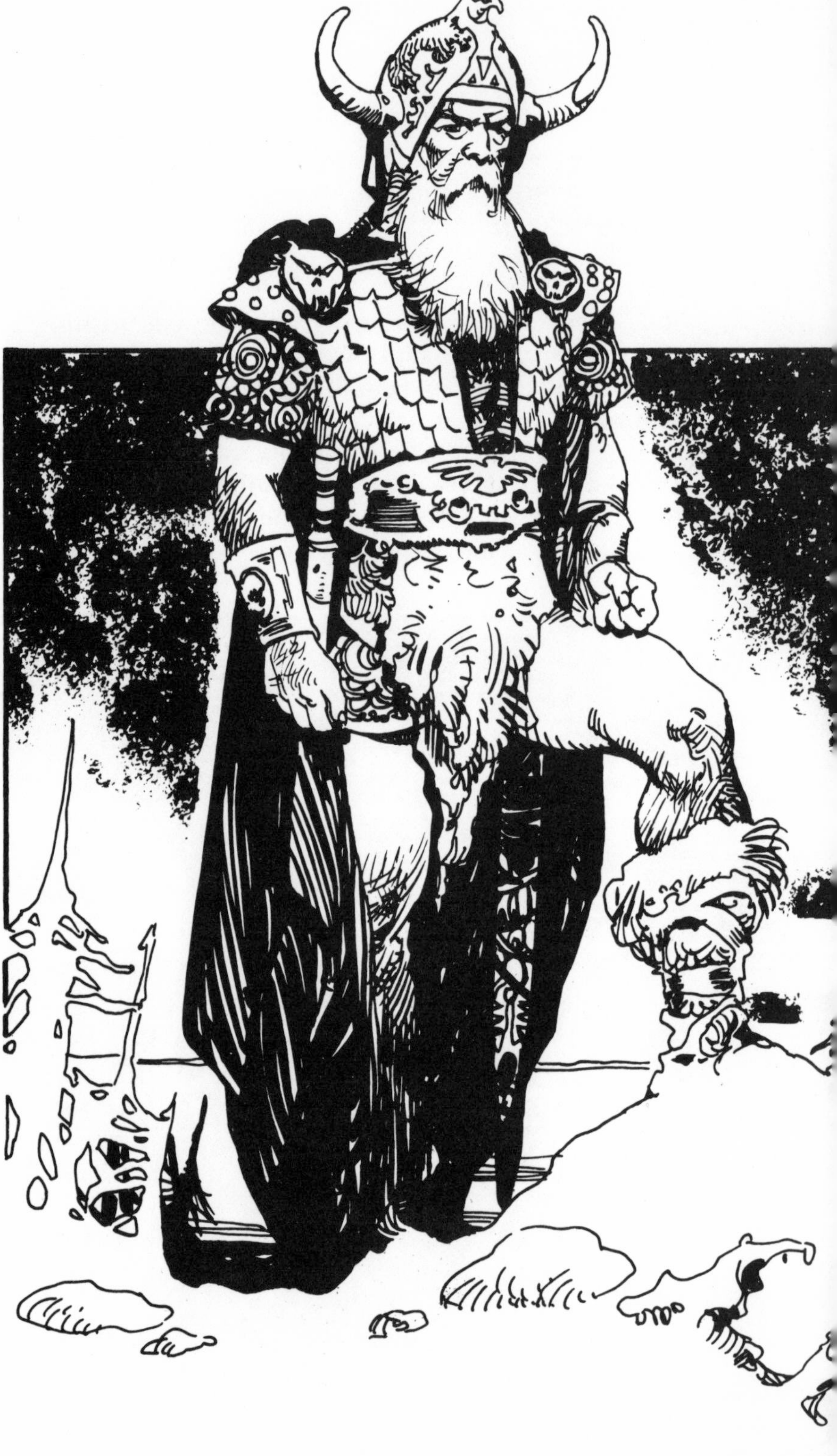

The Warlock spoke to him in Nordik. "Good landing. I never thought we'd live through that."

It seemed he wouldn't answer. Then, "I just got us down where I could. I thought I'd done a good job till *they* showed up."

"It's still better than failing to fly down. Where are you on a cloud when the magic runs out?"

The leader was a big man, strong enough to wear bronze armor without noticing the weight. White showed in his beard, and an old scar above one eye. He hadn't seemed to care if his prisoners lived or died . . . until now. Now he stared openly. "Were you actually riding on a cloud?"

"We traveled almost a thousand miles on that moving storm, thanks to Clubfoot's weather magic."

"What's it like?"

The Warlock suppressed a sigh of relief.

Mirandee could stay free. Her special talent would protect her, even here. Orolandes? They'd have to hope, and hope hard, because the swordsman was carrying Wavyhill. But Clubfoot and the Warlock could only expect to be questioned, then killed. Unless they could trade on their novelty value.

"Picture the most luxurious bed you've ever heard of," he said. "Not beds you've slept in, but beds from legend. Cloud-stuff is softer than that . . ."

Close behind him in the fog, a voice spoke to him. "Orolandes."

He jumped violently. He kept his sword high as he said, "Mirandee?" They might have captured her already —

"No, I stayed clear of them. Barely. There's a fog on my mind that's worse than this around us. Which way is the nearest mountain?"

"What about the others?"

She shook her head. Her leather garments had suffered, but Mirandee wasn't hurt; she didn't even seem rumpled. "We can't do magic here," she said. "For miles and miles around it must be nothing but old battlefields. Were you thinking of rescuing them singlehanded? Or teaching me to use a sword?"

"What do we do, then?"

"We get out of this dead area. Uphill. If Wavyhill can lead us to the 'god within a god', we'll just summon the others." She took the skull in both hands; her hair brushed Orolandes' cheek. "He doesn't look good."

"Was that a joke?"

She laughed. "Poor Wavyhill. Strap him to my shoulder, will you? Leave your arms free. No, I meant that he could be really dead. I'll have to do the spells all over again ... Orolandes? Do you remember Wavyhill's true name?"

"Not offhand."

That bothered her badly. "Try to remember. We can't do a revival without Wavyhill's true name."

"All right. The wind's that way," Orolandes said, "and that was the way the cloud was moving along the mountains. North. So we go east."

Orolandes didn't like the touch of Wavyhill: dry, dead bone, and just a trace of the smell of death. He emphatically didn't like strapping the skull next to the witch's ear. "Why can't we stow it in the pack? It'll be safe enough."

"Think of it as Wavyhill, our ally. The attitude is a large part of magic, love. He'll live more readily if I'm here waiting for him to advise me." She smiled at him, lovingly, and the skull grinned on her shoulder.

It became too dark to climb before they were barely started. They camped among half-seen trees. Mirandee's small crystal ball had shattered in the fall, and they spent some time shaking shards and slivers of crystal out of the blankets and the pack.

In the night the fog turned to powdery snow. They wakened chilled despite blankets and bruised by the hard ground.

The chill dissipated as they climbed, but Mirandee tired easily. Her hair was white again. She drove herself hard. By noon they had climbed above the fog.

Mirandee argued for going straight up the nearest peak. But even if Wavyhill revived, they'd only have to go down again; it was not on their path to the hump-shouldered magical mountain. Mirandee gave in to his arguments, possibly with relief.

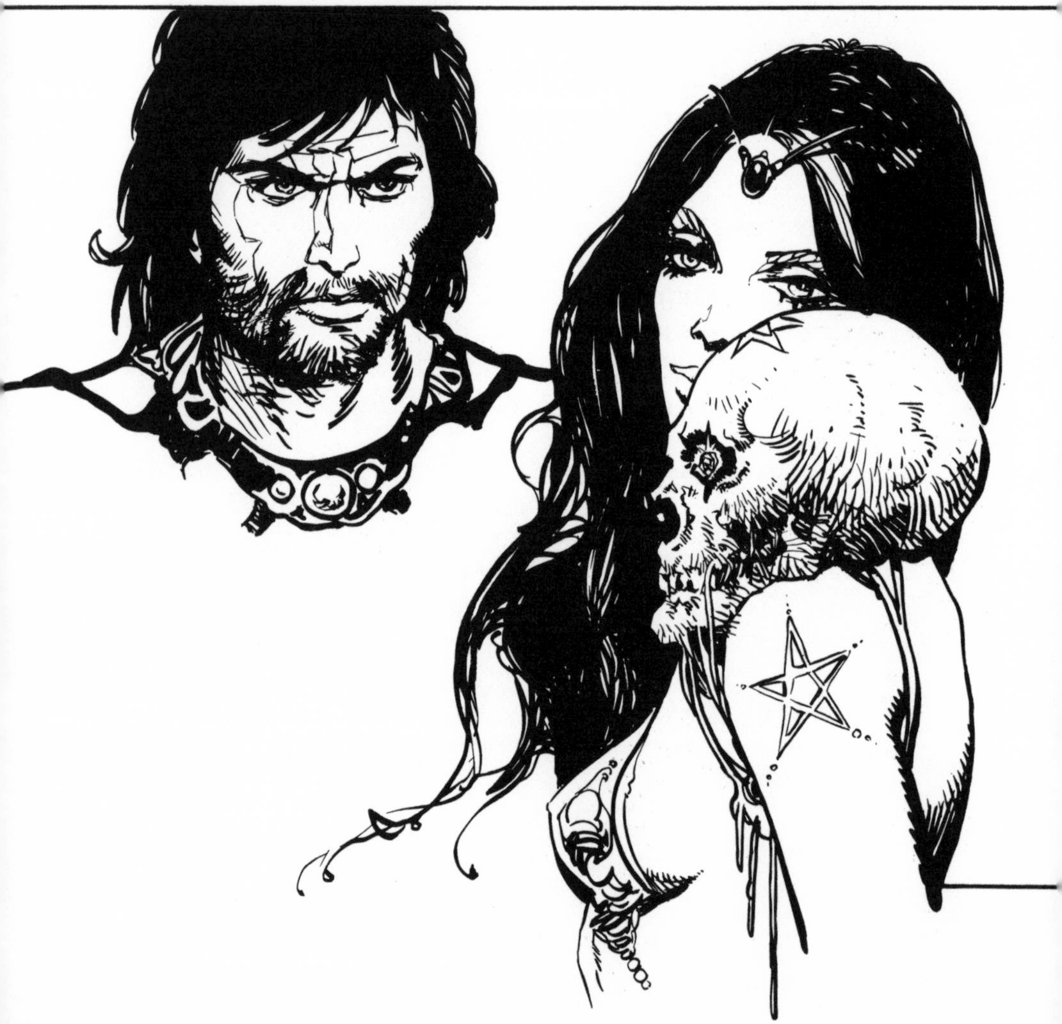

They went north and upward. They would stick to the ridges.

They had clean snow for water. They saw food, always receding at a good clip: a mountain goat, a small bear that shambled off although Orolandes shouted scathing insults at it. Orolandes wished for a bow and arrow, and settled for a stabbing spear made by using some of their rope to bind his sword to a straight sapling.

They didn't talk much. Each had private woes which they suffered in silence ... but Mirandee sensed her lover's shame at abandoning companions. What with the closing in of her own mind, the loss of youth and magic, she suffered for two. Orolandes wanted to comfort her. He had no skill at it, but her empathy spoke for him.

So it went until, at sunset of the third day, Orolandes saw an elk. It would have been enough meat to feed a village, but to Orolandes it looked just right for two. He started toward it, prowling, trying to determine windage. The elk cropped the sparse mountain grass with an eye constantly lifted toward danger.

Then, casually, it turned toward Orolandes and walked toward him, ignoring the grass, looking straight ahead ...

To a hunter Mirandee's voice was shockingly loud. "I've summoned it. Can you butcher it?"

The elk stood waiting for him to slash its throat. He did, feeling like a murderer. The sword cut through throat and spine with startling ease. The magic sword —

"I wish we knew its name," Mirandee said. "As it is, we're trusting someone else's magic whenever we use that sword."

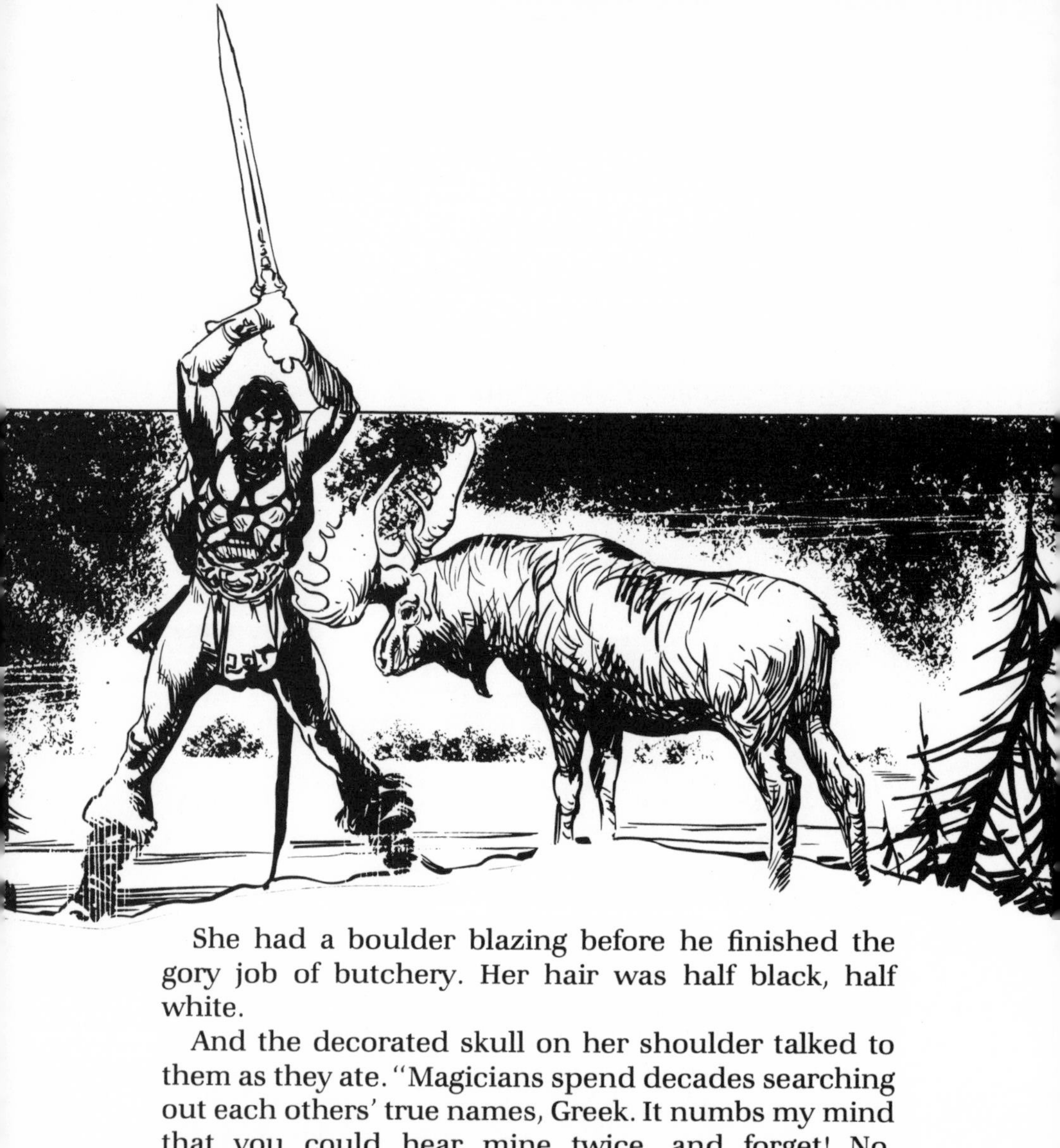

She had a boulder blazing before he finished the gory job of butchery. Her hair was half black, half white.

And the decorated skull on her shoulder talked to them as they ate. "Magicians spend decades searching out each others' true names, Greek. It numbs my mind that you could hear mine twice, and forget! No, Mirandee, I'm not going to tell you. Enough that the Warlock and Clubfoot can move me like a puppet. You would be one too many."

". . . biggest bird that ever lived. We thought they'd all gone mythical. Suddenly there it was, diving down on Mirandee." The Warlock's voice was thin and reedy, and he had to pause for breath . . . for air hotter than the atmosphere of Hell, that scalded his throat. It didn't matter. They listened. "Claws like eight curved sword blades. Eyes the size of your shield, Poul . . ."

The sauna was a big underground room with a wood stove glowing in the middle. There were benches along all four walls, on two levels; and thank the gods for that, for the Warlock was on the lower, cooler level. He'd have been on the floor except that it would violate Nordik custom. The village held more than two hundred, and half of them were in this incandescent room, sweating enough to fill a respectable river. They were all stark naked: men and women, older children and people so old they couldn't walk without assistance, and even some Frost Giant slaves, seven and eight feet tall, sitting on the lower benches with their heads near the ceiling.

The Warlock had seen strange peoples in his day. He knew how various were the ways of being human. He hid his surprise at sauna customs, and showed only the diffidence of a stranger who must be shown the rules. When Poul explained that they roasted themselves in this fashion to keep themselves healthy, he only nodded.

Clubfoot had guffawed when the Warlock told him that. (But they were alone then.) To the Warlock it was a disturbing sign of the times. Medicine was a branch of magic. Take the magic out of medicine, and what was left? *This?*

He wouldn't have been human if he hadn't shown some discomfort. And it was stranger than strange, to

see this many naked men and women crowded this
close together, pouring sweat, and none of them so
much as flirting! And every so often someone would
bolt and run for the river downslope. Ten minutes
later he'd be back, and if he brushed you in passing
his skin was icy, as if he'd been dead for days.

Yet they were paying him a signal honor, and it
behooved him to take advantage of it.

"Oh, Wavyhill was as evil a man as I've ever known.
He killed whole villages, and not by coming on them
with swords, but by stealth, by gaining their trust. He
sold them zombie servants that were dead men from

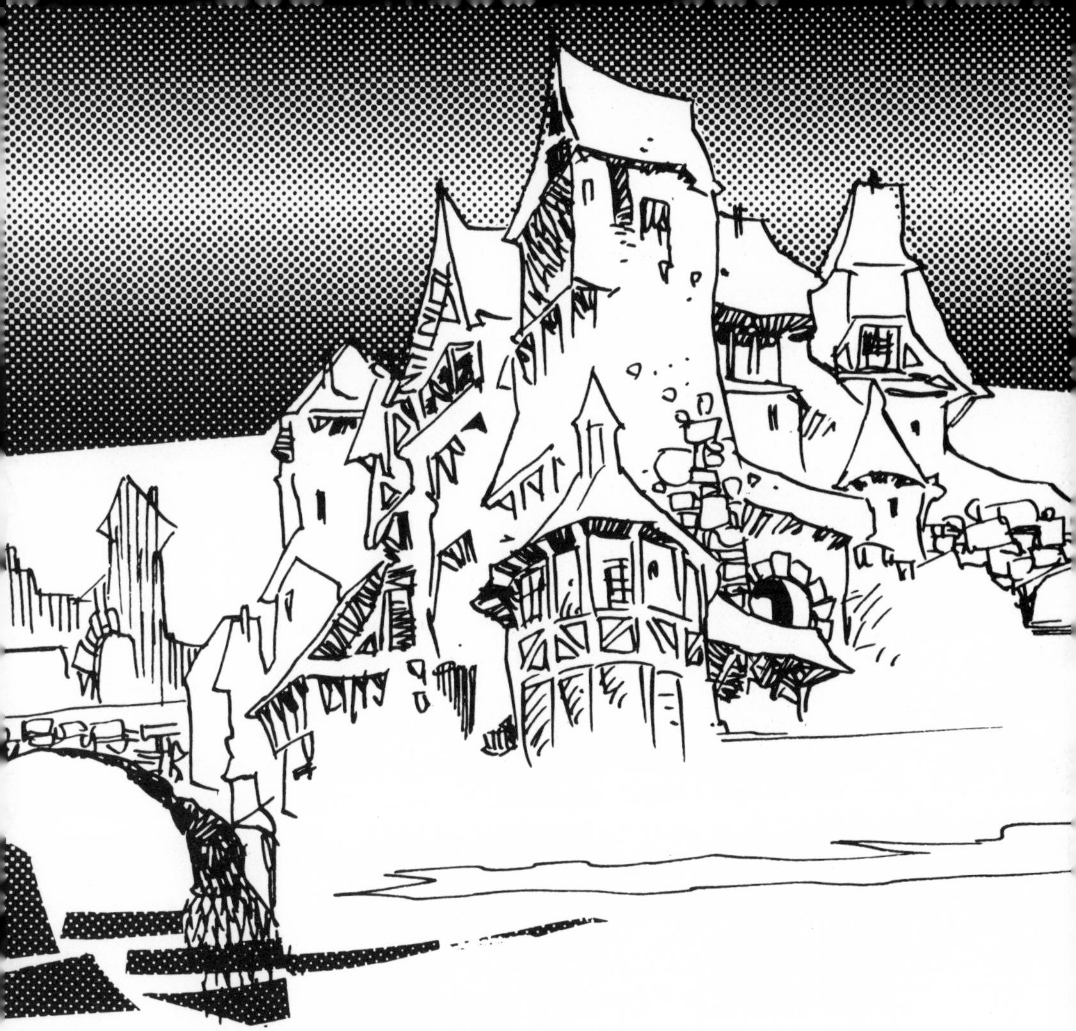

the last village he'd gutted, revived and hidden under the seeming of good troll slaves. One night the trolls would take up knives and . . ."

It had been very different three nights ago, when Harric reached Vendhabn Village with magicians as his prisoners.

Vendhabn was a place of stone houses with steeply peaked roofs and tiny windows lining both sides of a street of trampled dirt that curved like the cowpath it had once been. Houses of human scale, until you came to the great hall in the middle of town.

The Warlock was dopy with fatigue and sudden senility, and Clubfoot wasn't exactly alert, but they noticed the hall. It was tremendous. The stone blocks that made it were tremendous. The door was eighteen feet tall, and built of whole trees . . . and it was old. He wondered if it had been built by Frost Giants.

The night was dark and still foggy. Nobody was about. That was good; the Warlock had dreaded being put on show for a japing mob. The bronze-armored man named Harric led them past the great hall and into what had to be a jail: a hut built to the same colossal scale as the great hall, a single room with a roof eighteen feet high, and more recent stone partitions dividing it.

Their tiny room had a small window in the door. The guard outside was a tall, gangling warrior with big knobby hands. The Warlock was too exhausted to speak, to do anything but flop on the straw bedding and try to keep breathing. As Clubfoot bent over him, hurting with the need and the impossibility of curing him by magic, the Warlock had gasped three words.

"Keep them entertained."

Later that night he had awakened; but Clubfoot still didn't know that. The guard and Clubfoot had been pressed close to the window in the door. Clubfoot had been telling the guard about lovemaking on a so-lidified cloud, exactly as if he had done it him-self . . . exactly as his jealousy-fired imagination must have painted it. Certainly the Warlock had not been meant to hear.

In the morning he had felt stronger. He'd been able to eat some bread and drink some mead. Last night's guard had seemed friendly enough, and a bit awed by his prisoners. Clubfoot had introduced him as Poul Cloudscraper.

The magicians talked quietly on the straw bedding.

"We'd rather be guests than prisoners," the Warlock said. "What are the chances?"

"Maybe. I talked to Poul last night. Blamed the killings on Orolandes. If they get him I'll have to say I lied. I made out that we were kind of his prisoners."

"If they get Orolandes we can cut our throats. I'd like to give the impression we're taking their hospitality for granted. It just hasn't occurred to us that they might cut a wandering magician's throat —"

"Too late. I asked Poul about that. He can't protect us. He's a householder, but he only gets one vote in council."

"Oh."

"How's this? You're a loveable, trusting old man, and I'm your ex-apprentice who lives only to take care of you. It might stop your heart if you thought you'd been threatened by our hosts. Should anyone be so boorish as to raise the subject —"

"You insist that I mustn't find out. Good. Help me up."

Leaning heavily on the red man's shoulder, he peered out the small window. There were men and women dressed too lightly against the cold, moving to avoid puddles and patches of half-melted snow. Two giant women went past with a dressed ox carcass slung from a pole. They were both very pale of skin, and white-haired, though they seemed young, and they stood seven feet tall or taller. The Warlock glanced at Poul, their big Nordik guard, and caught Clubfoot's warning headshake; there was no good reason whatever to speculate on whether Poul was part Frost Giant.

"We need not mention our ally Wavyhill. Too macabre," said the Warlock.

"Right. But tell 'em about the duel, it's a good story."

"Fine. So you're the old man's loyal apprentice, and

you wouldn't dream of deserting him in these his remaining years. Once they're convinced of that they
may loosen your tether. If you get the chance, you
run."

"No way."

"I mean it. I'm out of the game. Here —" The Warlock slipped the sliver bracelet from his upper arm.
"This'll point out the mountain. Mirandee will head
there, and she'll have Orolandes and Wavyhill."

"Sure," said Clubfoot. He was certainly lying. He
helped the Warlock back to the straw to rest.

"We use the sauna once in ten days," Poul
Cloudscraper said. Poul was on an upper rack of
benches. His impressively big feet were propped
higher than his head, on a row of rails for that purpoe.
"We keep it only warm all the time. If one comes dying
of the cold, we can warm him quick."

"You certainly can."

"Then again, the sauna brings on a quick childbirth.
You would be surprised at how many children are
born in the sauna."

"Not at all. I'm about to give birth myself."

Poul was concerned. "Shall we dip in the river again,
or have you had enough?"

The river had been icy; he had thought it would
stop his heart. And now he was pouring sweat again.
"I've had as much ecstacy as I can stand," he assured
the guard.

The cooling-off room was next to the sauna itself. It
was crowded. The Nordiks would rest in here for half
an hour, then leave . . . but today they weren't leaving.
As the Warlock washed himself he tried to hear what
Clubfoot was telling them.

"None of us is old enough to remember what the

gods are like," the lame magician was saying. "Not even my friend the Warlock here. How did you like the sauna, Warlock?"

The Warlock smiled back. "A unique experience." He accepted a towel from a silent Frost Giant woman. She used another towel to dry his back.

"There are some interesting legends, though," Clubfoot said. "The god Dyaus-pita took a number of human women as lovers. Most of them came to grief. There was one who insisted that he show himself in his true form ... which was probably a mistake." The pleasantly shaped young woman next to Clubfoot was one the Warlock remembered: Harric's younger sister. Good. If Clubfoot could pacify the bronze-armored warrior ...

The time of the japing mob had come, of course. At midmorning Harric led them out. It was funny in a way, to see the villagers' embarrassed reactions to Harric's conquest: a cripple and a feeble old man. The magicians answered politely to some of the gibing questions put to them; they attempted to act like guests rather than captured freaks, and hoped that they would not therefore be taken for madmen. Harric put them back in their cell and went away angry, and the villagers went back to their tasks. The children remained.

There must have been a hundred children of all ages, maybe more. At first they only stared. The magicians began to talk to them. They gathered closer. Here and there you would see a younger one sitting on a teenager's shoulders. At the back, a few white-haired, white-skinned boys and girls stood like trees among saplings, straining to hear. Clubfoot and the Warlock took turns at the window to tell tales of dragon fights, wars of magic, ancient kingdoms, strange half-human peoples ...

Evening came, and most of them disappeared to their dinners. For those who stayed, the Warlock tried the spell he had used at the inn in Prissthil for the diners' entertainment. In the darkness the colors were dimmer yet, like the Northern Lights brought to earth. The children loved it.

The next morning brought a cluster of angry parents.

The Warlock was exhausted. He had to let Clubfoot deal with them. He lay on the straw with his eyes closed, listening to Nordik anger and Clubfoot's tones of bewildered hurt. He wondered what had gone wrong.

"... turn them into *magicians?* My son will grow up to be ..."

"... corrupting our children ..."

"... wiser to learn *our* customs before you ..."

"... too dazzled to do their work, now you've filled their heads with ..."

Came the noon meal, and they were left alone. "I wasn't a lot of help, was I?" the Warlock said miserably. "How much trouble are we in?"

But Clubfoot seemed thoughtful rather than worried. "Not as much as you'd think. I got one old woman talking for the rest of 'em. She's the ring-bearer's mother." The gift of tongues informed the Warlock that the ring-bearer was the lord of the hall, effectively the mayor. "Her name's Olganna. Warlock, a lot of the parents are delighted we've got the kids interested in something. And the children are all on our side, of course."

"What in the gods' names was *bothering* those people?"

Clubfoot's grin flashed. "Magic was always used against the Nordiks, never for them. They didn't have any. The tales they tell their children today are all about brawny Nordik warriors against evil magicians. Justice triumphed, and now there's no more magic."

"Oh."

"So now the kids are constantly bothering the Frost Giant servants at their work, and they don't do their own chores either. They want magic. Only Frost Giants make magic." Clubfoot dipped bread into stew, and said, "I learned some things. The Frost Giants really did have a god named Roze-Kattee, and his powers did hold off the Nordiks for a hundred years or so. Then the god's powers waned, and the Nordik berserkers swarmed all over the Frost Giant warriors."

"So that much was true, at least. What else did you find out about Roze-Kattee?"

"Olganna couldn't seem to tell me what the god was *doing* to the Nordik armies. I think it's been forgotten. Maybe they never knew. One thing, though. Do you know what a berserker is?"

"Not by that name."

"A berserker sort of goes insane before battle. He froths at the mouth, he chews his shield, he charges the enemy and keeps going until he's actually hacked apart. He doesn't notice wounds, even lethal wounds. What I want to know is, did the Nordiks have berserkers when they were driven out of the Fertile Crescent?"

"Yes. A lot of tribes developed that technique when it got to be so difficult to raise actual zombies."

"Well, the Nordiks didn't use berserkers until the actual last battle. Olganna said so and they all backed her up."

"That's funny. I wonder why...god of love and madness?"

Clubfoot nodded vigorously. "That's what I thought. The Nordiks couldn't fight because Roze-Kattee kept bringing the Nordik berserkers to their senses. One more thing. The Frost Giants still worship Roze-Kat-tee."

"What? But they're slaves!"

"Interesting, isn't it?"

They emptied their stew bowls and set them aside. Presently the Warlock said, "Have you thought what will happen to these people if Wavyhill and Mirandee can bring back magic to the world?"

Clubfoot shrugged. "They're swordsmen."

"Well, yes ... Meanwhile we've got to cool off the irate parents somehow."

"We can change our tune. There are tales where magic really was used for evil. Wavyhill's zombie servants, and the demon-sword Glirendree, and the raising of the dead in the war against Acheron."

"That'll help. What about a magic show?"

"What?"

"Let the kids get it out of their systems. The adults too. I'm sure we can work something up."

"Maybe. I'll ask Olganna what she thinks."

The magic show had been a huge success. The Warlock had pretended to call up the dead: phantasms that Clubfoot animated with his thoughts. Clubfoot had read minds, discreetly, and told the contents of locked boxes. The Warlock had told futures, again using some discretion.

But they were still in the cell when the day of the public sauna dawned.

He drowsed face down on the wooden bench while talk floated around him ... *sent a plague that killed most of his worshippers* ... His knuckles brushed dry earth. *Why? Stingy with their sacrifices ... understandable. Baal took every first-born child* ... The bench was harder than cloud and he was naked, but the air was

warm and dry and pleasantly scented with wood and woodsmoke. *Started as a war between men ... eventually split the whole pantheon, with gods fighting on both sides ... boredom. Sure, the gods had their squabbles, but it was boredom ... flattened both cities before ...* Clubfoot was still talking about gods. The Warlock dozed. *Mostly they worshipped out of fear. Why else would the ...*

Some phrase caught the Warlock's attention and pulled him awake. He sat up. He felt good, better than he'd felt in days.

"There's no mystery to it," Olganna was telling Clubfoot. Her hair was white and whispy-thin, she was small and withered and wrinkled, but she still looked like she could climb a mountain. Deep stretch marks on her belly told of her eight sons and eleven daughters. "They simply wouldn't surrender unless they were allowed to serve their god. Our forefathers could have killed them all, of course, but what for? This Roze-Kattee hadn't helped them. We let them have their way."

The Warlock sat up. Nobody seemed to think it strange that he had dozed off here.

"I wonder what makes them so loyal," Clubfoot said.

"Why, they just . . . are. Or stubborn," said Olganna. She seemed unaware that two Frost Giants, man and woman, were drying themselves on the far side of the room. "Once in my life and once before I was born, we got tired of their taking so much time off for their ceremonies. In my time it was a crop that had to be got in. We postponed the ceremonies. They stopped work, all work, till we gave in. It was a hungry winter."

"But don't you find that strange? All the old tales tell of gods striking mortals down for some casual mistake, or as part of some godlike game, or just for being proud of their own accomplishments. Sometimes the prayers and sacrifices were bribes for service, but usually they were just to get the god to let them alone: no more floods, no more plague, no more lightning, please. What did Roze-Kattee *do* for the Frost Giants?"

"I've wondered." Olganna frowned. She looked about her . . .

They might have been father and daughter, or uncle and niece, or man and wife; their ages weren't *that* different. White hair, pale skin, eyes the color of ice, spare frames seven feet tall: they looked very much alike. They sat together, with Nordiks comfortably close on both sides of them, in the egalitarian style of the sauna, and they rested in the peace that follows the heat.

Olganna called across the room, and the entire village must have heard her. "Gannik, Wilf, just why *do* you still serve a god nobody's seen in a hundred years?"

The old man flinched. Certainly he had not come to the sauna to be cross-examined. But some are more equal then others, and Olganna's son was the ring-bearer, the lord of the Hall. The pale young woman beside him didn't help matters; she was looking at Gannik as if she too expected an answer.

He shrugged and answered. "Those who do not worship do not marry, do not love, are not loved. It was always that way. If one loses faith after a long and successful life, his wife will desert him, his children will not speak to him, none will help him when he is sick and aged. If Roze-Kattee frowns on a man, he is impotent; on a woman, her lovers are impotent. We knew this long before you came to live in our land."

Clubfoot had been clever, telling his tales of gods. So now we have our answer, the Warlock thought. Roze-Kattee's power lay in the taking. He took the madness from a berserker, and the power of love from an apostate. But if the god himself had been impotent for hundreds of years . . .

With a thrill of horror the Warlock saw that it didn't matter. For thousands of years only the devout had had children. Roze-Kattee had bred the Frost Giants for loyalty to Roze-Kattee.

And while this flashed through his mind Olganna was nodding dismissal to Gannik. She was satisfied. To Clubfoot she said, "My nephew tells me that you came here to search out Roze-Kattee."

The Warlock flinched. Clubfoot said, "We came searching knowledge of Roze-Kattee. How could we not? Roze-Kattee may be the last living god, and knowledge is power to a magician. Usually." Ruefully, "This time it was a mistake. We have lost power."

The pair of Frost Giants seemed to have lost interest. But slaves had always been good at that.

THE CAVERN OF THE LAST GOD

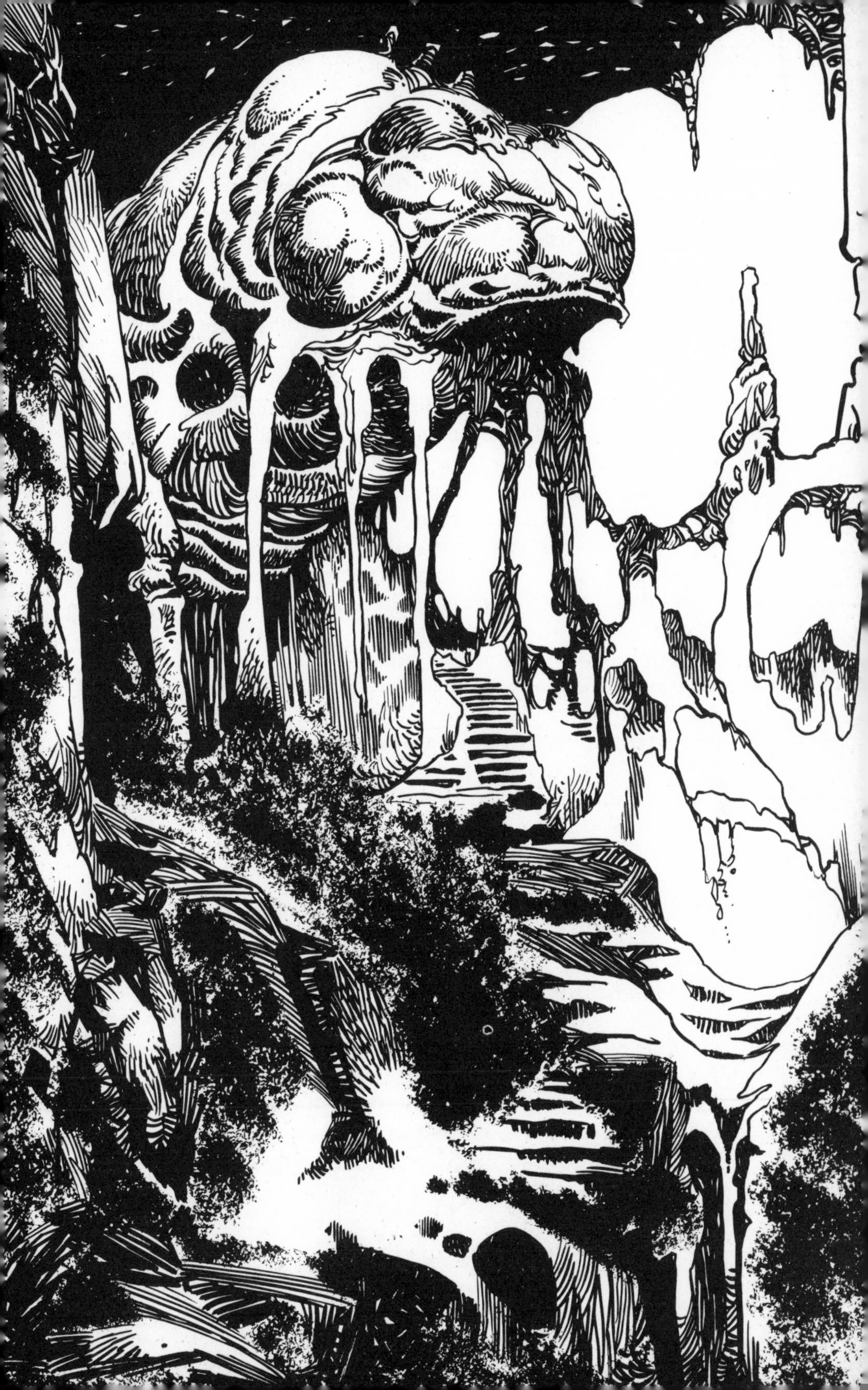

The ridged back of the mountain chain was an easier path than Orolandes had expected. These mountains were old, worn to smooth rock and rotted to soil that could hold the occasional grimly determined tuft of grass; and the towering peaks were all to the south, behind them. Mirandee's hair remained white, but she was strong.

Yet the journey had its difficulties. Their boots wore out, and they lost half a day summoning rabbits and skinning them for new boots. Always as they walked, they had Wavyhill for their entertainment. Unhampered by the need to draw breath, Wavyhill talked constantly of the ease with which magicians used to travel, and the precautions they could and should have taken to save this grueling walk. His life story was a chain of enemies made and defeated, and they had it all in detail, until Mirandee threatened to move his felt tongue to the backpack. "What makes you so garrulous?" she demanded. "You never needed company when you were living all alone in those fortified castles."

"Oh, blame it on the Warlock, dear. I was deaf and dumb and blind for thirty years. You'd want to talk too."

"He could have revived you earlier, if you'd told him your true name before the battle," she said, and Wavyhill chortled hollowly.

But he woke her that night by saying, "Kranthkorpool. It's Kranthkorpool. Just in case."

It took them six days.

The last few miles were the easiest, a wide, rounded ridge of smooth rock sloping gently downhill. Mirandee's hair went dark and light as if cloud-shadows were passing. It was late afternoon.

The slope dipped more drastically there at the end, until it was a vertical drop. "Wavyhill? This way?"

"Yes! Get us down there, Greek!" Wavyhill was almost indecently eager.

Orolandes motioned Mirandee back. He stood at the edge of the drop, looking around, taking his time.

From the lip it was thirty feet to flat dirt. The rock face must slant inward; he couldn't see it.

The drop could be made in two stages, by way of what looked to be a congealed river of lava. It was twenty feet high and thirty-odd feet wide, a rounded ridge of smooth gray rock with big potholes all over it, and it ran beneath Orolandes' feet. Ten feet down, then another twenty feet to dirt. But the lava river itself was rounded to vertical all along its length, and it ran further than he could see, twisting into the broken foothills.

"It'll be easier just to moor the line and climb down here. Here — " He showed Mirandee how to slide with the line around one ankle and clutched between the feet. He slid down first, then stood underneath, ready to break a witch's fall. She did fine. He caught her anyway, for pleasure.

They stood before the mouth of an enormous cavern, under the edge of the roof.

"In there," Wavyhill whispered. "I was right. I wasn't sure until now."

Orolandes dropped the pack and drew his sword. "Stay behind me, love."

Wavyhill laughed. "Do you have any idea what to expect?"

Orolandes boosted himself to the top of a chest-high buttress of stone. "Tell me."

Wavyhill didn't answer.

Orolandes pulled Mirandee up. They looked into the cavern.

"Don't go any further," said the skull.

The entrance was big, but it widened even further

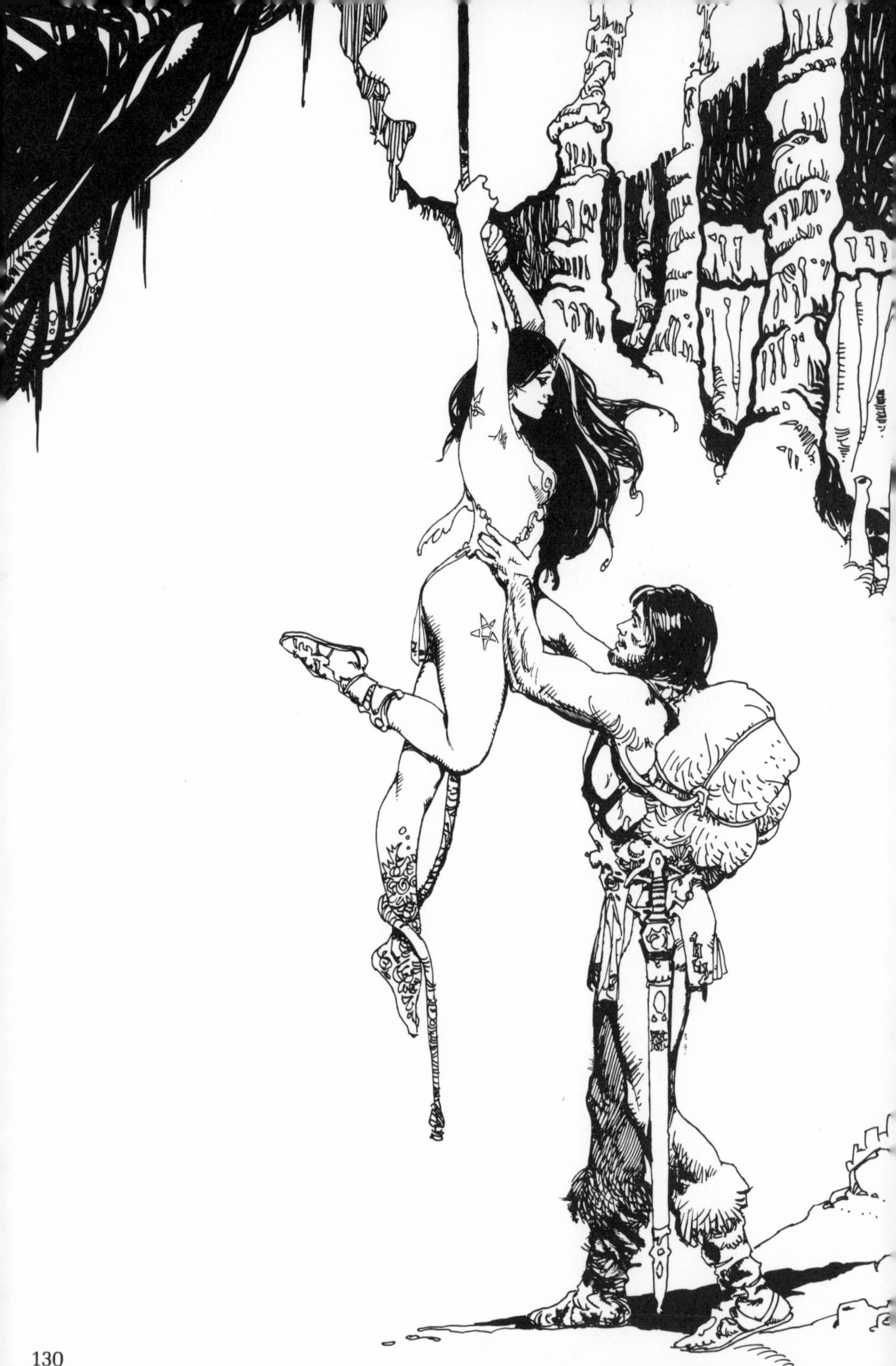

beyond the opening. In the darkness they could see vertical bars, stalactites and stalagmites of prize-winning size. The twenty-foot high river of grey stone ran deep into the darkness . . . or it had run out of there, glowing, long ago.

"It's big," Orolandes said. "Do you know what this dormant god looks like? How big it is?"

"Don't go any further. I mean it."

True, he'd been edging in. Mirandee asked, "Why not?"

"We have a decision to make," Wavyhill said. "Do we risk this without Clubfoot and the Warlock? Or shall we try a Great Summoning, now?"

"That's no decision at all. We don't have the power."

"I think there might be enough to —"

"Wavyhill, I'm surprised at you! The *mana* is here, but it's too diffuse. We need the last god first. You know what would happen if we tried a Great Summoning and failed."

Orolandes waited. He didn't have to trust Wavyhill. In one second his sword could split that skull, and without scratching Mirandee's shoulder.

"Mirandee, it only strikes me that we might not *know* enough between us to —"

"I will *not* try any Great Summoning until we have the power to do it. And you can't make the gestures."

Wavyhill gave a barking laugh. "You win. All right, Greek, put the sword down and go in and find the dormant god."

Mirandee said, "Alone?"

Orolandes said, "Put down the sword?"

"I said that, yes. Of course, neither of you *has* to take my orders."

It was dark in there. Menacing. The sword's weight felt comfortably normal in his hand.

"Leave it here. Otherwise it'll kill you. Snap out of it,

Greek, this is your big moment!"

He didn't like Wavyhill's obscene grin; but Oro-landes had made his decision long since. He set the sword on a boulder. He turned and walked into the darkness.

Stalagmites stood thicker and taller than he was. He had to duck the points of the longer stalactites at first, but then the cavern's roof became too high for that.

Wavyhill's echoless voice followed him. "I don't know the size or shape of what you're looking for. You'll find it on the other side of that stream of smooth rock, probably far back."

He turned and called, "All right."

It happened while his head was turned. Motion exploded around him. Things swatted his head from two directions. Orolandes threw himself flat and rolled over clutching for his sword. Things screamed all around him, their voices excruciatingly high-pitched.

Still fluttering, still screaming, they wheeled away from him. Dark shapes swarming around the roof. Bats. Orolandes got up and moved on, breathing heavily.

The lava flow ran along the side of the cavern. It ran the full length, back to a deeper blackness at the end. Orolandes' exploring hands found smooth rock marred with potholes. Strange to find potholes here where there was no rain. And in the sides, too.

Strange but convenient. He climbed the potholes, up the rounded side of the rock. Stalactites hung low over the top.

Between the back side and the cavern's wall was a three-foot gap. Orolandes walked toward the back, ducking stalactites, looking into the gap.

The deeper blackness at the back: could it be another cavern? He might have to search that too.

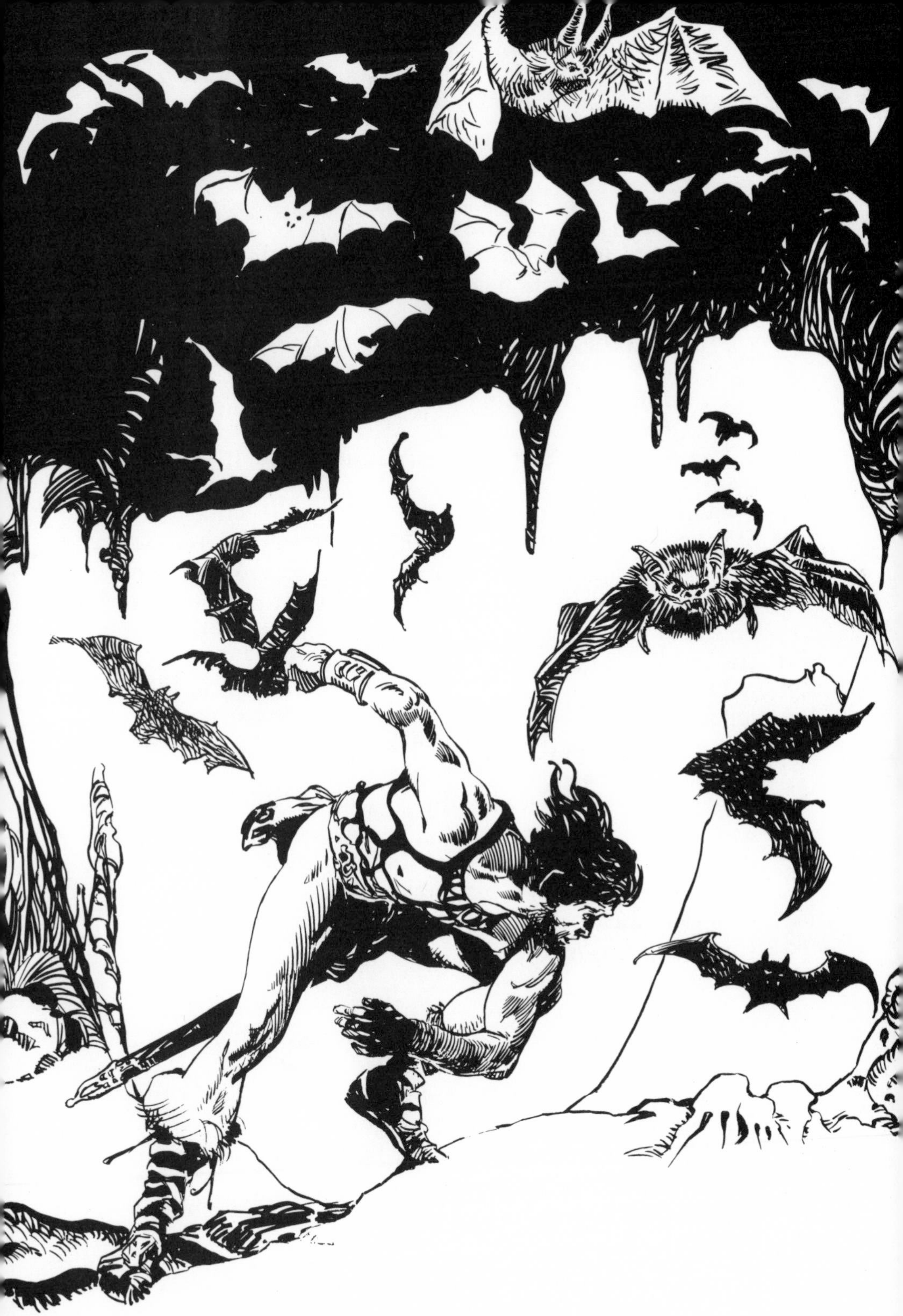

Should have brought a torch. But there was a shadow far back along the gap, a big shadow. If that was the god, it was too big to be moved. Even if it wanted to be moved.

From the beginning he had wondered if it would fight him.

Wavyhill's shout came jarringly. "Orolandes! Come back! Come back *now!*"

"What for?" Orolandes' own shout echoed around him.

"Now! Obey me!"

He didn't trust Wavyhill worth a troll's curse. But he trusted the panic and anger in that command. He dropped lightly from the lava flow, caught himself in a controlled roll, stood up and jogged toward the entrance.

The entrance flamed with daylight. Orolandes jogged around stalagmites with his eyes on the chancy footing and his head lowered to avoid the down-pointing spires.

Mirandee leaned casually against a smooth rock wall, seemingly watching him. It was hardly a scene of panic. Orolandes called, "What's the trouble?"

He knew that when his muscles locked. He teetered on a rigid forward leg, then toppled on his right side in running position. He tried to cry out, but his voice was locked too.

Mirandee didn't move, didn't speak, didn't blink.

The sword was on the boulder where he had left it, a tantalizing arm's reach away.

The skull on Mirandee's shoulder said, "I'm sorry. My mistake, and it was made right at the beginning." He raised his voice. "Piranther! Where are you?"

"I'm just over your heads."

Piranther floated like an autumn leaf into the bright entrance.

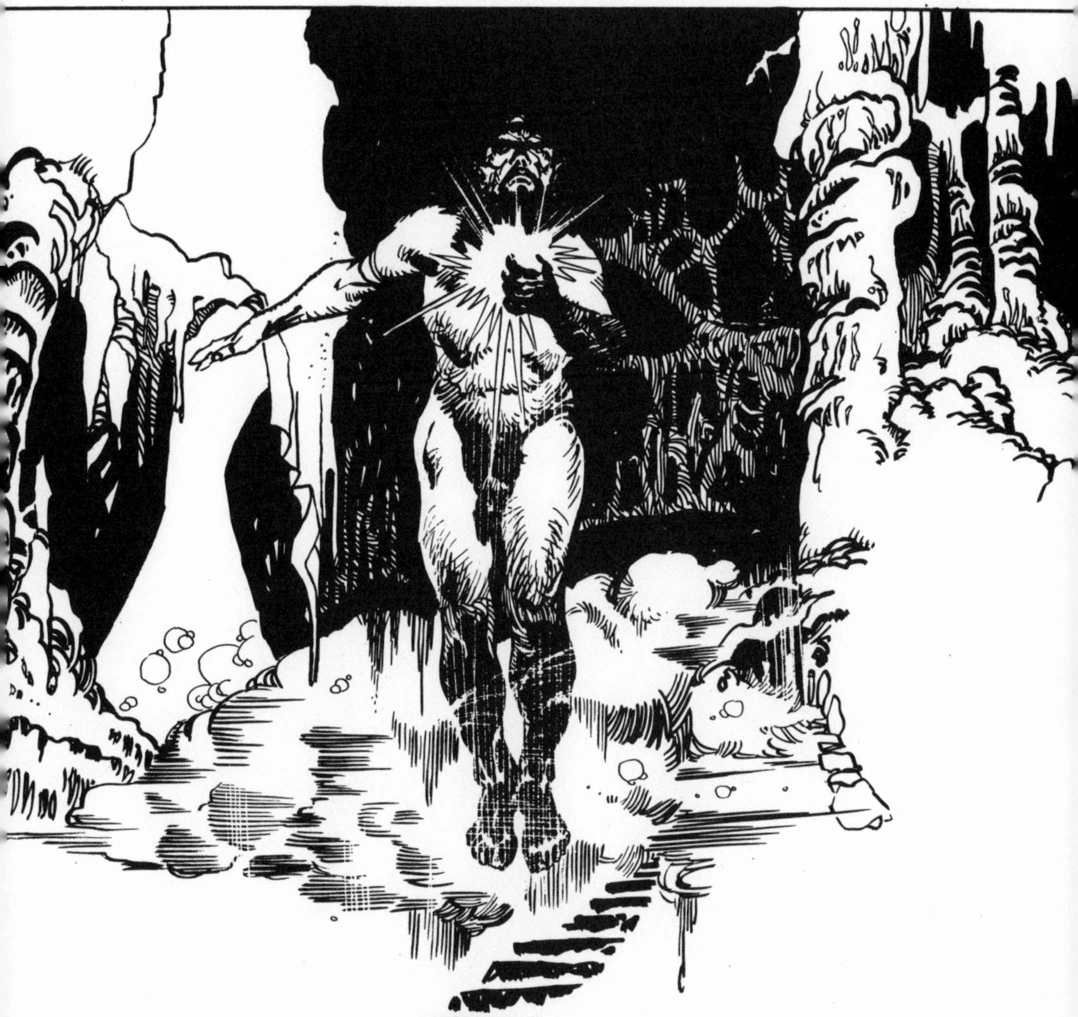

THE FROST GIANTS

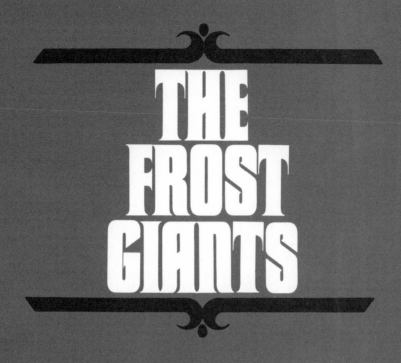

They should have have thought of it. Granted that
the Warlock was sick with age and Clubfoot was trying
to keep them both alive with old stories; there was
more to it. Sorcerers have a blind spot, and that blind
spot is —

" — swords. They keep appearing in your old tales,"
said Harric. The burly redhead was dressed casually
now, in leather and flaxen cloth. "Are these magic
swords all a thing of the past?"

Harric's invitation to dine at his table had surprised
the Warlock. Less surprising was the presence of
another guest, their young guard, Poul. Two other
men struck the Warlock as fighting men; their arms
were thick with muscle, they bore healed scars, and
they walked as if they didn't expect anyone to be
standing in their way. Now he began to understand.

"Wavyhill had a magic sword," Clubfoot was saying.
"It didn't help against the Warlock. And there was a
demon forced to the form of a sword: Glirendree. The
Warlock killed it. In fact . . . Warlock, I guess you're
our expert on magic swords."

The Warlock smiled. Oh, yes, he should have made
this happen earlier. "What would you like to know?"

"Where do they come from? What do they do?"

"Hmm . . . Glirendree doesn't count. He was an actual demon. Wavyhill's sword was enchanted to strike
always at the vitals of an enemy. You can do that, or
set it to block another's weapon, or make it sharp
enough to cut boulders, or all three."

"Can you do that to any sword?" Harric leaned
across the table.

"Mmm . . . I can, or could, if I were in a place where
magic works."

"All right, you've said that murder carries this magical power. There were battles fought all through
here — "

"No, no. Murder and war are not the same. The intent is different, and the intent counts for a good deal."

Harric settled back. The Warlock sipped mead and waited. Presently Poul said, "Kinawulf's barrow?"

"Yes, by the gods! Warlock, Kinawulf was a ring-bearer of our people who tried to practice sorcery himself. He had some success until Roze-Kattee turned his followers against him. They slew him after torture. His barrow is a place of ill fame, but with swords and magic to guard us we should be safe enough."

"It sounds perfect. How far is it?"

"Most of a day's walk...uphill. Mpf, we had best make you a litter. Are there materials you need?"

The Warlock asked for parchment and colored inks. "I'll send Clubfoot scouting for herbs. And bring the swords, of course."

They set out on the morning of the sixth day. The swordsmen were heavily laden: two to carry the War-lock, the others carrying half a dozen extra weapons in addition to the magicians' materials. In his present condition the Warlock wondered if he could pick up any one of those great metal killing-things, built heavy enough to slice through armor.

He was mildly disappointed, and mildly relieved, that Clubfoot had come back with the herbs. Hell, Clubfoot hadn't promised to run. Maybe there had been a guard. He didn't ask.

The trees thickened as they went, until Poul and the Nordik named Hathsson had to slide sideways to move the Warlock's chair between the trunks. The Warlock sighed and said, "I'll walk from here."

"It's not much farther. Bring the chair anyway," Harric ordered.

The forest smells were pleasant. Harric passed a fat skin of mead around, then discarded it. Clubfoot said, "I've been wondering what happened to this Kinawulf. We seem to have worked out that Roze-Kattee drove people *sane*."

"Selectively," said the Warlock. "Who attacked Kinawulf? Someone who had reason for hatred or jealousy?"

"His younger brother and a few followers, helped by Kinawulf's wife."

"I expect Kinawulf's problem was that none of his own followers were mad enough to stand in the way of a sword. That was Roze-Kattee's doing. The god wouldn't have touched Kinawulf himself; he might have surrendered. We may well find magic operating around the barrow."

"There — " Harric pointed.

The barrow was the peak of a small hill covered in green grass. It was clear of trees. "We want the top," said the Warlock.

He was behind the others as he climbed, puffing, leaning on Poul's arm. Why didn't he feel stronger, if this place was so rich in *mana?* There was *mana*, but not enough to power a youth spell, or to work a loyalty spell or a death spell on swordsmen. Or to do much to a metal sword. Now, how does one explain to a known berserker that one can't give him a dozen magic swords after all?

They heard Hathsson shout. Poul sprinted for the top of the hill, sword in hand. The Warlock struggled after him.

Even in this northern cold, Piranther went naked. His bright eyes searched for motion, for any sign that his spell of paralysis had failed. Nobody moved.

Piranther relaxed his grip on the leather bag at his

throat. He walked nonchalantly past Mirandee, inspecting her; then turned his attention to the skull.

"Kranthkorpool, speak to me. Did you find the dormant god?"

"Maybe." It was no more than the truth, but Wavyhill's voice was strained.

Piranther slit the straps that held the skull to Mirandee's shoulder. He lifted it down and looked at it, his fingers avoiding the gnashing jaws. "I could smash you," he said. "Or I could take away your senses and bury you here. Who would ever find you? Don't make me dig for information, Kranthkorpool."

Wavyhill said, "I think the Frost Giant priests must have put it behind that long, rounded wall of rock, far back. The Greek knows."

"Thank you. Why did you want him? You could have fetched it for yourselves."

"He's the only strong one among us. The god is bound to be heavy. Too heavy for you, too, Piranther. Can we deal on that basis?"

Piranther looked thoughtfully into the cavern. "But with the *mana* inherent in it, you could float it out. Why —?"

"Curse it, we can't afford the loss! We need all the *mana* the god has left to it. Don't you understand, this is the biggest thing anyone ever dreamed of!"

Piranther laughed. "Your big and foolish project. Your one solution to all the world's problems. Never trust such solutions, Kranthkorpool. I will take the dormant god back to the South Land Mass for our own use. It will serve our needs for some time to come." He set the skull down facing him. "I can leave it dormant for now. I do not need its *mana*. I have these."

Orolandes tried to make out what Piranther was holding. He saw intricate flashes of colored fire against the dark pink of Piranther's palm.

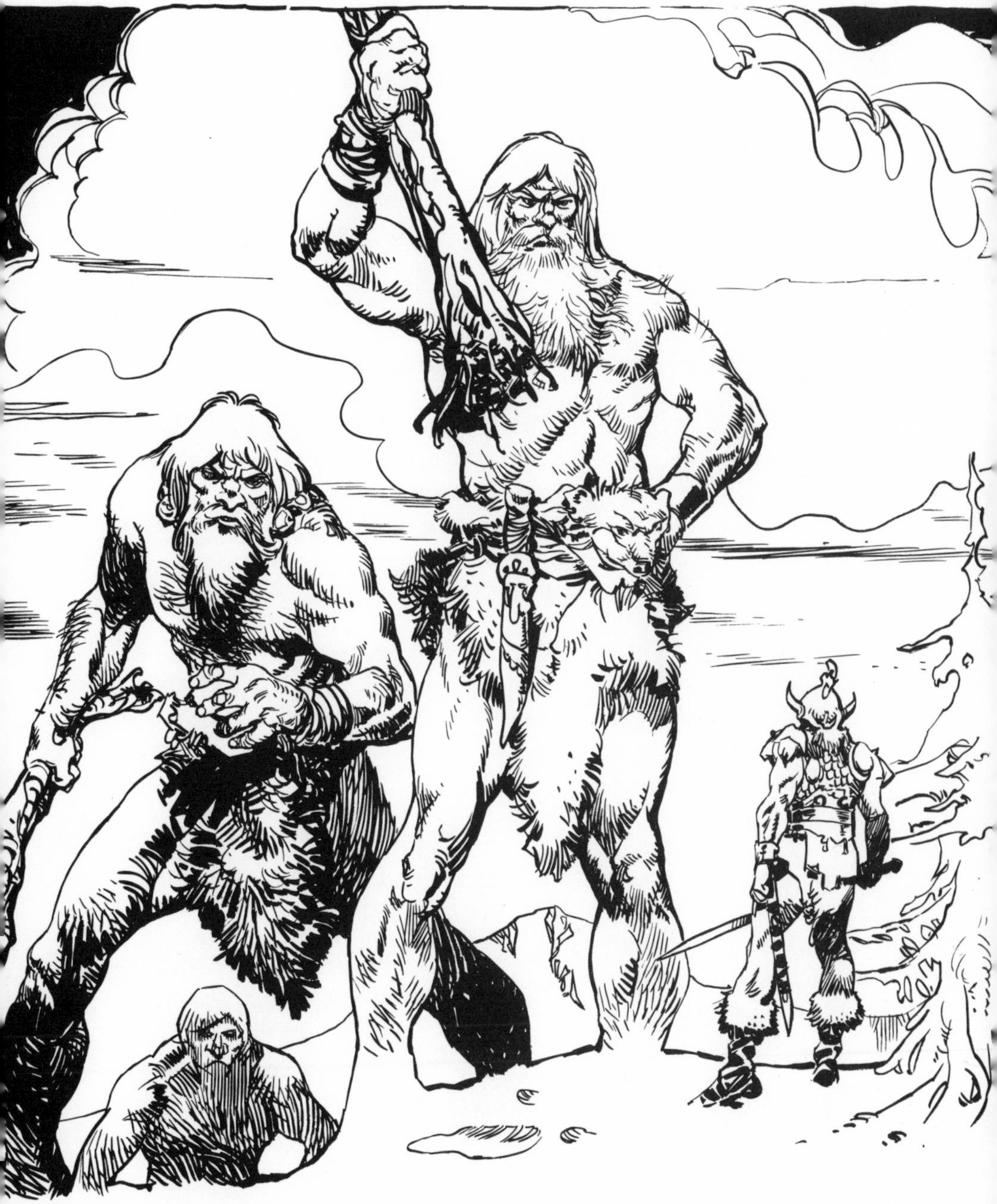

"Black opals. See how beautiful they are. Sense their power. There are more black opals in the South Land Mass than in all the rest of the world. Even so ... our numbers increase. These will not last forever. We must have the dormant god."

"You think small."

"Perhaps. Where are the others?"

"I don't know." Again Wavyhill's voice was strained.

"Must I dig for information?"

"Dig ... then. You say my ... name badly." Was Wavyhill *gloating?*

Piranther shrugged. He turned to Orolandes' backpack. "Certainly Mirandee carried a crystal ball. True, my dear? Let us look in on them." He upended the pack, and things spilled out: blankets, a smoked joint of elk, rope, pouches of dusts, the copper War-lock's Wheel, a few sharp slivers of crystal. "Could I be wrong? Kranthkorpool!"

"She smashed it falling out of a cloud." No mistake now, Wavyhill was gloating.

"Then we'll do it the hard way. After all, I have the power. If Clubfoot and the Warlock are trying to harm me ..." Piranther selected a fine, polished bit of many-colored fire as big as his toenail. " ... we'll just interrupt them."

The Nordiks had armed themselves. They were looking downslope to where three Frost Giants waited on the hidden side of the barrow hill.

A patch of snow behind them made them hard to see. Gannik and Wilf stood tall with a dignity they hadn't worn in the sauna. The third Giant was getting to his feet, taking his time.

It was worth the wait. The third Frost Giant stood seventeen or eighteen feet tall. He wore a fur about his hips, the skin of a white bear, and nothing else. His wild white hair and beard flared about his head; he was all white, even to the small tree that hung casually from one hand, with a knob of roots at the end to make an impressive cudgel.

Sword conspicuously in hand, Harric strode forward to call down the hill. "What do you want here?"

"Give us the magicians," the big one boomed.

"They are our guests. We hold the high ground."

The Warlock whispered to Hathsson, "What does he mean?"

"They have to come at us uphill," the blond Nordik whispered back. "Can you enchant our swords before they decide to charge?"

"No."

Meanwhile the big Frost Giant laughed boomingly and cried, "We are the high ground! And we must have the magicians. May Wilf come to speak to you without being hurt?"

"Yes."

If the Frost Giant woman was afraid, she showed none of it. She walked up without haste to join them. Harric opened conversation by saying, "Nordiks have fought Frost Giants before."

"We must have the magicians. Why must any of us die? You argued whether to kill them yourselves."

Interestingly, Harric did not deny it. "They are to do us a service. But even that is less important than this: Nordiks do not take orders from Frost Giants."

The Frost Giant woman looked down at Harric. "Have we not worked willingly for all of our lives? Have we refused you anything but one thing? These men threaten our god."

Clubfoot tried to interrupt, but Harric gestured him to silence, and answered her himself. "Your god had lost nearly all its power when you buried it."

"He kept enough," Wilf said wistfully. "I've heard the

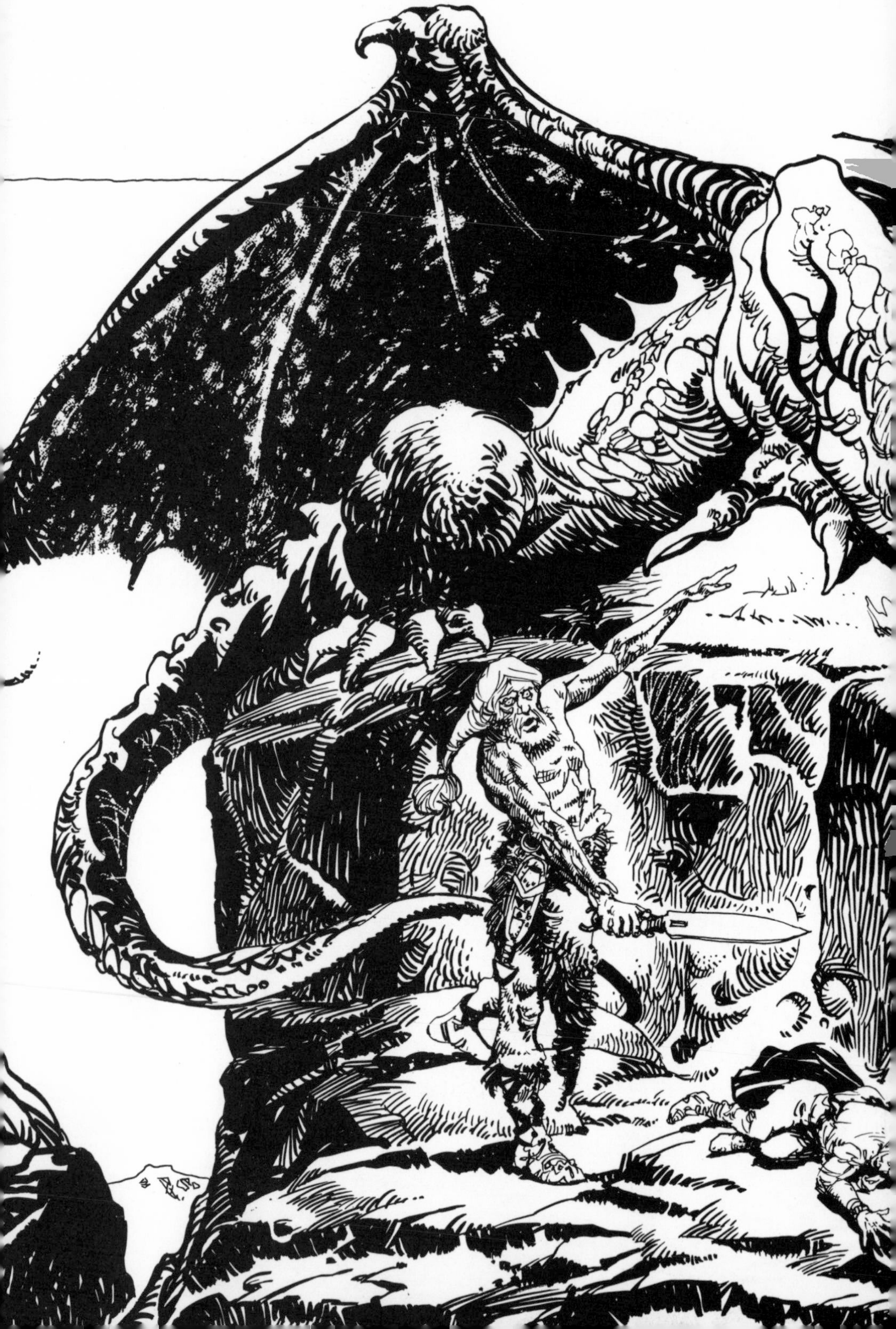

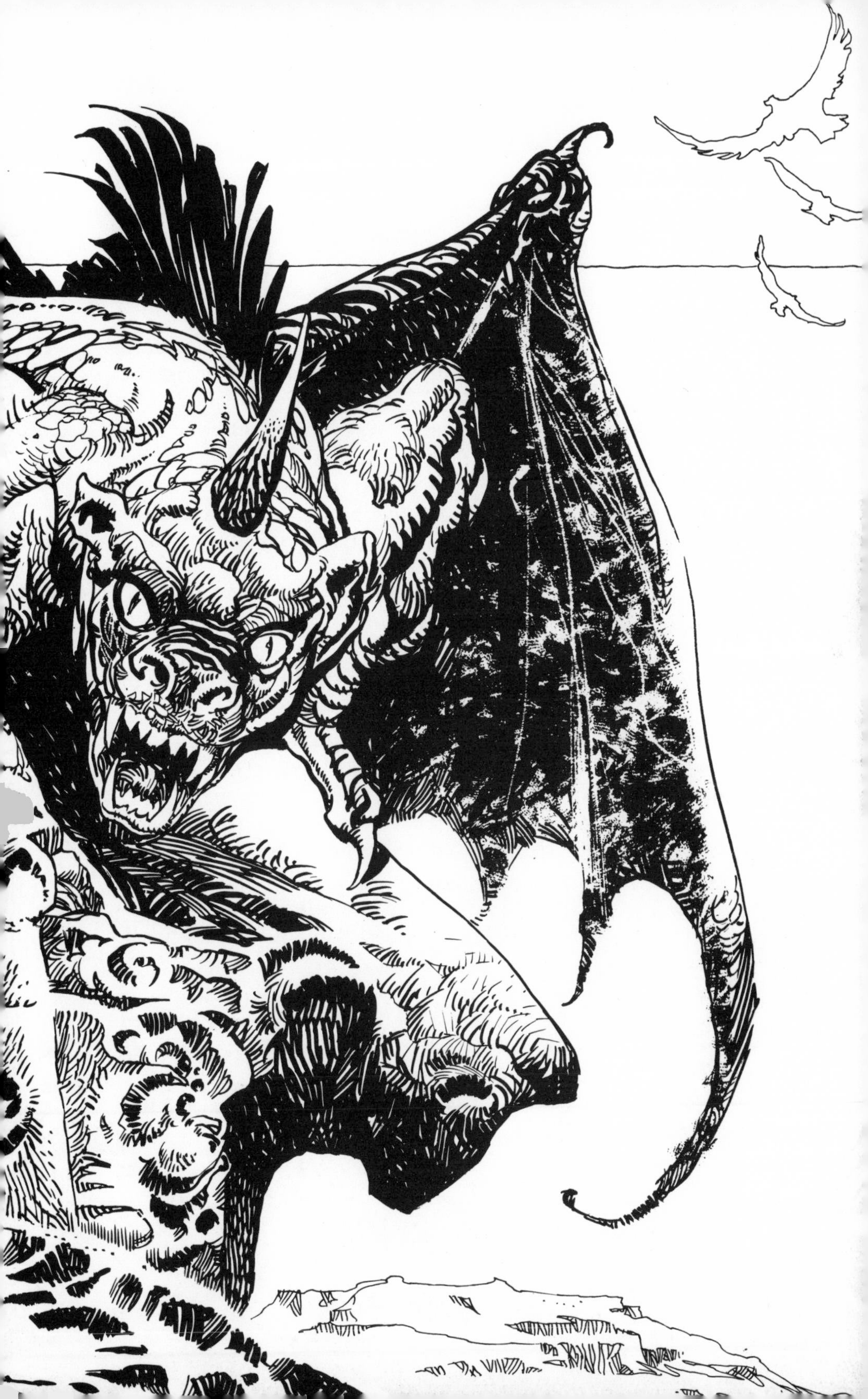

old ones talking. Even today, while the god within a god sleeps ... first love always ' fades. Marriage goes from adoration to companionship. My own lover turned to another woman for mere variety. If the god truly died — "

"We do not threaten your Roze-Kattee!" Clubfoot shouted. "Tell the big one that we want to bring the god back to life"

The Warlock saw sidelong glances between the Nordiks. *Curse!* But Wilf's reaction was stranger. The woman was blushing: pink blood beneath the white of cheek and throat. She wouldn't look at the magicians. It was suddenly obvious that the Frost Giants preferred their god dormant.

Harric asked, "Who is this tall Frost Giant who threatens us?"

"Tolerik is my father's cousin. He ran away when he was eleven; you may remember. He's lived here ever since. Sometimes we bring him things he can't get here." All in a rush she said, "We must have the magicians. If you give them to us, Tolerik will work for you for a year."

The local *mana* had allowed a Frost Giant to reach his full height, but it was too low to let a magician defend himself. They could only wait.

Poul said, "But by law he is already —"

Harric's voice easily drowned him out. "Very well. Take them."

Clubfoot dived for the pile of swords. Hathsson's foot hooked Clubfoot's twisted ankle. As Clubfoot sprawled headlong he felt a sword's point pressing the small of his back. Clubfoot froze.

Poul said, "But the swords! Wilf, will Tolerik let the magicians enchant our swords first?"

"Don't be a fool. We can't trust them now," Harric said.

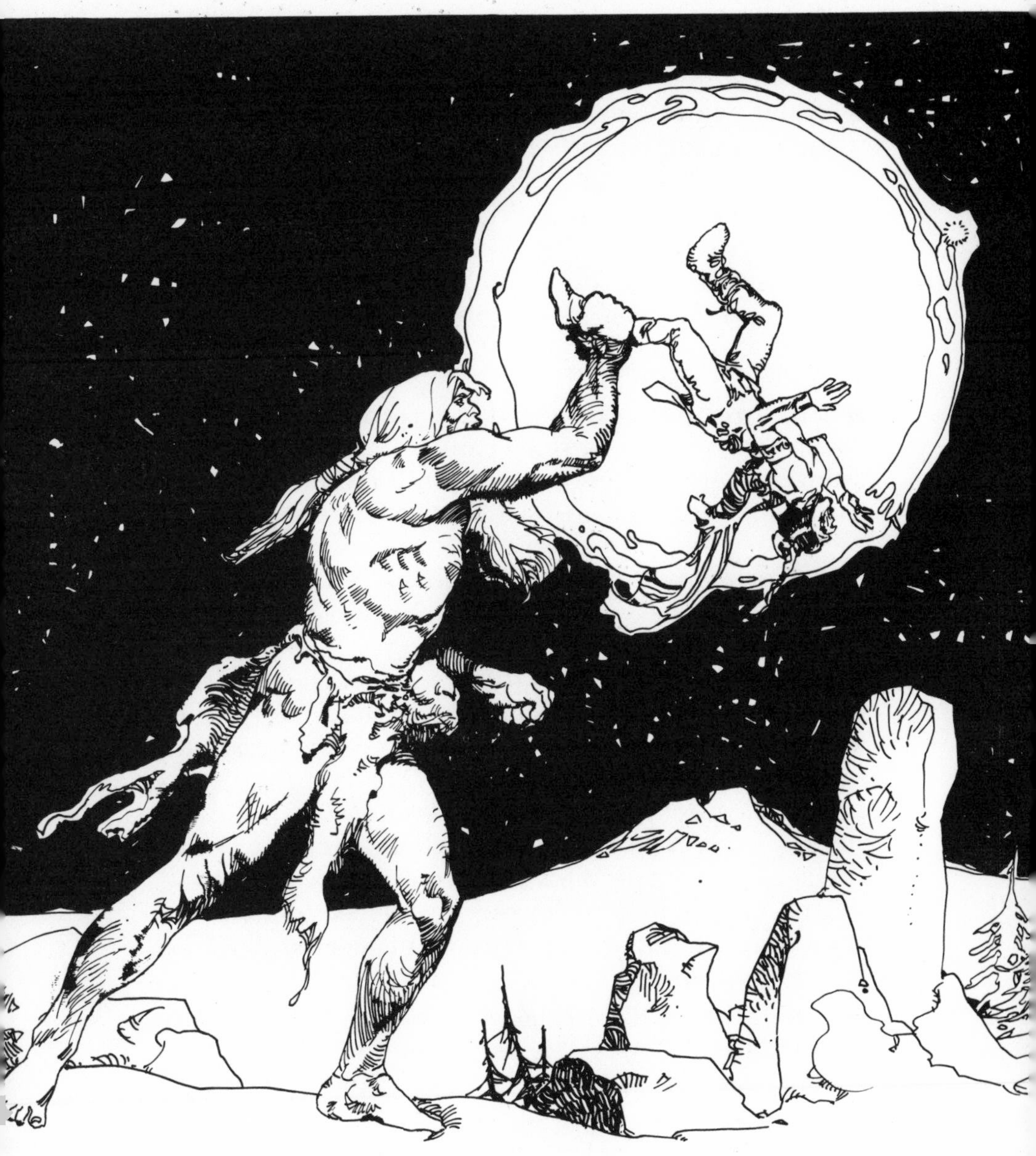

Wilf gestured downslope. Her father and his huge cousin started up. The Warlock was cursing himself for that moment of stunned surprise. Surprise, that warriors would betray a magician!

What kind of threat would cow an armed man the size of a big tree? The Warlock raised his arms. A fantasm, a great red-and-gold dragon stooping, slashing . . . if the Giant dodged, if he fell downslope, his height alone might break his neck . . .

The Giant's hand closed around Clubfoot's ankles and lifted him.

Colors formed in the air, tinges of red and gold. Harric frowned and rapped the Warlock's skull with his spear haft. The Warlock sank to his knees with the pain. He saw Clubfoot writhing in the Giant's hand as the Giant prepared to dash his brains out against a rock.

Darkness rippled around Clubfoot, swallowed him, swallowed the Giant's hand to the wrist. The Giant yelled and tried to pull away.

The Warlock sagged on the grass. It was all right. He saw the darkness closing around him and knew it for what it was: a Great Summoning. Mirandee must have found the god-within-a-god.

The hillside disappeared, and he was on dusty stone. Strength flowed into him, the strength of youth spells reviving. The Warlock stood up, saying, "W —"

And every muscle locked in place, locked him standing with his hand extended, his eyes smiling, his lips pursed on a W.

Clubfoot was on a rock floor with a great severed hand holding his ankles. Beyond him, Orolandes lay awkwardly, like a toppled statue. Mirandee leaned casually against a wall. Piranther —

Piranther returned the Warlock's smile. "I must remember to ask Clubfoot about that hand. What kind of allies were you gathering against me?" He dusted his hands together; the dust fell like motes of colored fire. He turned to the decorated skull sitting on a rock behind him. "Or did you trick me? Did I rescue them from a greater danger?"

"Revive them and ask," Wavyhill suggested.

"I like them better the way they are. Well, let us see your dormant god," said Piranther. He stepped delicately across Orolandes.

"If —"

Piranther turned.

"Nothing," said the skull. "Just a thought."

"Well?"

"You still can't move him."

"I'll decide that." Piranther turned and walked into the cavern.

Orolandes lay frozen in a frozen world. Behind him Piranther's footsteps were casually erratic, growing faint and blurred with echoes.

Wavyhill spoke low. "I hope you're not dead. If you're all dead, then I'm in serious trouble."

The skull chuckled softly. "He's deep in the cavern now. Warlock, if you can hear me, I claim a vengeance foregone. I could have suggested that he take you with him, for advice. He could have bound you with a loyalty spell, and you would have walked in with him. Warlock, Clubfoot, do you remember what you did to me, do you see what I am now? Mirandee, do you remember suggesting that I wasn't worthy to join you?"

The rock softened under Orolandes' rigid elbow. The light grew pink; or was the rock itself changing color?

The roof of the entrance descended.

Behind Orolandes came Piranther's echoing

scream. Wavyhill laughed shrilly, madly. A warm wet wind blew against Orolandes' back. It stank like the breath of a thousand wolves. Piranther's scream ended as if muffled.

The roof above him had dropped low enough to touch the Warlock's head.

Wavyhill ended his cackling. "Well? Am I right? Did I have your lives in my grasp? Isn't it a *marvelous* hiding place for the last god? Greek, you probably still don't understand. Have you heard of the World-Worm, the snake that circles the world and swallows its own tail? The Alps and the Andes and the Rocky Mountains all form a part of its body. And you lie within its mouth."

Orolandes said, "Uhn!"

"Oh, ho! You're alive, are you? That paralysis won't last. I could free you now, if I could make the gestures. I don't think Piranther did anything fancy; he just bulled through our ward-spells with the power in his black opals.

"Marvelous, isn't it? The World-Worm is a strange beast. Of course it couldn't possibly live by eating its own flesh. The tail used to have flanges of bone behind those huge pores. It sweeps up all kinds of things: turf, birds' nests, the dens of animals that lair in the pores, even full grown trees growing in the dirt the flanges sweep up. It grows very slowly this tail. And of course anything that wanders into the mouth gets eaten. I should be talking in the past tense, really," said the skull. "The fins are all weathered away. The World-Worm is like all magical forms of life; it turns to stone when the *mana* runs low. Like dragon bones. Like that statue in front of the Prissthil gates. What fooled Piranther was the tail. Running back into the mouth like that, it changes the shape so the cavern isn't mouth-shaped any more."

Teeth, thought Orolandes. I was jogging through a forest of spike teeth. He said, "Uhn!" The calf of his leg kicked suddenly, painfully.

The roof of the cavern was rising . . . and changing in color, greying to the look of stone.

"Can talk," Clubfoot said. "Can't move yet. Anyone?"

The Warlock grunted. "Spell should wear off soon."

"Got us with those black opals," said Clubfoot. "We couldn't know. Wavyhill. Why here?"

"Why, it's obvious! Look: nobody who knows what this place is would come here. The World-Worm must have been nearly dead for centuries, but who'd risk it? If a mundane wandered in here all unknowing, nothing would happen. But if a magician came here looking for the dormant god — " Wavyhill chuckled. "There's *mana* in magic. The power of their spells hovers around magicians. Put a *mana* source in the World-Worm's mouth and what happens?"

"Poor Piranther," said Mirandee.

"It wakes up for a snack," Clubfoot said callously.

"I think it would have done that even without the opals. Any time a magician comes calling . . . or a swordsman carrying a sword stolen from a place where gods once lived. In the meantime, whatever *mana* is still with the World-Worm is there to keep the dormant god alive. If our luck holds."

Clubfoot had called up a pair of hares: an old and simple magic, still potent almost everywhere. He had started a fire and cleaned the hares and was now roasting them. In his stiff back there was a rejection of the quarrel now going on in the cavern entrance.

"I won't let him go," Mirandee said. She sat with her back to them, her legs dangling over the stone buttress . . . over what must be the World-Worm's lower lip.

Orolandes came up behind Mirandee. He moved

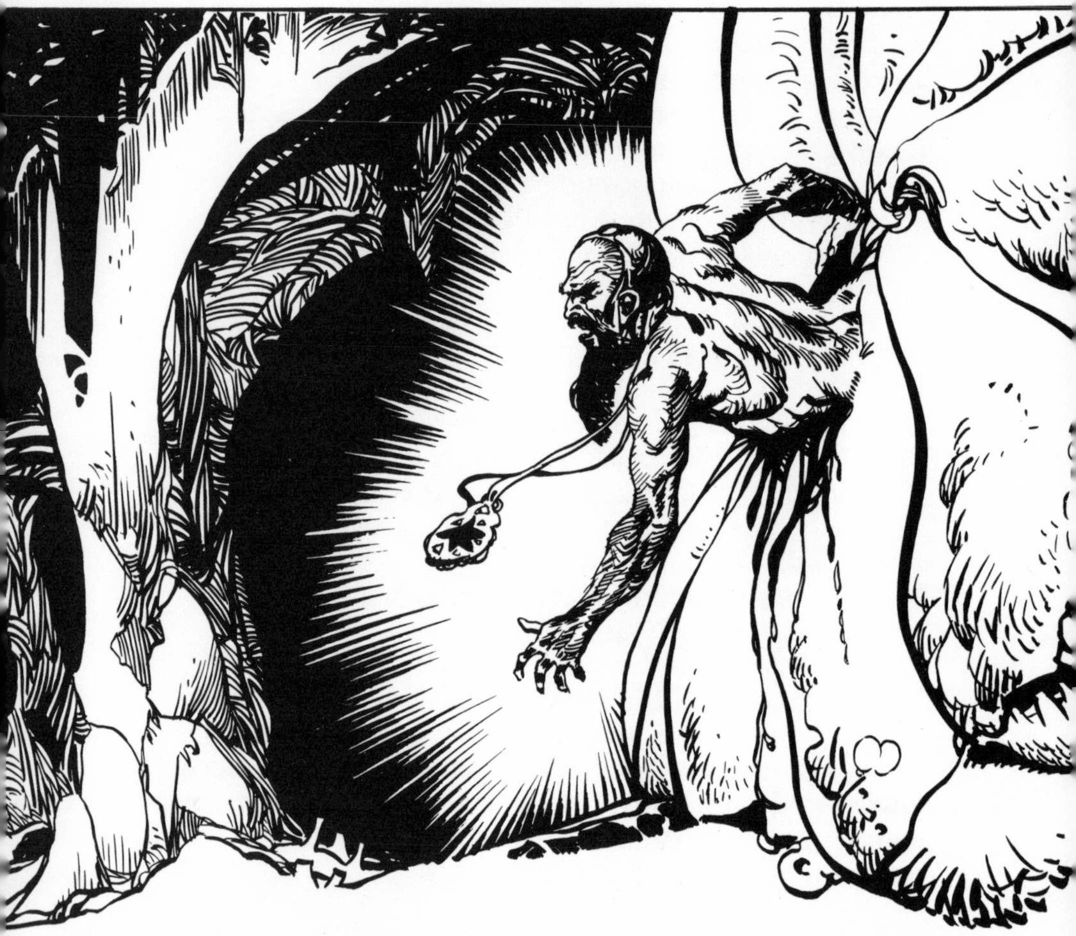

stiffly. They were all sore from the cramps that had followed their paralysis. He put his hands on her shoulders, ignored their angry shrug. "It is what we came for."

"Idiot! It's eaten a powerful magician *and* his black opals. It may not sleep again for years! Wavyhill, tell him! It eats things that wander into its mouth!"

"It may have gone dormant again," the skull said

comfortably. "It was *mana*-starved for generations. It's a big beast; it needs nourishment."

"Father of trolls!" she spat.

"Retired."

"Mountain goat," the Warlock said without turning. He stood at the corner of the cavern's mouth, a little apart.

He was ignored. The skull on the rock said, "Listen, girl. I gave up my vengeance against these, my murderers. I am willing to risk a swordsman to the same high purpose."

The Warlock began singing to himself.

"Well, 'Landes? You heard him. You can't throw away your life after that. What about me?" Mirandee demanded.

Floating bodies, myriads of bodies, shoals of bloated human bodies turned in the waves, bumping gently against each other and against the wooden raft on which Orolandes lay dying of thirst beside the decaying body of a centaur girl. Did they thirst for vengeance? They had the right...and if Orolandes walked out of the cavern alive, there were lives still to be saved. There were centaur and satyr tribes in Greece. He said, "I have to."

"If you die I'll die!"

He was startled. "You'll die? Because you read my mind?"

"Yes!"

Wavyhill said, "She's lying. Think it through. Piranther read your mind too. Would he have taken that risk?"

Orolandes looked at her. Her eyes did not drop. "I mean it. I won't live without you."

A clattering of hooves startled them. They turned as a mountain goat bounded up on the World-Worm's lip and stood gazing up at the Warlock.

"Any of you idiots could have thought of this," the Warlock told them. He turned back to give the goat its orders.

Stiff-legged and blank of eye, the goat walked into the cavern. They watched it blunder into stalagmites and stumble on until it had reached the entrance to the inner cave . . . the World-Worm's gullet.

Clubfoot spoke grudgingly, it seemed. "You can wait till morning. Have some dinner."

"No."

Mirandee sat stony-eyed. She did not look up as Orolandes stroked her hair, turned and walked after the goat.

The smell of broiling meat followed him and made it hard to go on. He circled teeth taller than himself. He climbed the soil-gathering potholes in the side of the long, long tail. He walked along the top of the tail with his torch casting yellow light into the gap.

He heard only his own footsteps. The bats . . . the bats must have been eaten along with Piranther. The flickering flame made motion everywhere. How would he know when the roof began to descend?

Far at the back, the tip of a stalagmite tooth showed above a whitish mass that enclosed it.

The last god was no bigger than Piranther, made of nearly translucent marble. It sat with its arms and legs wrapped tight around the base of a tooth. Its slanted eyes glowed yellow-white by torchlight. Its face and ears were covered with fur. In the triangular shape of its face there was something cat-feminine.

It took some nerve to wrap his arms around the stalagmite and, throwing all of his weight into it, try to move the tooth. It was solidly fixed.

"There's no way to get it loose from there," he told the magicians. "Your Roze-Kattee was a coward,

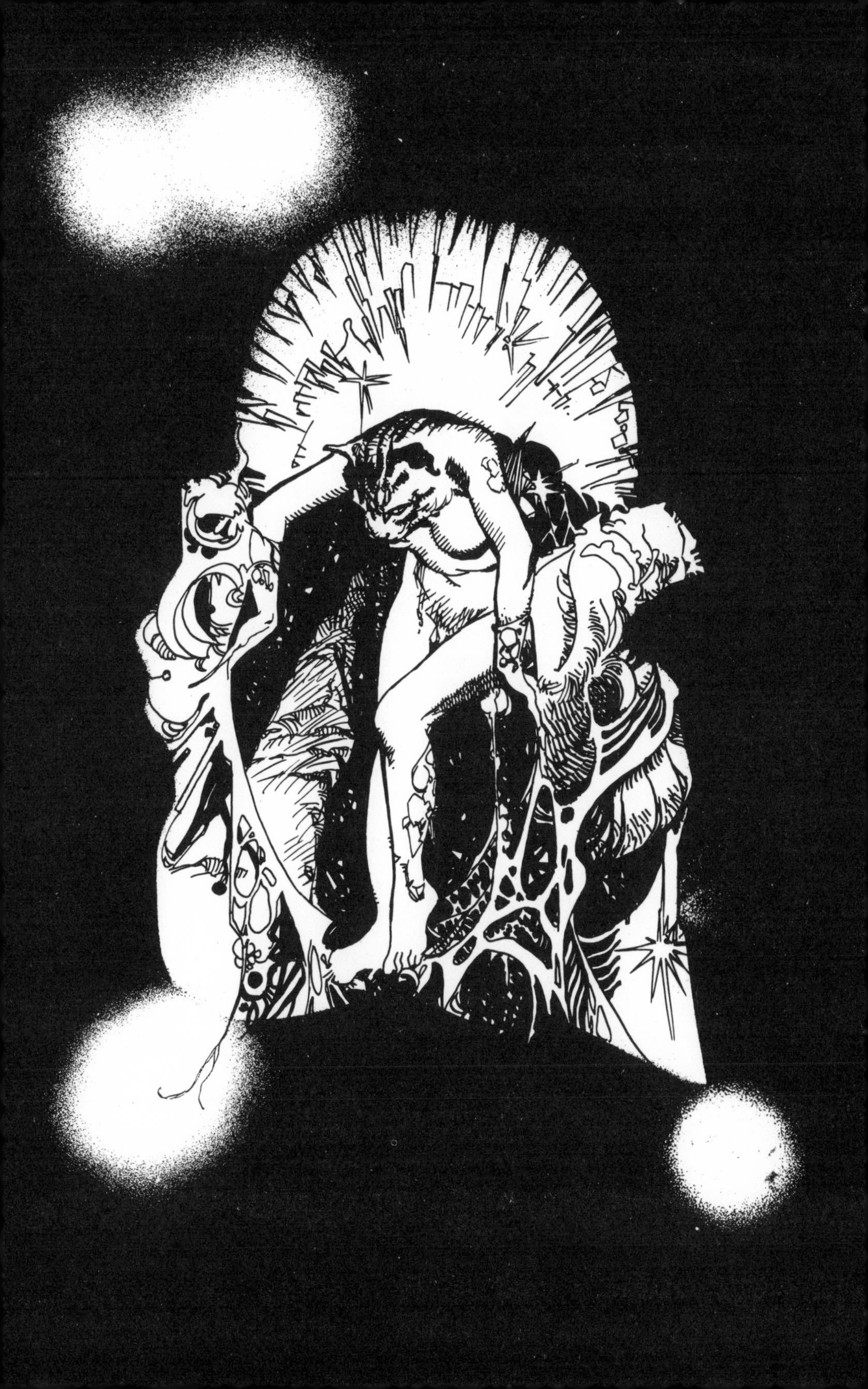

Wavyhill. It's got a death-grip on that tooth." And he sat down to eat hot disjointed hare, one-handed, with his other arm around a weeping Mirandee. He had been ready to die in there; he had come out alive, and he was famished.

When there was nothing left but bones, Wavyhill said, "It sounds bad."

Orolandes grunted. "Would you consider chopping through one of the god's arms?"

"No."

"Then we'd have to chop through the tooth at the base, then have a team of men pull out tooth and statue together. Work for an army. Can we hire some of the Nordiks? They live close enough to — "

The Warlock chopped at the air. "The Nordiks won't help us. Even the Frost Giants seem to prefer their god dormant. Curse them and their coward god."

"And my lost vengeance," said Wavyhill.

Clubfoot sat hugging his knees. "I don't believe it. We came all this way, and now . . . No. There's an answer. We've got meat to be called and snow for water. We'll stay here until we find an answer."

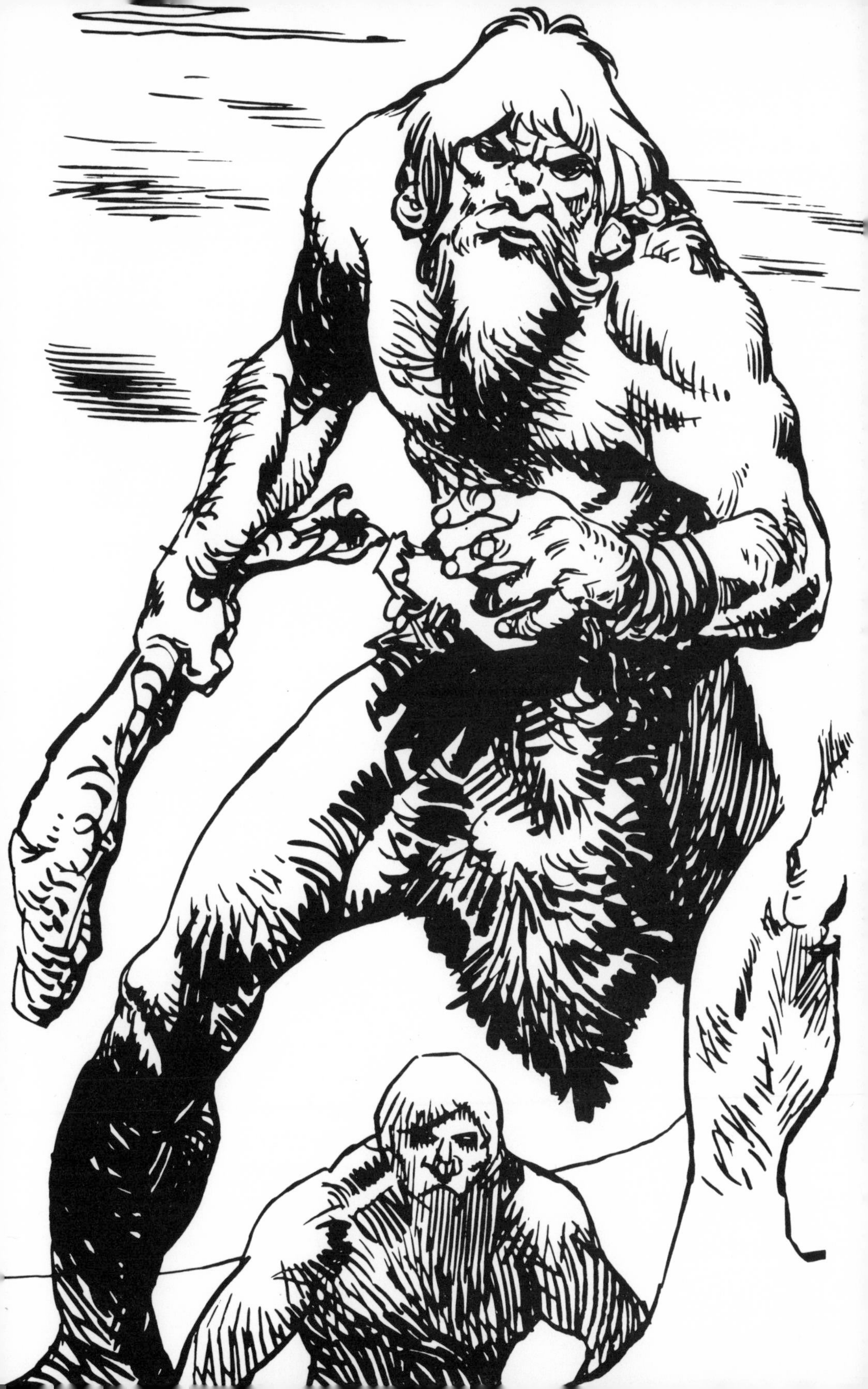

THE GOD OF LOVE AND MADNESS

Fourteen thousand years have garbled all the details.

The last god is remembered in diverse legends. Roze become Eros, Kattee become Kali and Hecate, their qualities radically changed. Now only children hear of the Warlock's great project. They learn of a foolish frightened hen who ran screaming to tell the world that the world was ending. Some she convinced. In a desperate effort to salvage something, she led them into a cave.

The solution was in the cave. So close . . .

"We *can* get close!" A bellowing voice cut deep into the Warlock's dreams.

He rolled over, blinking. He heard rustlings and grunts of annoyance around him, and saw Clubfoot looming over him in gray pre-dawn light. Half asleep, he struggled to sit up.

Clubfoot was shivering with excitement. "Wavyhill, do you remember that gesture-spell, the variant on the Warlock's Wheel? The one that cancels *mana*."

"Remember it? Sure. I designed it. Nearly killed the Warlock with it, too. Shall I teach you the gestures?"

The Warlock said, "Wait a minute. I'm still trying to wake up. Clubfoot, have you really got something?"

"Yes! We can't get into the cavern, right? But we can get close! Roze-Kattee is just inside the World-Worm's cheek!"

Orolandes woke late, to the smell of roasting rabbit and the pleasant sound of Mirandee's humming. "Eat," she said gaily. "We've got work to do."

"Work? That's good. Yesterday it was all a dead end. Where are the others?"

"Already at work. Today it's different. I had a dream."

"So? Or do you dream the future? You're so much a

man's ideal woman, I keep forgetting what else you are."

She kissed him. "Sometimes I dream the future. It's not dependable." Her brow wrinkled. "This one was funny. I guess it means success. I dreamed the sky was falling."

Orolandes laughed. "That sounds scary."

"No, I wasn't frightened at all. And it is what we're after, isn't it?"

"Maybe, but it sounds scary as Hell when you put it like that. What *did* you feel, watching the sky fall?"

"Nothing."

After breakfast they walked on bare earth, swinging their linked hands. On their left a sloping wall of stone rose out of the earth, higher and higher above them as they walked on. The stone was smooth, worn by the wind, until only a suggestion of scales was left to show that this was the side of the World-Worm's head.

They came to where a patch of the smooth rock turned to crumbly sandstone. Here was a hole in the the rock, head-high, and sand spilled beneath it. Orolandes paused to look, but Mirandee pulled him on.

The second hole was higher and larger, big enough for a man to crawl through. Clubfoot and the Warlock waited as they came up. The magicians had piled rocks as stepping-stones to reach the hole. Orolandes climbed the pile and looked through.

It was black as a stomach in there. Clubfoot coaxed the end of a branch into flame and handed it up to him. By firelight Orolandes saw that he was ten feet away from the marble statue of Roze-Kattee.

"How did you break through? We don't have so much as an ax."

"We cursed it," said the Warlock. "Wavyhill evolved

a gesture spell that uses up the *mana* in whatever he aims it at. He used it on me once. We don't use it much these days. It's wasteful."

Wavyhill spoke from his accustomed perch on the Warlock's shoulder. "This isn't just rock, after all. It's a great brute of a dying god."

Orolandes nodded. "What's the next step? Can you revive Roze-Kattee through that hole?"

"We think so. The next step is tricky, and it involves climbing," said the Warlock. "That leaves it up to you and Clubfoot."

Clubfoot nodded, but he didn't look happy.

And Mirandee was frowning. "Why, no. I climb better than you, don't I, Clubfoot?"

"Well, there's more to this than — "

"And I'm as skilled at magic. Unless this is weather magic? Just what have you in mind?"

Clubfoot answered in the Guild tongue.

They talked for some time. Whatever they were discussing, it was complicated, judging from Mirandee's frequent questions and the way Clubfoot waved his arms. Orolandes could see that Mirandee didn't like it. He edged closer to those inseparable colleagues, Wavyhill and the Warlock, and asked, "What's going on?"

"Necromancy," said the skull. "Very technical. Can you climb that rock with a pack?"

"Yes. But why is Mirandee — "

"We didn't discuss it with her before. She didn't know what was involved."

"Then — "

"No!" Mirandee snapped. "If it has to be done, I'll do it. Otherwise I wouldn't let you do it either. Orolandes!" She turned her back on Clubfoot, whose face was a study in mixed emotions: sorrow and relief. Mirandee was biting her lower lip.

Orolandes went up alone, barefoot, using as fingerholds and toeholds those crevices and irregularities whose pattern just hinted at serpent-scales worn smooth. There were potholes in the great smooth expanse of the World-Worm's head: real potholes this time, worn by rain pooling to dissolve rock. Orolandes chopped with the sword point — the blade was uncannily hard — until he had joined adjacent potholes into a knob that would hold the line.

Mirandee toiled up the line. There was nothing Orolandes could do from up here except hurt for her, fear for her. The slope wouldn't kill her if she slipped, but it would remove skin and the flesh beneath, and she might break a leg at the end . . .

But she arrived intact, panting. She said no word to Orolandes. She spilled the pack he had carried up. She selected a chain of tiny silver links and arranged it in a circle. She drew symbols with a piece of red chalk. She looked up.

"Give me your sword," she said.

Orolandes didn't move. "What's it all about?"

"I don't think you want to know."

"Tell me, love."

She sagged. "Necromancy. Magical power derived from death, from murder. We need enough power to waken a half-dead god. We're going to get it by murdering the World-Worm."

"Oh. More death. Isn't there any other way?"

"I tried to think of one. Don't you believe me?"

"Yes, of course. Of course I believe you."

"Curse it, Orolandes, the World-Worm is dead *now*. The land has shifted and broken its back in places; it's not even the shape of a snake any more. The wind has worn it away, scales and skin and flesh. If we revived it completely, right now, it would die almost immediately. It's *dead*, but it doesn't know it yet, and we can take advantage of that. Give me your sword."

He did.

"Stand well back," she said, and turned to her work.

The song she sang was unpleasant, grating. Orolandes felt numbness in his toes and fingers and a black depression creeping into his soul. He watched as the dusty stone within the ring of silver turned dusty pink.

Mirandee raised the sword, holding the hilt tightly in both hands. She brought it down hard. Still singing, she pounded on the hilt with a rock until the blade was entirely sheathed.

The mountain shuddered. Orolandes flattened, gripping rock, ready for the next quake. Far back along the mountain chain to the south, he saw motion and churning dust.

The mountain shuddered and spilled Clubfoot's little pile of stones. The Warlock cursed in his mind, but

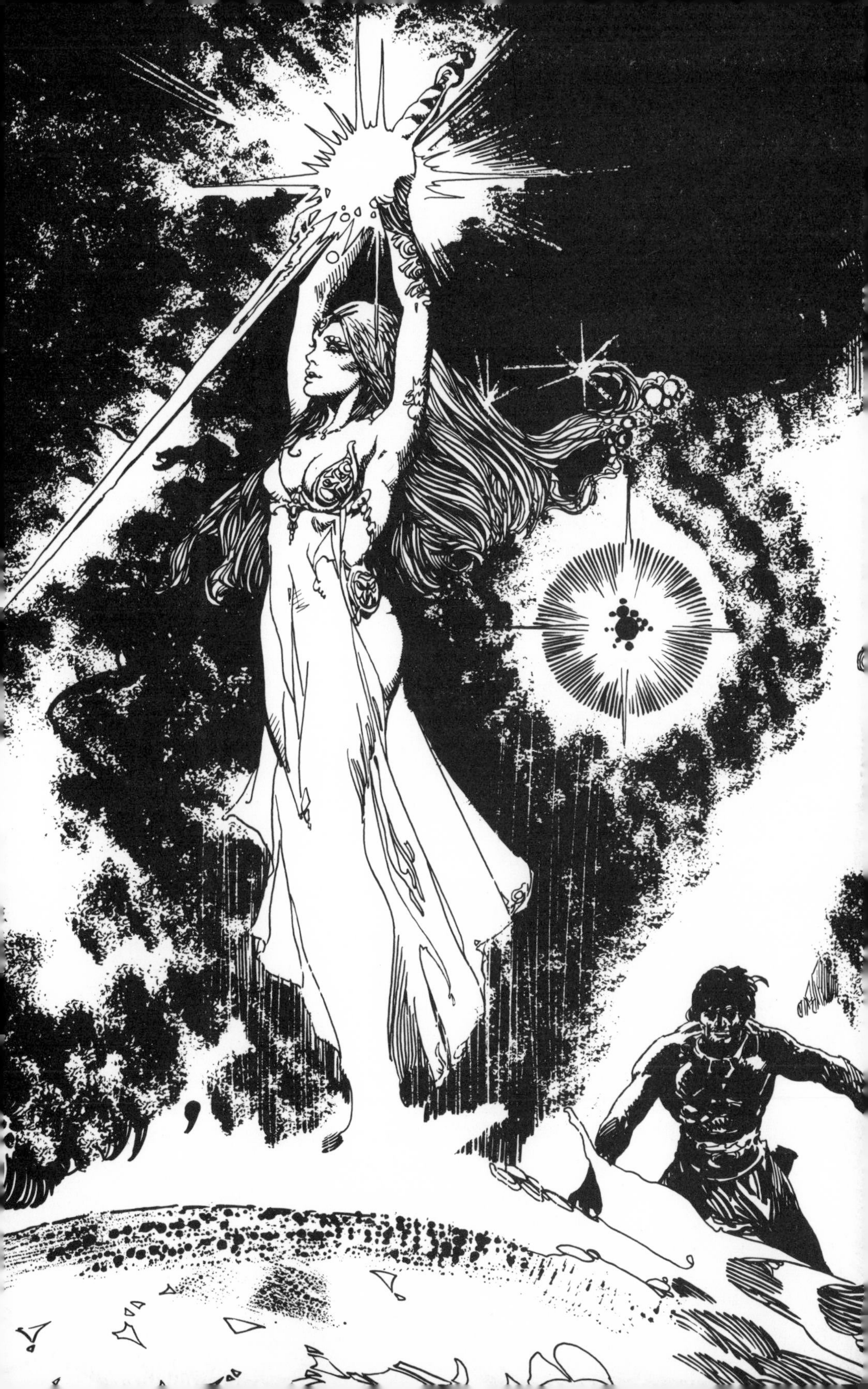

he started chanting immediately. *Let my enemy's heart be mine, let my enemy's strength be mine* — Wavyhill sang the counterpoint next to the Warlock's ear, while Clubfoot worked at moving rocks.

It was hard work, and Clubfoot was in haste. Without the ladder of stones, they could not aim their spells into the cavern. Sweat ran down his cheeks and his neck,. and he hurled his cloak from him and kept working. Poor Clubfoot, he couldn't even curse. The Warlock sang on and watched the rock pile grow.

High enough. Clubfoot mumbled over a dry branch until it blazed, hurled it through the hole and went up the rocks after it. The Warlock followed more slowly, accepting Clubfoot's assistance. He could feel the power in him now. The World-Worm's life had fed him.

The last god seemed to move in the firelight; but it was illusion. Its marble arms gripped the World-Worm's tooth as tightly as ever.

Wake and see the world ... They sang the spell he and Clubfoot had sung for Wavyhill, the song for reviving the dead. Wavyhill's voice quavered and shifted. Wavyhill was frightened, and rightly. This could cost him his own not-quite-life. The Warlock could feel the *mana* leaving him.

In the middle of the chant his voice left. him. He managed to finish the phrase, then signalled Clubfoot with a very ancient gesture, a finger across his throat. Clubfoot moved in smoothly. Wavyhill sang on, in an echoless voice that did not pause for breath.

The tree limb had almost burned out. The statue's eyes picked up the firelight like cat's-eye emeralds. The Warlock made his exaggerated passes, and worried. *Let your heart beat, let your blood flow* ... Would a spell worked to revive men revive a god?

The song ended.

The marble statue did not move.

At last Clubfoot sighed and turned from the black opening. He stumbled down the ladder of stones. The Warlock followed. He was exhausted. The soreness in his throat felt permanent.

"I feel rotten," said Orolandes. Shoals of shifting corpses floated past his memory. He sat slumped with his chin on his knees. He could not think of a reason ever to move again. "We killed the World-Worm. How could anything be worth that?"

"It's the spell," Mirandee said. "I feel rotten too. Live with it."

"I'm glad I'm not a magician."

"No, you don't have what it takes."

"What does it take?"

Her black hair was a curtain around her, rendering her anonymous. "It takes another kind of courage. You know what I can do, given the power. Cause solid rock to flow like soft clay in invisible hands. Walk on clouds. Read minds, or take them over, or build illusions more real than reality. Kill with a gesture: one moment a hale and dangerous man, the next a mass of meat already decomposing. I can wake the dead to ask them questions. All those things, and other things I know how to do: they make a hash of what a mundane would call common sense. What scares the wits out of the mundanes is knowing how *fragile* our reality is. Not many can take that." She shifted a little, but the tent of hair still hid her. "Swordsman, I think we made a mistake, getting so involved with each other."

He nodded. In retrospect it seemed almost ridiculous, how dependent he had been on this woman. "It's no basis for a lifelong love affair, is it? I'm glad you said it first."

When she said nothing, he added, "You read my

mind by accident. You must know a spell to break you loose."

"I do."

The sun was warm and bright, and here they sat on the biggest corpse in the world. He had felt so good this morning. Where had it gone?

The witch-woman said, "You're around thirty, aren't you? A child, no more. I'm over seventy. The boy and the old lady, the witch and the swordsman. They don't go," she said sadly. "That's not to say we should give up sex. That was good."

"You pulled me out of a bad period. I guess you know I'm grateful."

"You're just not in love any more. Nor am I."

"Right."

Mirandee seemed to drift off into a private reverie of her own.

Orolandes was feeling better. The awful death-wish depression was leaving him. It was good to end a love affair this easily, with no hatred, no recriminations, no guilt . . .

He saw her stiffen.

She stood abruptly. "Let's get down."

"Not so fast," he said as she wound the line round her waist and backed toward the drop. "You're in too much of a hurry. Curse it, slow down, you'll get killed that way!"

Mirandee ignored him. She went down backward, properly, but too dangerously damn fast. "Slow down!" he ordered her.

"No time!"

Huh? Well, it was her neck. He watched her descend.

"I think I've chanted my last spell," the Warlock whispered. His throat felt dry as dust.

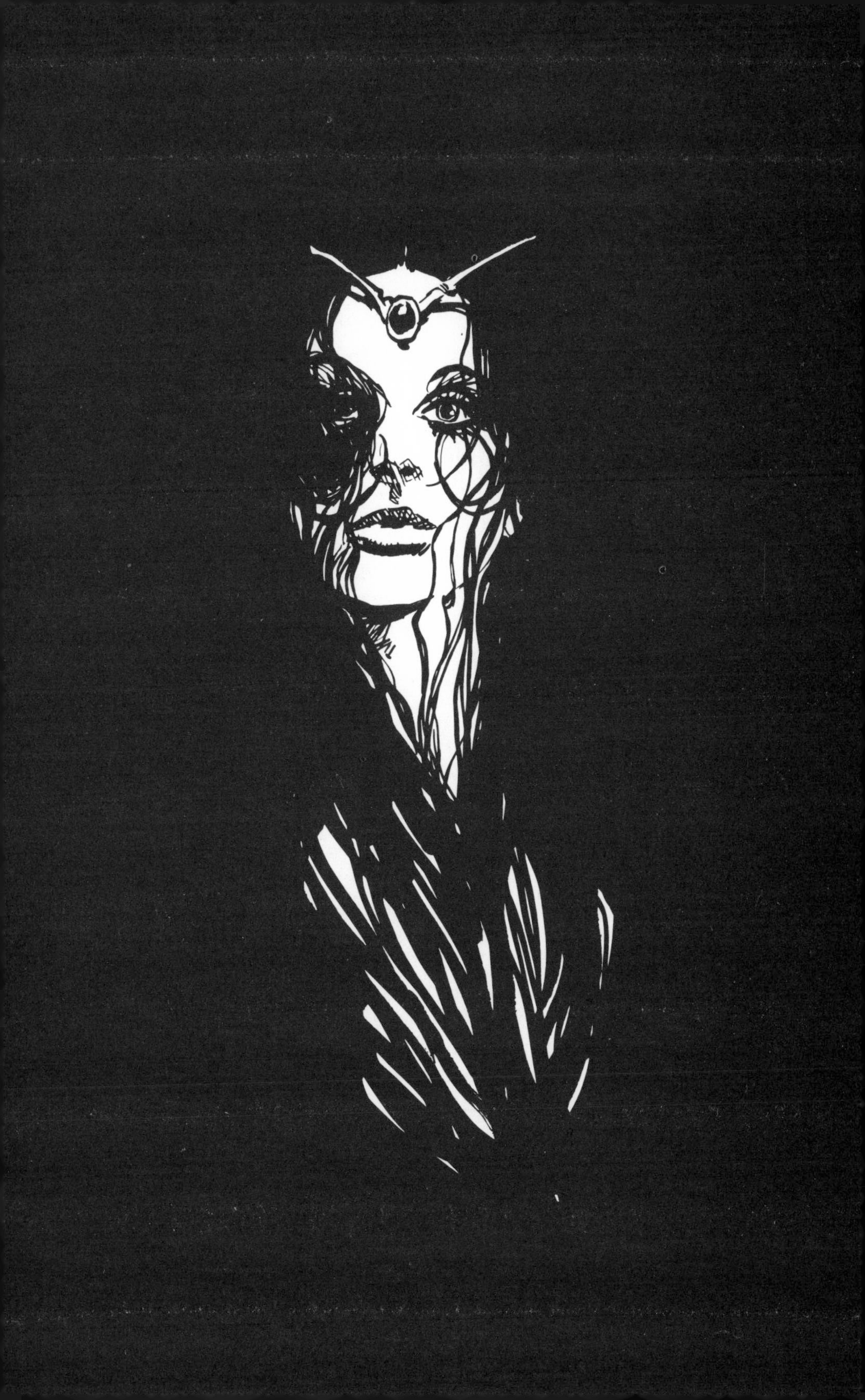

"This isn't the end," said Clubfoot. "Only the first attack. We'll talk it over with Mirandee. Figure out what went wrong. Try again."

"Sure."

"I chanted youth spells for you once. I can do it again," said Clubfoot, "once we land the Moon." He paused. "That sounds insane."

"Maybe it is."

They sat slumped against the corpse of the World-Worm. It felt like sandstone now, crumbly soft rock that the winds would wear away. The magicians were exhausted, even Wavyhill, who had not spoken in minutes.

"No maybe about it," Clubfoot said suddenly. "It's crazy. How long have there been men in the world? A couple of thousand years at least, right? Maybe more. Maybe a lot more. But the *mana* was still rich in the world when some unknown god made men. And they used it."

"Of course they did," said the Warlock. "Why not?"

"The names of the great magicians come down to us. Alhazred, Vulcan the Shaper, Hera — Look, what I'm getting at is this. There were a couple of thousand years of *mana* so rich that none of us, no magician of these last days, has the skill to use it. His spells would kill him. Do you believe that nobody in those last two thousand years ever tried to land the Moon? *Nobody?*"

"Why should they?"

"Because it's pretty! And not all those old masters were completely sane, Warlock. And some of the sane ones served mad emperors, like Vulcan served Trillion Mu."

"All right. They tried. Certainly they failed. Maybe they weren't desperate enough."

"Maybe. Another thing. If we don't know what keeps the Moon up, we sure as Fate don't know why. One of the gods put it up, maybe; or many gods; or even a being of unknown power and unknown nature, something that doesn't live on a world at all. If we don't know why the Moon was put there, how can we dare call it down? We don't even dare drain it of *mana*, because we don't know what ancient spells that might ruin."

"You make sense," the Warlock said with some reluctance. "I've even been wondering if it matters to anyone but us."

"Well, of course it matters ..." Clubfoot trailed off.

"Are you sure? Animals die. Classes of animals die. Civilizations die. New things come to take their places. Take Prissthil. The sky-stone is gone, but is Prissthil hurting? It's a thriving village, a trade center. The guard: his grandfather was a magician, but he's not hurting. The Nordiks had captive magicians, and what did they want from them? Magic swords, and nothing else! Even the Frost Giants are happy enough with their god dormant. The strong ones adapt."

"I wonder what Mirandee's in a such a hurry about? She's coming down awfully fast."

The Warlock didn't hear. He said, "Maybe Piranther was right. We use Roze-Kattee directly, get what good we can out of the last god. Wavyhill, what do you think?"

"I want to die," said Wavyhill.

"What?"

"It's not worth it. Another ten years of life, another hundred, and so what? People die. Even World-Worms die, and gods, and magicians."

"Wavyhill, what's got into you?"

"Nothing. Nothing's got into me. What could get into a dead man? I don't feel good, I don't feel bad. I guess I like it that way. Turn me off, Warlock. Use the spell we used to break through the World-Worm's cheek. It won't even hurt."

"Are you sure?"

"I'm sure," Wavyhill said without regret.

Mirandee found them that way, apathetic and dreamy-eyed, when she reached them out of breath and still trying to run. "Where is it?" she demanded.

The Warlock looked up. "What? Oh, the god. It sleeps on."

"Troll dung it does! Can't you *feel* it?"

"Feel what?"

"Why, it's soaking up all the love and all the madness it can reach! *Feeding* on it!"

The Warlock stood up fast. Of course, he'd been stupid, they'd all three slipped into sanity without noticing! Sweet reason and solid judgement and philosophical resignation, these were not common among sorcerers. As he scrambled up the piled stones behind Clubfoot, he wondered what had tipped off Mirandee, who *was* stable and sensible. Then he remembered the Greek swordsman.

Clubfoot put his head in the hole. His voice was muffled. "Curse, we forgot to bring a torch! Mirandee, would you — "

The sandstone wall next to them fell outward. A splinter of rock nicked the Warlock's cheek; another struck Wavyhill, *tok!* Slabs of rock fell and smashed to sand, and behind them the last god stepped forth.

God of love and madness, was it? Roze-Kattee seemed a god of madness alone. It was shaggy with coarse hair, hair that covered its face and chest, baring only the eyes. Its eyes blazed yellow-white, brighter than the daylight. Orolandes had called it small, but it wasn't; it was bigger than the Warlock . . . and it was growing before their eyes.

Its pointed ears twitched as it looked around at its world. Already its head was above the magicians, and

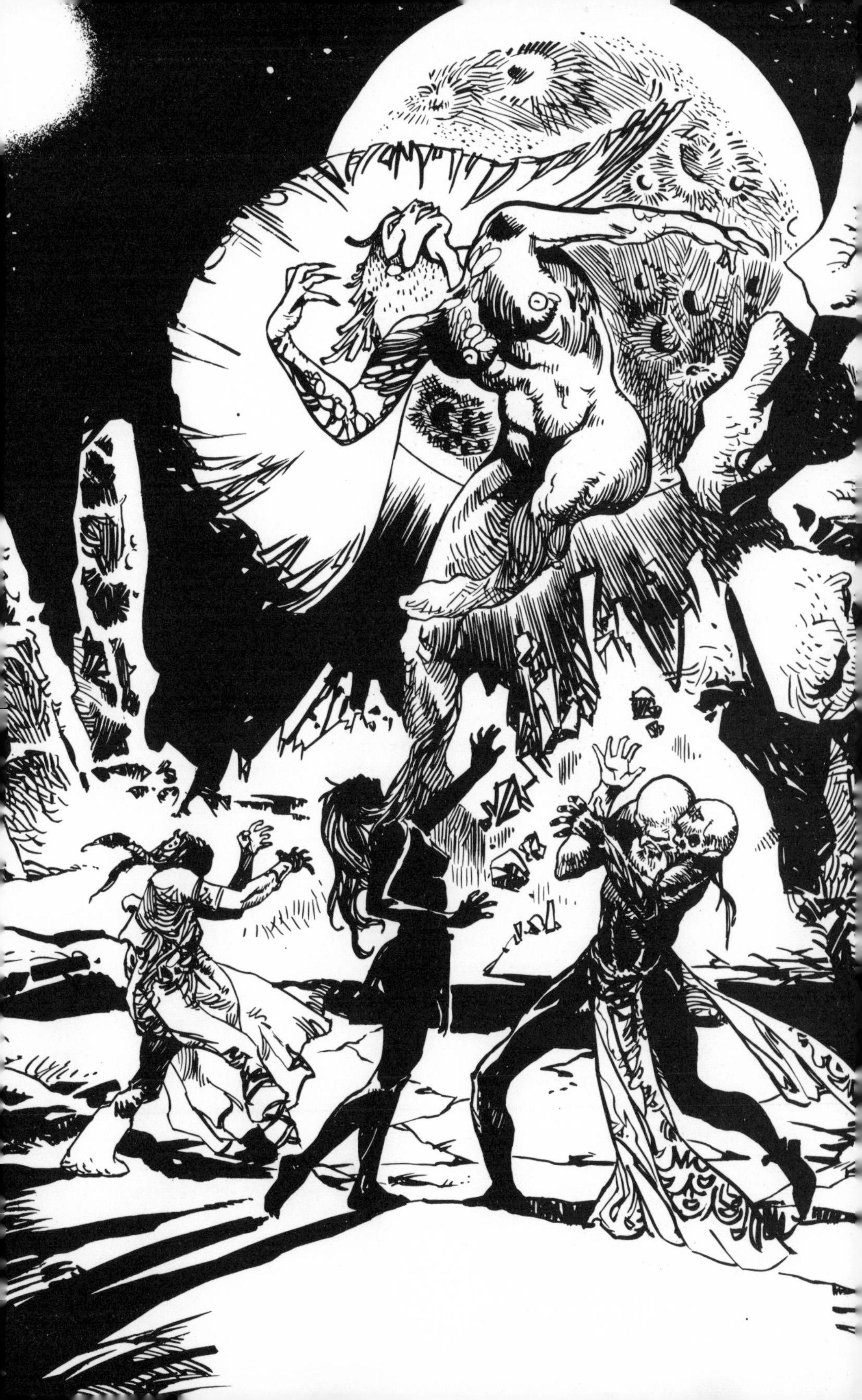

it did not see them. Alien thoughts formed in the War-lock's mind, crushingly powerful.

ALONE? HOW CAN I BE ALONE? I CALL YOU ALL TO ANSWER, YOU WHO RULE THE WORLD...

The last god was male and female both. Its male organs were mounted below and behind the vagina, in such a way that it could probably mate with itself. And this was embarrassingly clear, because the magicians were now looking up between the tremendous hairy pillars of its legs. It was still growing!

How? Where did it find the power? Roze-Kattee's range must be growing with its size, with its power. The Warlock had never anticipated this: that as the last god, Roze-Kattee was beyond competition. Every madman and every lover must now serve it as a wor-shipper.

Wavyhill snarled in the Warlock's ear. "Get hold of yourselves! Clubfoot, quick, what's your true name? Warlock, wake him up!"

Mirandee and Clubfoot were still gaping. The War-lock shook Clubfoot's shoulder and shouted, "Your true name!"

"Kaharoldil."

Wavyhill sang in the Guild tongue. *My name is Kaharoldil, I am your father and mother...* The War-lock joined, making Wavyhill's gestures for him. After a moment Clubfoot joined them. It was the old loyalty spell they were using, a spell the Warlock had once rejected as unethical. It decreased the intelligence of its victims. But now he only wondered if it would work.

They had come ill-equipped, and moved too fast. Too much had been forgotten about the gods. Perhaps nobody had ever known enough.

Roze-Kattee was a hairy two-legged mountain now. Its head must be halfway up the World-Worm's head.

And still it grew. The Warlock imagined chill sanity engulfing the Frost Giants and their Nordik masters, sweeping over the Greek islands, crossing Asian and African mountains; wars ending as weaker armies surrendered to stronger, or as farmers-turned-soldier dropped their spears and returned in haste to harvest their crops; husbands returning to wives, and wives to husbands, for remembered fondness and remembered promises, old habits and the neighbors' approval. Already Roze-Kattee had changed the world.

Orolandes lay on his back on the crumbly rock, looking up at the sky.

He had tried a drug once. Something an American was carrying. The red man had burned leaves in a fire, and Orolandes and some of his troop had sniffed the smoke. He had felt like this, then. Abstracted. Able to view himself, his friends, his environs, from a godlike distance and with godlike clarity.

It had not seemed worthwhile to follow Mirandee down the mountain. Whatever she and the others were planning, it could hardly be worthy of his attention.

Even the guilt was gone. That was nice.

There was a muffled booming somewhere far away. He ignored it.

Then a section of rock the size of a parade ground, not far from where he was lying, settled and hesitated and dropped away. Thunder sounded below him.

The corpse of the World-Worm was decomposing.

Orolandes moved by reflex. He swept gear into his pack (leaving gear on the battlefield could get you killed next time), donned the pack and went backward down the rope. He tried to keep his weight on the rock, not on the line. The knob of rock could crumble. His life was at stake, and Orolandes truly did not have

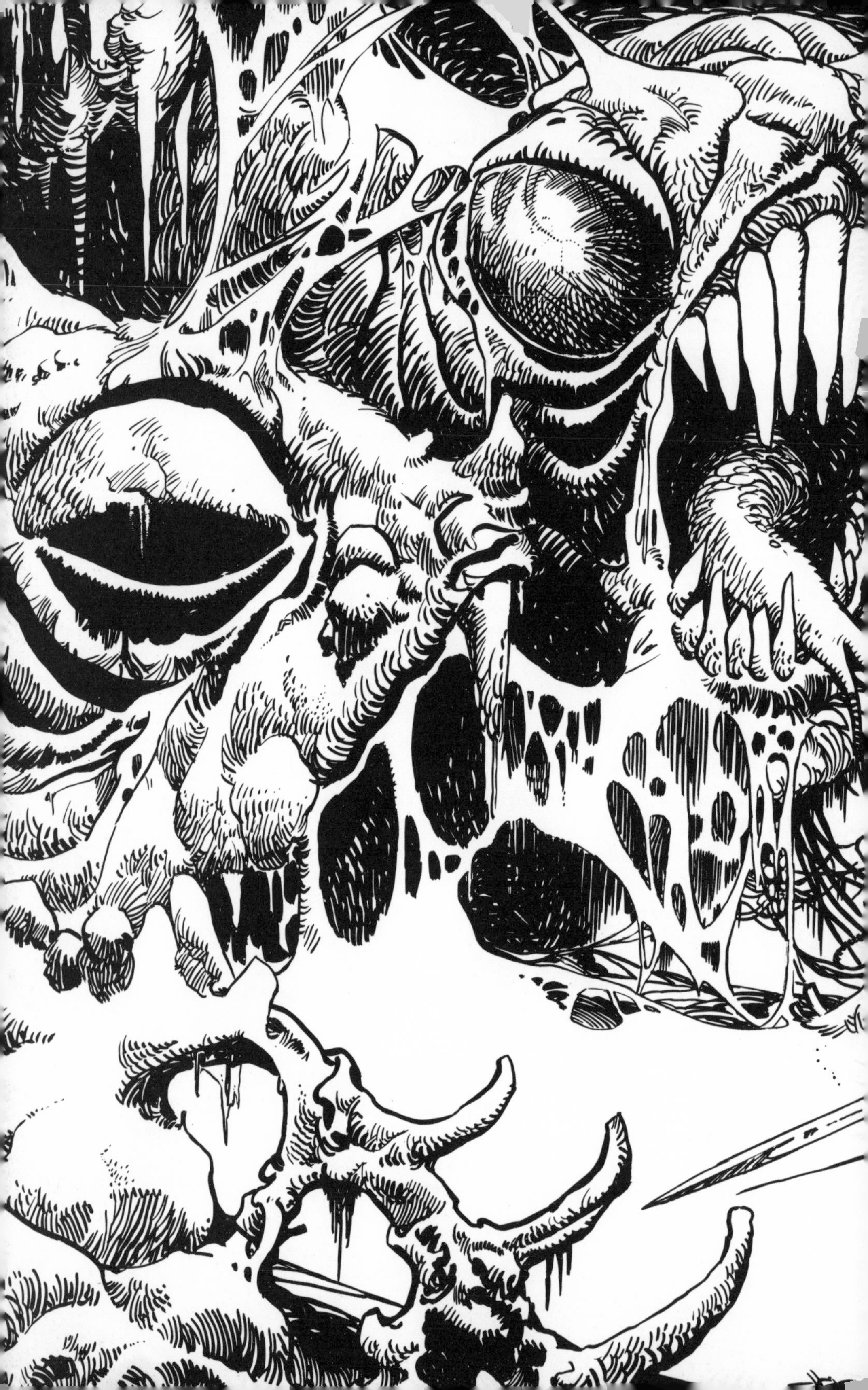

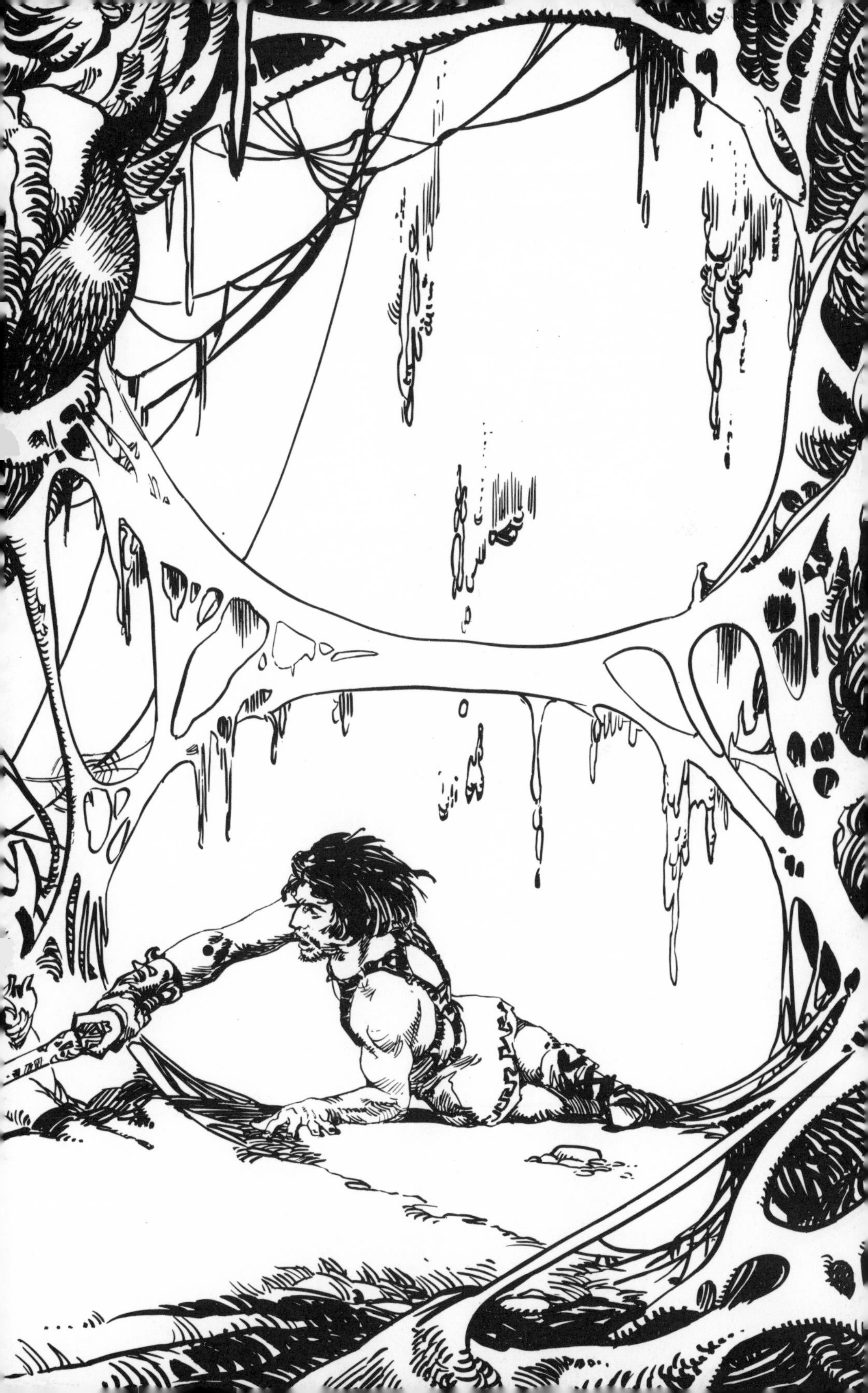

the gift for abstraction.

I CALL YOU TO ANSWER, YOU WHO RULE THE WORLD . . .

Orolandes stiffened. Those were *not* his thoughts. He looked around.

He was then halfway down the slope, several hundred feet up. He saw a beast-thing with glowing yellow eyes, eyes level with his own. The great eyes locked with his, considered him, then turned away.

Orolandes continued to descend.

Certainly it would have been easy to let go. His muscles ached from the strain of climbing . . . but the hurt didn't seem to matter either. It was easier to follow his training.

I am Kaharoldil, your teacher and your wet-nurse and your ancestors' ghosts. I tell you things for your own good. Wavyhill and Mirandee and Clubfoot sang, and the Warlock's fingers made patterns in the air.

Roze-Kattee heard.

The tall ears twitched, the head swiveled, the blazing yellow eyes found them clustered on the ground. Roze-Kattee dropped to knees and hands, the better to observe them.

Wavyhill said, "Ah, never mind."

Right. What did it matter? Clubfoot had stopped singing too. Roze-Kattee covered the sky; its yellow eyes were twin suns. The Warlock sat down, infinitely weary, and leaned back against crumbling rock to watch the last god grow.

A thought formed, and tickled. Roze-Kattee was amused.

YOU WOULD USE A LOVE-SPELL ON ME?

Why, yes, a loyalty spell was a form of love spell. They'd been silly.

SILLY AND PRESUMPTUOUS. BUT YOU HAVE

WAKED ME FROM MY DEATH SLEEP. HOW MAY I
REWARD YOU?

The Warlock thought about it. Truly, he didn't
know. What must be would be.

YOU WISHED TO BRING DOWN THE MOON? Again
the thought tickled. PERHAPS I WILL.

"Wait," said Clubfoot, but he did not go on.

Now the Warlock imagined a fat sphere, blue and
bluish-brown and clotted white. He sensed a watery
film of life covering that sphere . . . and he sensed how
thin it was. Remove the life from the world, and what
would have changed?

This resignation, this fatalism, this dispassionate
overview of reality went far beyond mere sanity,
thought the Warlock. Roze-Kattee had practiced his
power long before men ever put names to it. Now he
imagined a smaller sphere, its rough surface the color
of Wavyhill's skull. It cruised past the larger sphere in
a curved path. Now it stopped moving, then began to
drift toward the larger sphere. Now the spheres
bumped, and deformed, and merged in fire. A sticky
cloud of flame began to cool and condense.

IS THIS WHAT YOU WANTED?

"No," Mirandee whispered.

"No!" Wavyhill shouted. "No, you maniac! We didn't
know!"

BUT IT IS WHAT I WANT. I CAN LIVE THROUGH
THE TIME OF FIRE. I NEED THE . . . STATE OF THINGS
THAT LETS GODS LIVE, THAT WARPS DEAD REALITY
TO LIVING REALITY. WITH THE DEAD MOON'S AID I
WILL PEOPLE THE CHANGED EARTH WITH MY
CHILDREN. BECAUSE YOU HAVE SERVED ME, I WILL
CREATE EACH OF YOU OVER AGAIN.

The last god had grown so huge that Orolandes
couldn't even find it at first. He stepped back from the

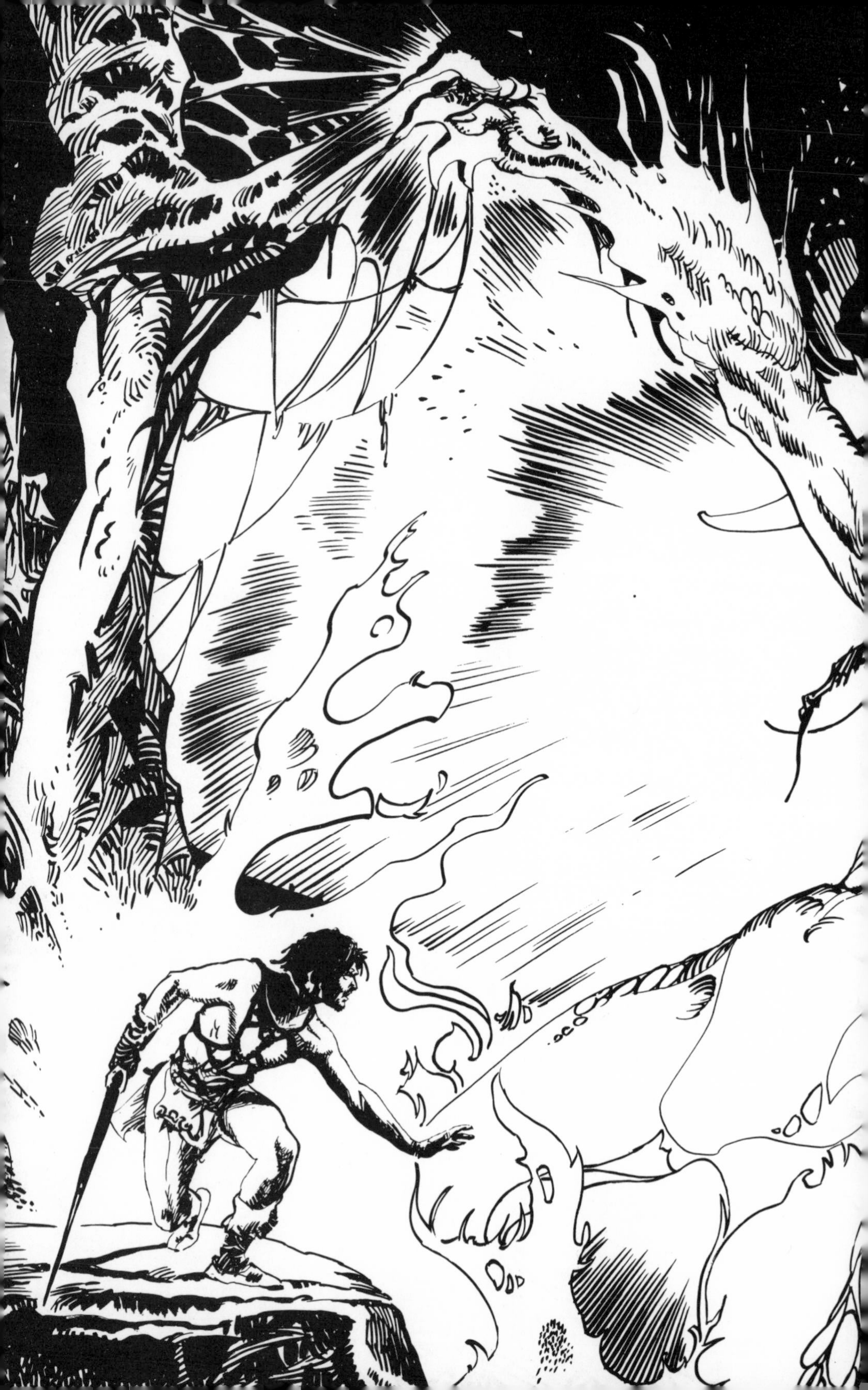

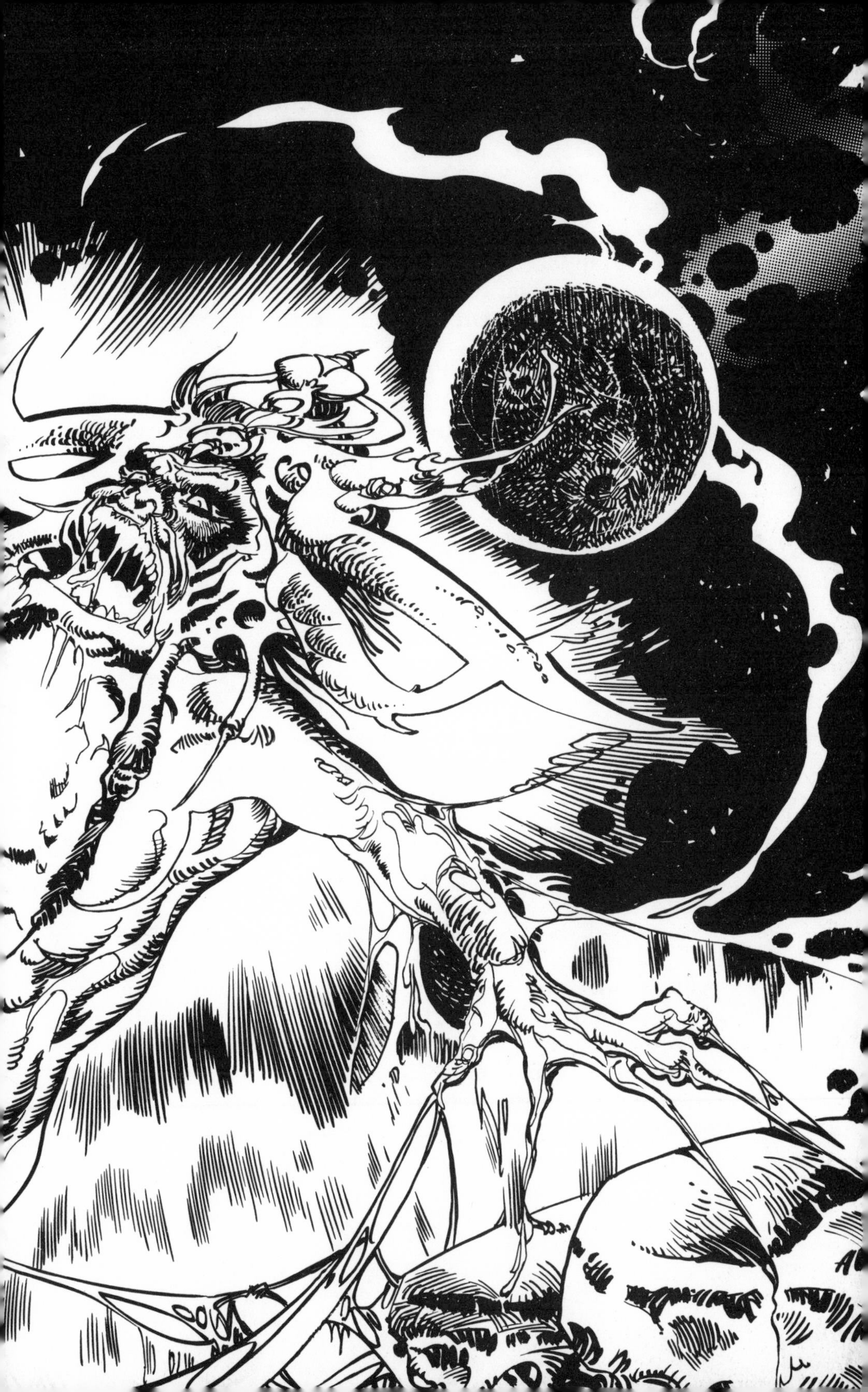

rope and looked around him. There were the magicians, a good distance away, doing nothing obvious
about the menace. There, what he'd taken for a mountain became a pillar of coarse pale hair . . . leading up
into a hairy torso . . . Orolandes froze, trying to understand.

Then pictures invaded his mind and sent him reel-
ing dizzily against the rock wall.

Nobody had ever told him that the world was
round. After the daydream-pictures stopped flitting
through his mind, he remembered that. He remembered that everyone was about to die. But the pictures
he had understood so well, grew muddled now, and
faded . . .

Never mind. What to do next? Orolandes thought of
fleeing; but he wasn't frightened.

HOW CAN I STOP THE MOON IN ITS COURSE? YOU
WHO WORK IN A LAND THAT IS ALMOST DEAD, YOU
MUST HAVE CONSIDERED THIS. The question came
with crushing urgency, and Orolandes thought frantically. How would a Greek soldier go about stopping
the Moon? Then his head cleared . . .

Well. The last god was proving very dangerous.
Perhaps it would be best to kill the thing, Orolandes
thought. The magicians seemed in no position to do
so, and killing wasn't really their field.

He pulled the silver chain from the back pack. He
found the red chalk too, looked at it . . . but he had
paid no attention to Mirandee's symbols. Nor to the
arm-waving. Best stick with the chain and the sword.

And still he wasn't frightened. It was strange to be
thinking this way, as if Orolandes had no more impor-
tance than any other man or woman. He had lost even
love of self. This was no drug dream. It was like battlefield exhaustion, when he had fought and killed
and run and fought until even his wounds no longer

hurt and dying meant nothing but a chance to lie down. Thrice he had known that terrible death of self. He had not stopped fighting then.

YES, GOOD. I CAN DO THAT, he thought; and he imagined himself stretching into the sky, growing very thin and very tall.

But it was Roze-Kattee that stood upright and reached skyward. Roze-Kattee's furry legs grew narrow, and the knees went up and up; but Roze-Kattee's torso receded much faster, up through a stratum of broken clouds and onward.

There was no way to reach a vital spot now. Well . . . Orolandes marched toward the last god's foot.

There was now something spidery about Roze-Kattee. The eyes were tiny dots of light, stars faint by daylight and right overhead. The fingers of both hands seemed thin as spiderweb strands: a web enclosing a pale crescent moon. The feet had spread and flattened as if under enormous pressure, and Orolandes had no trouble stepping up onto the foot itself, though it must cover several acres.

At no time did he picture himself as a mosquito attacking a behemoth with cold-blooded murder in mind. Orolandes' sense of humor was stone dead.

He jogged toward the slender ankle. His skin felt puffy. He guessed that the sensation came from Roze-Kattee, and ignored it. He never guessed its origin: most of Roze-Kattee was in vacuum.

The last god's ankle was like an ancient redwood, slender only in proportion. Orolandes looped the silver chain and held it against the furry skin. He thrust through the loop. The blade grated against bone. He withdrew the blade, moved the loop and thrust again. The point scraped bone, found a joint and sank to the hilt. He grasped the hilt in both hands and worked the blade back and forth. Roze-Kattee was

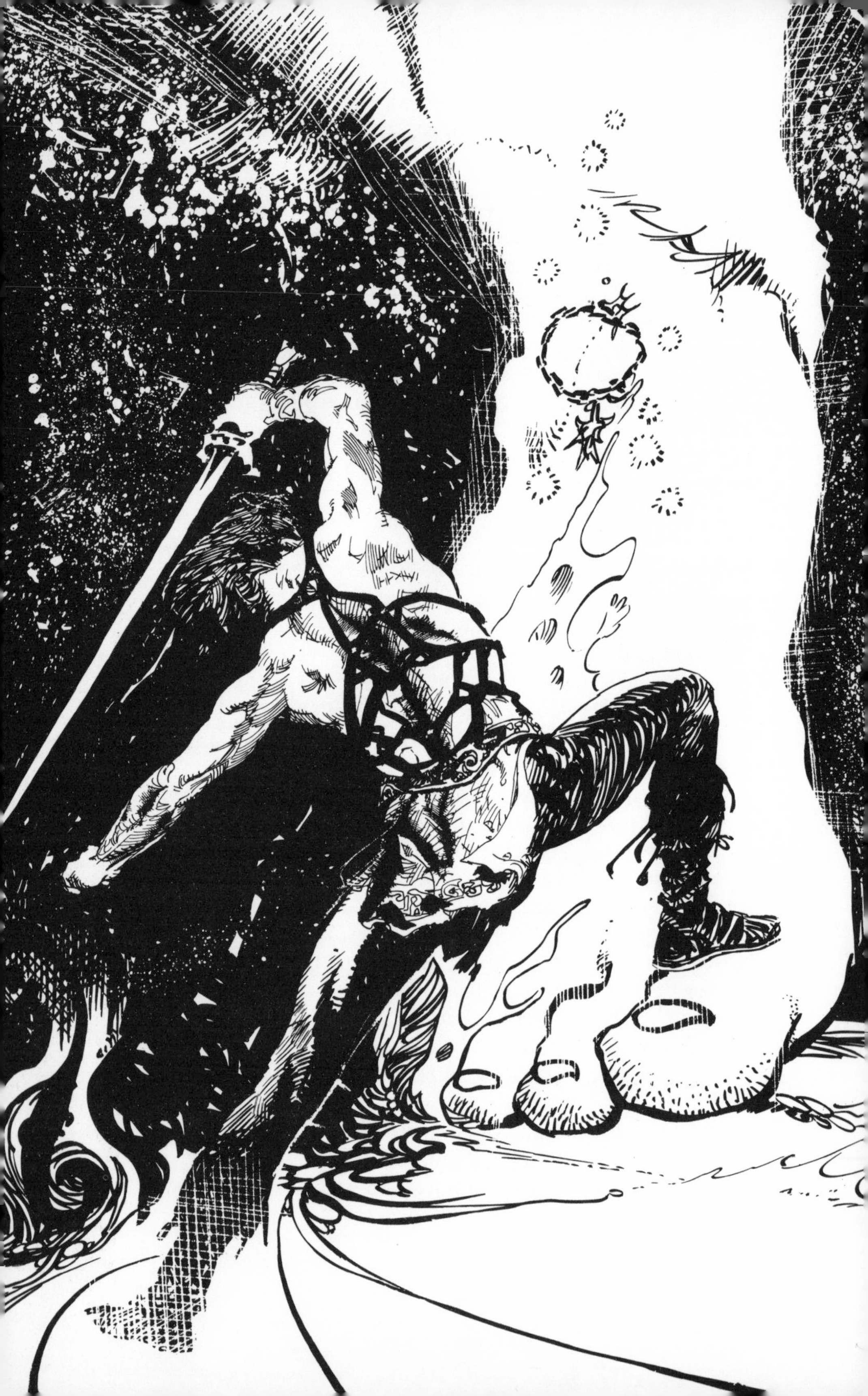

slow to respond. Without impatience he withdrew the blade and stabbed again.

HURT! Orolandes yelled and grabbed his ankle. It felt like a snake had struck him. He found no wound ...but he would not be unwounded long, because Roze-Kattee's spidery hands were descending in slow motion.

Something else had changed. Suddenly it mattered very much whether a Greek swordsman survived. Orolandes ran limping across the last god's foot, swearing through clenched teeth.

The Warlock said, "What?" exactly as if someone had spoken. He shook his head. Now what had startled him? And how had he hurt his foot? He bent to look, but the scream stopped him.

"Orolandes!" Mirandee's scream.

It was a puzzling sight. Roze-Kattee was spread across the view like a child's stick-figure drawing defacing a landscape painting. The scrawled line-figure stooped as if to tie a bootlace. And Mirandee was running toward where a flea seemed to be scuttling across the thing's foot ...

Then it jumped into perspective, and the Warlock saw Orolandes running for a gap in the World-Worm's cheek. He snapped, "Wavyhill!"

"Here. Somewhere we have lost control."

"He had us controlled till Orolandes distracted him."

"Suggestions?"

"Kill it."

Wavyhill didn't like the taste of that. "How?"

"The Warlock's Wheel."

"You built another one? Why?"

"I was trying for a prescient dream. Success or failure for the Guild meeting. I took the right drugs, and I slept in the right frame of mind, and I had a nice, peaceful, dreamless sleep. Understand? Where I was trying to look...no *mana.* So maybe I'd be using a Warlock's Wheel."

Now the swordsman was somewhere inside the World-Worm's mouth. Roze-Kattee reached with spidery fingers into the hole a much tinier Roze-Kattee had broken through the sandstone.

Clubfoot was on the ground, his arms over his face, his body clenched like a fist.

"That's suicide for us both. There's got to be a better way. Warlock, there's *mana* in god-murder. If we can kill it and take its power —"

"How?"

"Mirandee's vampire spell!"

"She'd be cremated, or turned into something shapeless. Could you hold that much power? Could I? Poor Clubfoot's already had more than he can take."

"I hate it. All our work, lost! That's the world's last large source of *mana,* and you talk of burning it out to save a swordsman!"

"To save the world," the Warlock said gently.

"Even Roze-Kattee can't bring down the Moon by *pushing* on it!"

Pain stabbed at the Warlock's hand. Roze-Kattee howled in their brains...and was suddenly quiet. It turned to look at them, to study them.

The cavern was black. Orolandes stayed on his hands and knees. Stalagmites he could feel his way around, but a drooping stalactite would take his head off. His foot hurt like fury. He turned left, toward the cavern's main entrance.

Marble pillars tipped with claws blasted their way through the wall and began feeling their way around, knocking World-Worm teeth in all directions.

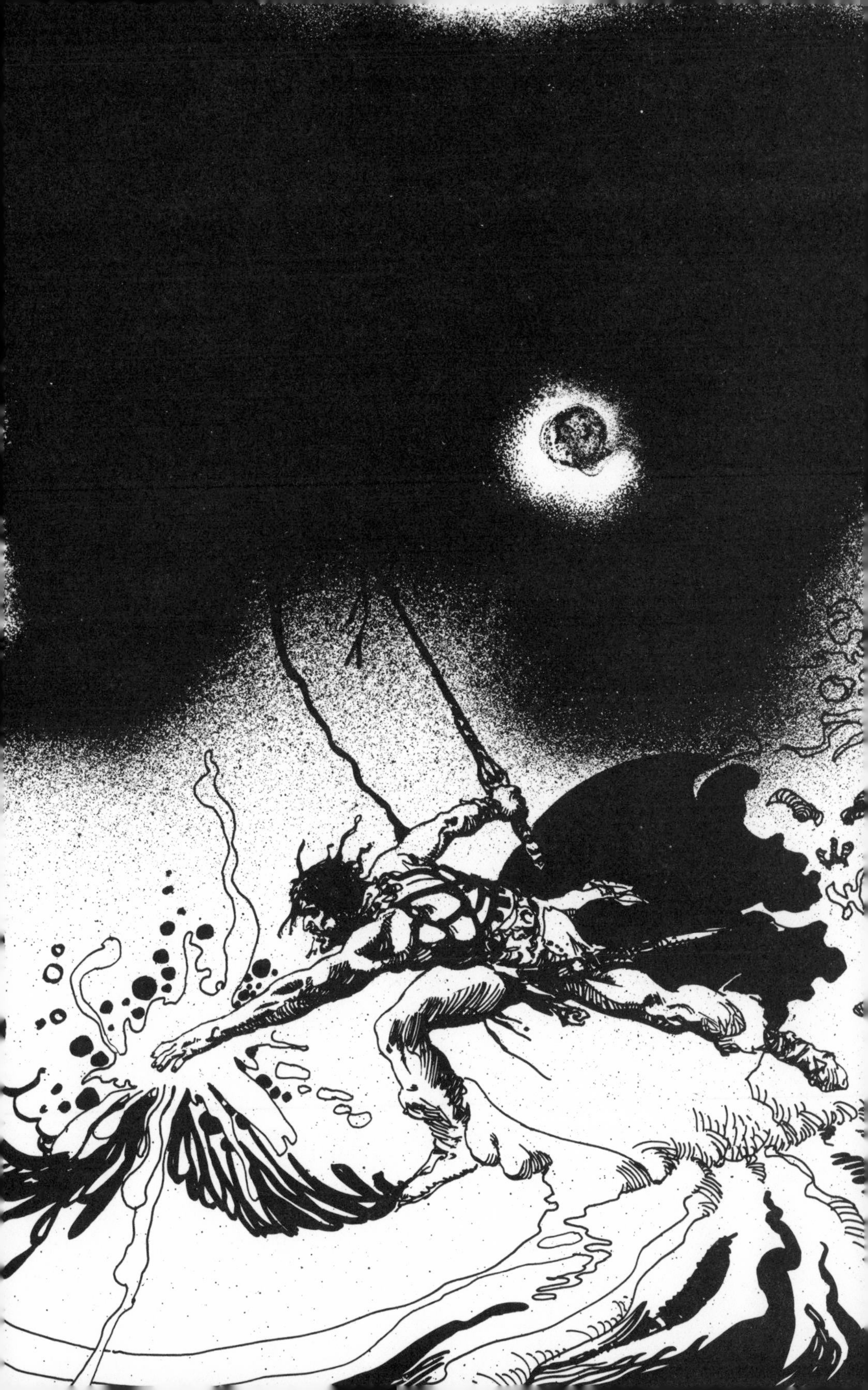

Now there was light. Orolandes waited.

The hand paused as if bewildered.

Orolandes sprang. He slashed at a knuckle, howled, set himself and slashed again. He ducked under the wounded finger and slashed at another. Nobody who loved Orolandes would have recognized him now, with saliva dripping from his jaws and his face contorted in murder-lust.

The hand reacted at last. It spasmed. Then it cupped and swept through the cavern gathering spires of rock. It gathered Orolandes. He stabbed again, into a joint. Then closing fingers squeezed the breath from him. His eyes blurred . . .

Wavyhill was shouting, "But what about *us?*" when the god's blazing yellow eyes found them. "Never mind," he said. "I think I see."

Those eyes: they could make you not care; they could make you lose interest. But they guaranteed a dispassionate overview and a selfless judgment.

"I don't care if it can bring down the Moon or not. It's got to die," said the Warlock. "The world belongs to the gods or it belongs to men."

"I said I understand. Go ahead."

The Warlock's legs wouldn't hold him. He started to crawl. Orolandes' backpack was yards away, and his knees and hands hurt. Roze-Kattee's vast spidery hand emerged from the cavern.

"Come *on.*"

"This is my top speed. Hell, at least I did it to myself."

"What?"

"This is where it ends, the killing of Glirendree. Maybe I made the wrong choice. It was a long time ago . . ."

The young magician had had to leave his
home ... again. Somehow his spells lost power. It
happened to everyone. Irritated, but curious too, the
Warlock had devised an experiment.

He had made a simple copper disk and set two
spells on it. One was simple and powerful: it held the
metal together, gave it near-infinite tensile strength.
The other spun it. He put no upper limit on that spell.

And when the Wheel had destroyed itself, he knew.

He had kept the secret for more than a century. But
the demon-sword Glirendree had come to challenge
him ...

"I didn't have anything else that would kill it." The
Warlock spilled the pack and picked a copper disk out
of the litter. "I couldn't let Glirendree run loose, could
I? Then the secret spread like a brushfire. The battle
made too good a story."

"You and your damn Wheel."

"The magic goes away and never comes back. All the
magicians panicked. You made a whole discipline out
of murder and resurrection. Piranther and his band
scrambled for a place of safety. Rynildissen City barred
magicians —"

"Do it. Before we're stopped."

The Warlock spoke a word in the old Guild language
and let go fast. The Wheel hovered in the air, spinning.

Roze-Kattee reached for them.

The Warlock heard a humming, rising in pitch.
Sudden weakness dropped him on his side, limp. The
disk glowed dull red. Roze-Kattee's fingers disappeared into the glow, stretching and thinning like
smoke in a draft. The Warlock felt no pain from the
god, only the god's amazement changing to horror.

Roze-Kattee set its feet and pulled back. Now the
disk was yellow-hot. Bursitis, arthritis, kidney stones,
all the agony of a body that had lived too long flared

and faded, and the Warlock's strength and his senses faded together. His eyes blurred. The disk was a blue-white sun, and Roze-Kattee was pulled into it. The god's panic was thick enough to touch ... and then that faded too.

Mirandee came picking her way delicately through fallen rock. Her face was above Orolandes when he opened his eyes. "It's all over," she said.

Orolandes sighed. "I've been thinking of giving up magic."

What should have been a joke only made her nod soberly. In daylight spilling through the smashed cavern wall, her hair glowed white. On her shadow-darkened face his caress found roughness and wrinkles.

The daylight was dwindling as they left the cavern. Orolandes saw no trace of Roze-Kattee. He saw a scar of burned and melted rock, and smelled vaporized copper.

It was possible to imagine that the mountain range to the south had the shape of a serpent, or that the earthquake-shattered cavern had some of the symmetry of a snake's mouth. But really, the landscape was quite ordinary. Where magicians had made their last stand, they found the red man curled up and apparently asleep beside what seemed a human skeleton with two skulls.

Mirandee stooped with difficulty. She put a large-knuckled hand on Clubfoot's shoulder and said, "Kaharoldil, speak to me."

"I couldn't handle it," Clubfoot said without moving.

"You can't go mad. Roze-Kattee saw to that. Come on, sit up. We need you."

Clubfoot rolled over and opened his eyes. He touched the two skulls beside him, almost caressingly.

"Nice, wasn't it?" he said, perhaps to the skulls. "Knowing how to grant wishes instead of working for them. Must have been bad when the gods were alive, though. They might grant your prayer, they might grant your enemy's, but they'd certainly grant their own. A god's wishes wouldn't have anything to do with what human beings wanted." Clubfoot looked up at last. "Mirandee, love, we should have remembered what the gods were like. Whimsical. Wilful. They wiped out humanity at least once, and made us over again. These last thousand years were a golden age. We got our prayers granted, but not often, and not too far granted, and it took some skill to do it."

"It's over," Mirandee said.

"Are you both all right?"

Mirandee nodded. Orolandes said, "Nothing broken, I think. I'll have some interesting bruises. I'd have been crushed if the Warlock hadn't distracted the god's attention."

"What do we do next? We're stranded on a mountain with no magic."

"We'll spend the night in the cave," Orolandes said.
"Get out of here in the morning. We'll be hungry. You
probably summoned all the game in this area. So I'll
put my spear back together, and we'll put the pack on
you, Clubfoot; it'll be empty anyway. You won't want
your tools now. What about the skulls?"

"Might as well leave them. I wish —"

"What?"

"Nothing."

—ABOUT—
★BORIS VALLEJO★

Born in Lima, Peru in 1941, Boris made his first sale at the tender age of sixteen; by the time he was twenty-three he decided he was ready for bigger things and migrated to the United States. Unfortunately he was to face several years of protracted struggle before his talent was finally recognized by Ace's Art Director, Charles Volpe. Since that first cover for Ace (I AM A BARBARIAN, by Edgar Rice Burroughs) Boris's popularity has increased almost geometrically until today he is one of the most sought-after commercial artists in the world.

Though forced by his enormous popularity to turn down many assignments, Boris says he will always have a special feeling for Ace—just one reason he is delighted to be involved in Ace's Illustrated Series of Science Fiction and Fantasy.

—ABOUT—
★ESTEBAN MAROTO★

Born in Madrid in 1942, Esteban Maroto began his professional career as an assistant on the illustrated series THE ADVENTURES OF THE FBI. His first independent work was on comic strips such as BUCK JOHN, and since 1963 he has concentrated largely on illustrated features for the English-speaking market. He is presently affiliated with Selecciones Illustradas, located in Barcelona.

Maroto definitively established his strong personality and unique graphic style with his series FIVE FOR INFINITY, followed by THE TOMB OF THE GODS and two exceptional heroic fantasies, WOLFF and MANLY. At present Maroto's artistic powers are focused on Ace Books' Illustrated Series of Science Fiction and Fantasy, including CONAN AND THE SORCERER and THE MAGIC GOES AWAY, soon to be followed by THE ILLUMINATED DORSAI by Gordon R. Dickson.

Maroto has received many awards, both in Europe and in the United States, and is considered by many to be one of the finest illustrators in the world.

THE MANA CRISIS

by Sandra Miesel

Picture the story you have just read as the graph of a mathematical function. Its vertical axis is emotion, its horizontal one, reason. Larry Niven has plotted the poignant issue of fading wonder against orderly extrapolative thinking to produce a smoothly swelling curve of fiction. It is a relentlessly logical process. Magic no longer exists in our world. But if, as all traditional cultures assert, it ever existed, then why has it disappeared? If magic vanished because its driving energy was depleted, what caused the shortage? And above all, how did people react to the crisis?

Such mixtures of imagination and hard logic have always been the special mark of Niven's fantasies. *The Magic Goes Away* is the direct descendant of his first effort in the genre, "Convergent Series"/"The Long Night" (1967), which finds a mathematical escape hatch from a diabolical pact. Niven approaches both fantasy and science fiction with a view to providing entertainment. As he describes his intention: "I'd like to train my reader to play with ideas for the sheer joy of it." He can extrapolate equally well from possible or impossible premises. Or as one editor put it, he "can write on both sides of the science fiction fence."

Furthermore, Niven's matter-of-fact way with marvels makes him the remote — but legitimate — descendant of Chaucer, Dante*, and other medieval writers. According to C. S. Lewis, "the Middle Ages favored a brilliant and exuberant development of presentational realism . . . the art of bringing something close to us, making it palpable and vivid, by sharply observed or sharply imagined detail." However unrealistic its content, medieval literature abounds in lifelike touches, as a glance at *The Canterbury*

Tales will speedily confirm.

Thus Niven's pot-bellied Warlock is truer to medieval tradition than Andre Norton's gothic-robed witches. Norton's romantic art evokes — but never fully explains — shadowy enchantments. On the other hand, realist Niven works his spells by daylight according to strictly rational patterns. His imagination is tightly focused at all times to record those concrete details (like the texture of enchanted clouds) which make the improbable plausible. As the author himself explains: "I want [my reader] to daydream in color and three dimensions, with sharp edges and internal consistency."

Niven's zeal for consistency and realism places him in the school of logical fantasy which he likes to call "rivets and sorcery." L. Sprague de Camp and Fletcher Pratt are perhaps the most famous members of this circle which flowered in the pages of *Unknown* magazine forty years ago. Logical fantasy is distinguished by its playful attitude towards the fantastic. It stresses ingenuity more than glamour and comedy more than melodrama. It is informal, sometimes to the point of flippancy. It may treat serious matters but without solemnity. The enterprise is fundamentally an intellectual game. Lightness alone does not qualify Roger Zelazny, Thomas Burnett Swann, or even Niven's favorite, James Branch Cabell, as logical fantasists.

Another way to characterize logical fantasy is to contrast it with other categories. High fantasy as practiced by writers like William Morris, Lord Dunsany, E. R. Eddison, J. R. R.

*Niven and Jerry Pournelle reworked Dante in their 1975 novel *Inferno*.

Tolkien, and Ursula K. Le Guin is laden with mythic significance, but logical fantasy treats myths simply as one kind of data among many. The eldrich horrors dear to H. P. Lovecraft, Clark Ashton Smith, and August Derleth are too dim and diffuse — logical fantasy names its horrors. The sword and sorcery of Robert E. Howard and his imitators is too robustly muscular. (Pratt, like many logical fantasists, reportedly "hated heroes who simply batter their way out of traps by means of bulging thews, without bothering to use their brains.") However, these classifications carry no value judgments. Good work can appear in any of them. Versatile talents like de Camp, Poul Anderson, and Fritz Leiber have written more than one variety brilliantly.

Similarly, Niven's own special traits show up best in contrast with the work of his fellow writers. Here are a few of the principal authors and stories: de Camp and Pratt's *Incomplete Enchanter* (1941: projection into the worlds of Norse myth and *The Faerie Queen* via symbolic logic), de Camp's "Wheels of If" (1940: an alternate America split between modern Norse and Indian nations), Pratt's *Blue Star* (1952: systematized hereditary magic in an empire resembling eighteenth-century Austria), Anderson's *Operation Chaos* (1971: domestic magic in an alternate version of present day America), Randall Garrett's *Too Many Magicians* (1967: forensic magic in the contemporary Anglo-French Empire), and Gordon R. Dickson's *Dragon and the George* (1976: an alternate Middle Ages featuring intelligent dragons).

Some of the stories just listed transport characters to other realities. Others stay exclusively within imaginary realms. But all are alternate world/parallel universe tales because this has traditionally been the most popular type of logical fantasy, from Lewis Carroll onward. Niven used the transit approach in his Svetz series, reasoning that since time travel is scientifically impossible, expeditions in time are actually fantasy journeys into parallel worlds. *The Magic Goes Away*, part of Niven's Warlock series, takes the other approach. It remains in the distant past on one time line that can be considered an alternate universe. (Niven also uses the parallel world device in "Wrong Way Street," 1965; "All the Myriad Ways," 1968; and "For a Foggy Night," 1971.)

The physical impact of effective magic is a major element in all these stories. Niven's Warlock series is distinguished by its emphasis on the physics and metaphysics of the Art. Niven is less interested in the technology or utility of magic than Garrett or Anderson although these aspects are not totally ignored — magic provides the industrial base for the Warlock's world. He is most especially indifferent to the showy, pyrotechnic possibilities of magic. He condemns the wastefulness of tricks like: " 'Castles floating in the air. Dragons with golden scales. Armies turned to stone or wiped out by lightning.' " Niven's sensible world with its mules and rug merchants is anything but a "purple and gold and crimson universe where anything can happen."

In the examples cited, Niven is neither as sociohistorical as Pratt nor as domestic as Anderson. His briskness also excludes Anderson's lushness. Garrett is coy and Dickson, de Camp, and Pratt have their farcical moments but Niven's humor is distinctly wry and tart. (Niven prides himself on

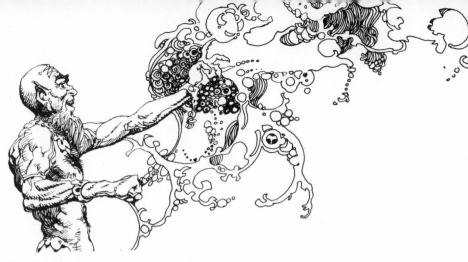

having "learned my projected societies so thoroughly that I could see the 'humorous' parts, and thus write about them.")

Nevertheless, Niven, like Anderson and Dickson, applies the conventions of logical fantasy to serious subject matter. He treats ecology (the Svetz series), the rivalry between brains and brawn ("Not Long Before the End," 1969), pacificism ("What Good is a Glass Dagger?" 1972), and theology (*The Magic Goes Away*). As the author himself puts it: "A fantasy story self-admittedly has no connection with any specific reality. Thus the writer is obligated to talk in universals. Otherwise he's not talking about anything."

Niven always writes by the extrapolative method "in which ideas are tracked to expose their implications." He is guided by two principles when writing fantasy: (1) It must be internally consistent, and (2) It must not be taken at face value. The latter rule separates his fantasy from his much-admired, rigorously factual hard science fiction.

Niven applies these principles to hilarious effect in his Svetz stories (collected in *The Flight of the Horse*, 1973). Their logic is madly plausible and their naive hero tumbles into one pitfall after another because he believes in everything he sees. Hanville Svetz, a browbeaten thirty-first century bureaucrat, is assigned to retrieve extinct animals from the past for the amusement of the drooling idiot who rules his world as hereditary U.N. Secretary General. But his expensive ("several million commercials per shot") trips into the past are, in fact, sideways jaunts across probability lines. As his superior muses:

'Did you know that time travel wasn't even a concept until the first century Ante Atomic? A writer invented it. From then until the fourth century Post Atomic, time travel was pure fantasy. It violates everything the scientists of that time thought were natural laws. . . . Every time we push an extention cage past that particular four-century period, we shove it into a kind of fantasy world.'

Svetz unquestioningly accepts fantasy phenomena as real partly because his civilization has so little knowledge of previous eras and partly because he himself is so stupid. "We've forgotten so much about the past that we can't separate legend from fact." He brings back a medieval unicorn instead of a horse and a Chinese dragon instead of a gila monster ("The Flight of the Horse"/"Get a Horse," 1969), Moby Dick for an ordinary sperm whale ("Leviathan," 1970), and a werewolf instead of a wolf ("There's a Wolf in My Time Machine," 1971). Then he is entangled in transforming an ostrich into a roc and altering his own time line by the removal of Henry Ford's first automobile ("Bird in the Hand," 1970). Finally, he wrestles with Death personified and renders his own world illusionary ("Death in a Cage," 1973).

Earnest, timid, and frail, Svetz is a kind of anti-Walter Mitty — a man thrust into exciting adventures he neither wants nor understands. Niven satirizes big government and small-scale human frailty through his inept flounderings. But some of the humor is a bit heavy-handed (e.g., the unicorn tamed by a "frigid bitch" staff member at the Institute) and by the last story the medium has peeled away from the message.

The Svetz series is a vehicle for environmental warnings. Svetz' ravaged world is home only to man, food yeast, and a few zoo animals.

> Once the ocean teemed with life, Svetz thought. Now the continental shelf is as dead as the Moon. Nothing but bubble cities. Once the whole continent was all forest and living desert and fresh water. We cut down the trees and shot the animals and poisoned the rivers and irrigated the deserts so that even the desert life died; . . . . We've wiped out most of the forms of life on Earth in the last fifteen hundred years, and changed the composition of the air to the extent that we'd be afraid to change it back.

Living in Southern California makes Niven especially sensitive to the problems of air pollution. He uses this as a plot point throughout the series. Over the centuries people have adapted well to chemical fumes and high carbon dioxide levels; exposure to the clean pre-industrial atmosphere would kill them. Svetz has to wear an air filter to shield himself from the "heady poison" breathed by past generations. Likewise, the animals he retrieves require special sealed environments in captivity.

Since Svetz was born into a world virtually devoid of non-human life, he hates animals and all alien creatures. His hunting assignments would be agony to fulfill even if he managed to complete them without injury. The captured animals reciprocate. The unicorn, dragon, whale, roc, and werewolf all try to kill him. (Only the deadly polluted air saves him from the angry roc.) Ironically, the zoo's only benevolent large animal, the elephant, is devoured by the roc and the friendly, viable dogs have to be caged for their own protection. "The dogs were behind glass because people were afraid of them. Too many species had died. The people of 1100 Post Atomic were not used to animals."

The Svetz series is worth studying for the light it sheds on the artistically superior Warlock series. It gave Niven practice in writing fantasy, a genre he initially found difficult, and contributed a few clever notions to the other series (large flightless birds as neotenous rocs, *Homo habilis* as the troll, and werewolves as wolves transformed into humans rather than vice versa).

The stories of the Warlock are better than those of Svetz in all respects. Their humorous and serious parts fit together as smoothly as if laminated. Their concepts are grander, their characters livelier, and their prose finer. During the course of the series Niven develops a firm yet relaxed fantasy voice that suits him well. By the final installment he has perfected an unadorned language that combines both dignity and vigor.

There are four items in the series but "Unfinished Story #1" (1970) can be disregarded. It is merely an excuse for a pun on the Maxwell's demon analogy in physics. But "Not Long Before the End" and "What Good is a Glass Dagger?" are directly related to *The Magic Goes Away*.

The setting of the stories is 12,000 B.C., "an age when miracles were somewhat more common." It makes no real pretense of being our own pre-historic past — the anachronisms are too obvious. It might as well be considered an alternate universe. Niven apparently chose a period as remote as Howard's Hyborian Age in order to underscore his

own distaste for the "slash and screw" or "fur jockstrap" brand of fantasy.

"Not Long Before the End," Niven's earliest venture into sword and sorcery subject matter, was written as an independent story. Niven had no further plans for its premises beyond inverting some mighty-thewed barbarian clichés. (In comparison, Anderson's "Barbarian" and de Camp's Jorian stories poke fun at Conan more affectionately.) Then Niven saw further possibilities in his material and more episodes followed. However, no further sequels should be expected. *The Magic Goes Away* is a "story to end all stories."

Fantasy assumes that magic works. Logical fantasy assumes it works according to consistent, discoverable laws. These laws have been traditionally formulated as Contagion and Similarity. Contagious magic works through objects that have touched or been a part of one another: one makes a love charm from a lock of the beloved's hair. Sympathetic magic, on the other hand, relies on models or symbols: one pricks a mannikin to harm a man. To these, Niven adds a third law — Poetry. This subjective principle says that enchantments depend on belief and symbolic appropriateness: the Moon is magical because everyone agrees that it is.

Niven goes beyond most fantasists and explains *why* magic works. He postulates that magical work requires "mana" just as physical work requires energy. Mana is the Melanesian term for the inner essence of things, the intangible quality that makes them "really real." As Mircea Eliade describes it, "Everything that *is* supremely, possesses mana; everything, in fact, that seems to men effective, dynamic, creative or perfect." Historically, the same concept occurs under other names (*orenda*, *wakan*, *megbe*, *ngai*, etc.) throughout Oceania, North America, and Africa. Andre Norton calls mana "power" and puts it to authentic use in her Witch World series.

Niven may have encountered the earlier definition of mana as "an impersonal force." This may have influenced him to think of mana in measurable terms. " '*Mana* can be used for good or evil; it can be drained, or transferred from one object to another, or from one man to another. Some men seem to carry *mana* with them. You can find concentrations in oddly shaped stones, or in objects of reverence or in meteoroids.' "

He sees mana as the preternatural analog of energy. This allows him to speak of it quantitatively as well as qualitatively, with a considerable gain in plausibility. But if mana corresponds to energy, then it, too, can be added or subtracted from a system. The idea of mana as a finite, exhaustible resource is Niven's unique contribution to fantasy. Magical and physical powers have conventionally been seen as having a reciprocal relationship: one waxes, the other wanes but neither totally extinguishes the other. Negative factors like cold iron block rather than annihilate magic.

Then Niven draws the realistic conclusion that mana's disappearance is inevitable. Since the supply can be depleted, it will be depleted. Conservation can postpone the day of reckoning, but not indefinitely. Thus the Warlock's world is threatened by a "mana crisis" comparable to our

own energy crisis and its response is as inadequate as ours.

The existence of this crisis is first revealed in "Not Long Before the End," more than a century after its discovery by the Warlock. " 'The power behind magic is a natural resource, like the fertility of the soil. When you use it up, it's gone.' " He had not intended to disclose his findings but no secret can be kept forever, no knowledge can be permanently suppressed. A duel to the death wrecks his secrecy.

"Not Long Before the End" is a droll reworking of heroic fantasy ingredients: luscious lady, doomsword, demon servant, and, of course, the requisite thick-headed barbarian. The last is described as "powerfully muscled and profusely scarred. . . . It seemed strange that so young a man should have found time to acquire so many scars." But the wise, honorable wizard is the hero here, not the dumb, treacherous warrior. He prevails through superior intelligence instead of superior power. The Warlock destroys Glirendree, an invincible demon masquerading as a sword, by exhausting the mana on which its existence depends. Then he slays the barbarian with an ordinary, unenchanted steel knife, the last kind of weapon his foe expected.

But the victory was costly, as "What Good is a Glass Dagger?" shows. "Now it was out, spreading like ripples on a pond. The battle between Glirendree and the Warlock was too good a tale not to tell." People react to the Warlock's secret in various ways — none of them prudent. The greedy master sorcerer Wavyhill is determined to prosper whatever the cost, even if it means inventing necromancy and practicing the mystical equivalent of slash-and-burn agriculture. The Warlock must stop him, not only to save lives but to preserve the dwindling mana supply. Dead areas already exist which are as fatal to magical beings as our own oil slicks are to seabirds.

The Warlock's other problem is to make an Atlantean werewolf named Aran appreciate the magnitude of the common peril and the urgency of meeting it instead of scheming to save the world from war by cancelling military spells. Aran's transformation from a naive student Peacemonger (" 'We want to change Atlantis, not destroy it' ") to cautious paterfamilias is a neat parable of maturation. The folly of pacifism is gorily exposed when Aran in wolf form has to savage Wavyhill in order to save himself and the Warlock. Even the most peace-loving being can be driven to violence when threatened: if he "could work on and on, stripping the living flesh from a man in agony, taking a stab wound for every bite. . . . then neither the end of magic nor anything else, would ever persuade men to give up war."

The answer to the question posed in the story's title is this: a glass dagger, whether imaginary or actual, is as dangerous as any other kind. A dagger in the mind can compel behavior as effectively as a dagger at the breast.

Such is the background to the situation in *The Magic Goes Away*. Niven repeats and expands the themes of his earlier stories, this time avoiding intrusive terms like hula hoop and telephone. To begin with, he replays the wizard-warrior rivalry which he had previously likened to "the natural antipathy . . . between cats and small birds or between rats and men." This antagonism is ancient and perennial. Scholar-priests are ever at odds with fighting

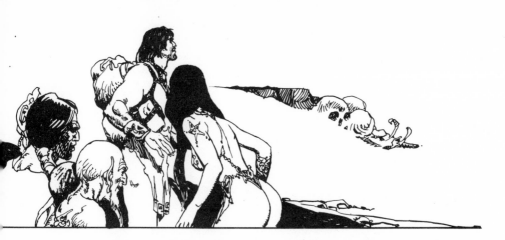

men. Indo-European myth and history are filled with examples, from the bickering between Thor and Odin to the medieval political struggles between Empire and Papacy. Nor are tensions confined to any one culture: the book prevailed in China, but in Japan the sword.

Niven repeatedly demonstrates that "'magicians and swordsmen go together like foxes and rabbits.'" Atlantis drowns, conquerors preen, questers quarrel. The currents of jealousy and condescension swirling around the protagonists are vividly traced, but perhaps the cleverest touch is having Nordik youths rebel against their parents by dabbling in magic.

One prime arena of conflict between the two parties is bed. That women, even witches, find swordsmen attractive irritates magicians: "'Would you tell me what the hell Mirandee sees in that bloody-handed mundane?'" asks Clubfoot. The Warlock knows there is no rational answer. But he also realizes it is no evidence for the natural superiority of warriors. His wife's regret over the barbarian's death in "Not Long Before the End" is merely sentimental foolishness. Mirandee is influenced by pity and lust: Orolandes' neediness helps make him desirable. Yet sorcerers should not try to imitate their rivals. Wavyhill's sword in "What Good is a Glass Dagger?" is an admission of impotence.

Niven sides with the wizards, even to the extent of transforming them into storytellers, but he does not ignore their ruthlessness (Wavyhill) and selfishness (Piranther). Wavyhill's crimes are worse than Orolandes' although the latter caused more deaths. ("'Murder and war are not the same.

The intent is different and the intent counts for a good deal.' ") The arrogance of power is deadly whether the basis of that power be one's right arm or right grimoire.

The wizards deplore the coming triumph of the warriors (as much for its boredom as its barbarism). Warriors likewise fear a resurgence by the wizards. (Where would the Nordiks be in a world full of magic?) Nevertheless, Orolandes and the sorcerers are able to overcome their resentments and make common cause when the fate of humanity hangs in the balance. They are people before they are functional roles.

Niven's other recurring theme is the fading of wonder, a traditional concern of fantasy writers (for example, Tolkien, Anderson and Swann). The prevalence of this subject reflects one of the world's oldest myths, what Eliade calls "nostalgia for Paradise." In every era and culture, men have mourned for some vanished Golden Age. Whether it is an Australian aborigine recalling the splendors of the Long-Ago Dream Time or a middle-aged American yearning for the Good Old Days, the phenomenon is the same. Transferring the Golden Age to the future, as Marxism does, is a relatively recent innovation in human thought. Be it wishful thinking, blurred memory, or perception of entropy, people continue to maintain that the past was better, even in the face of contrary evidence.

Myths usually explain the change from glorious Then to grubby Now as the result of some specific mistake, accident, or sin (e.g., the Biblical Fall of Man). But Niven makes it a long-term, gradual process, a foreshadowing of the eventual heat death of the physical universe.

The dearth of mana affects life at all levels: Atlantis sinks, dream castles decay, guardian devices falter, fabulous creatures "go mythical," amoebae shrink from monstrous towards microscopic size. Even "mundanes" remember better days: " 'My grandfather used to fly half around the world to attend a banquet. . . . Poor old man, none of his spells worked, there at the end. He kept going over and over the same rejuvenation spell until he died.' " Mirandee envies the mana-rich Australians. " 'I watched apprentice magicians duel for sport, with adepts standing by to throw ward spells. It was like stepping two hundred years into the past. I watched a castle shape itself out of solid rock. . . .' " The surviving magicians will soon be reduced to performing stage magic, telling tales, or shaping metal.

Most people would prefer to ignore the mana crisis gripping their world. A few urge conservation. (Aran gets laws passed to restrict the use of magic in his home town.) Piranther and his followers try to build a secure enclave for themselves. Their efforts are destined to fail. Eventually " 'the swordsmen will come to find small black people in the barren center of the continent, starving and powerless, making magic with pointing-bones that no longer work.' "

Only the Warlock thinks of a positive solution. His grand scheme to tap the Moon's mana bears more than a passing resemblance to the current space program with its potential for alleviating energy shortages. The cautious arguments used by the Warlock's associates sound much like those raised against space. (And to which Wavyhill replies: " 'You think too small' ") Notice that cloud-walking and real Moon-walking require a similar modification of stride. The

209

analogy is further reinforced by the novel's planetary models. Sadly, the Moon remains beyond their grasp — and they make sure it remains beyond Roze-Kattee's as well. Their decision to halt the project is brave and responsible. (What if orbiting solar collectors or the like prove to be intolerably dangerous and therefore unusable power sources?) Better a world impoverished than no world at all.

However, the most important implications of the mana crisis are theological. Basically, *The Magic Goes Away* is the battle report of a theomachy, a war against the gods. Niven discusses the nature of his world's gods and weighs the merits of worshipping them. He concludes that their nature is vicious and their worship vain.

Niven sews a crazy quilt of mythology — one rarely sees the Titans of Greece, Purusha of India, and Joshua of the Bible patched together as they are here, but the overall design of the myths is clear enough. At the beginning of time, when the mana supply was richest, the gods created themselves out of the primal chaos which they commemorated in their "children," the amoebic *goo.* They made men and other creatures to provide them with the one thing they lacked — worship. They were divine tyrants who often tormented, even destroyed their creations. They rarely bothered to bless those who adored them for " 'a god's wishes wouldn't have anything to do with what human beings wanted.' " Roze-Kattee could not protect the Frost Giants although they succeeded in protecting it. Gods need men, not men gods. Not men but gods are doomed by mana depletion.

The Magic Goes Away dramatizes and applauds the ex-

termination of the gods. (Extermination is the proper word here because the deities behave like parasites.) This process is scarcely novel, although historically it has most often been directed at other people's pantheons. One culture's god is another culture's demon. (Medieval Christians viewed Christ as blotting out the living gods of their ancestors.) Clubfoot and the Warlock succeed in proving that men are well rid of their divine masters. They make cynical comments on temple ruins and preach a rationalist gospel to the Nordiks. They pointedly observe that only the enslaved are devout. Even before experiencing the full intensity of Roze-Kattee's malice, they argue that the gods are cruel, fickle, and dependent on the subjective faith of their worshippers.

Men will be far better off without these dangerous beings. There can be no compromise. " 'The world belongs to the gods or it belongs to men.' " Final liberation from the gods compensates for the loss of magic. Men can manage their lives independently. The houses of Prissthil, "held up not by spells spoken over a cornerstone, but by their own strength" are models of the future.

Orolandes, the one mundane on the quest, lets go of both gods and enchantments. At the beginning of the story he fears both priests and magicians. Guilt drives him to surrender his own will. But he rejects magic implements ("Best to stick with the chain and the sword,") attacks Roze-Kattee and thus regains his self-possession. As C. S. Lewis once said, "The process of growing up is to be valued for what we gain, not for what we lose."

Men outlive the gods and outlast the mana. Human ties

and traits survive the changing of the world. People are attached to their work, their homes, one another. Niven shows this by tracing patterns of relationships between equals (lovers and enemies) and unequals (local-foreigner, leader-follower, adept-incompetent, master-servant). The ability to form personal bonds of some kind is a precious human talent. All the gods understand is exploitation.

The questers are surprised that Roze-Kattee combines the attributes of love and madness. The two qualities are not necessarily opposed, for sometimes love *is* madness. Moreover, life needs a bit of both for seasoning. For instance, Clubfoot's admirable devotion to the Warlock transcends self-centered rationality. The Frost Giants' god can produce only negative effects. It can annul both love and madness. "Roze-Kattee's power lay in the taking. . . . But if the god himself had been impotent for hundreds of years. . . ." Men, on the other hand, maintain courage, tenacity, loyalty, and mercy even under stress. These traits bring them victory over the last god.

The novel ends in sadness but not in tragedy. Niven's message is never futility. His characters are strong, positive, adaptable people. As his friend and collaborator Jerry Pournelle observes, he never writes of "grey folk thinking grey thoughts" because he "finds this marvelous universe a place to have fun." Ingenious situations and lively characters plus thoughtful content and crisply witty prose yield superior entertainment. Niven has plotted this function called a story upon our minds and hearts. Upward and outward flows the curve. *Its* magic does not go away.

Bibliography

Svetz Series (in logical order)

"The Flight of the Horse." as "Get a Horse." *The Magazine of Fantasy and Science Fiction.* October, 1969. (hereafter as F & SF)

"Bird in Hand." F & SF. October, 1970.

"Leviathan." *Playboy.* August, 1970.

"There's a Wolf in My Time Machine." F & SF. June, 1971.

"Death in a Cage." *The Flight of the Horse.* Ballantine: New York, 1973. (This collection contains the entire series.)

Warlock Series (in order of publication)

"Not Long Before the End." F & SF. April, 1969.

"Unfinished Story #1." F & SF. December, 1970.

"What Good is a Glass Dagger?" F & SF. September, 1972.

About Larry Niven

Born April 30, 1938, Larry Niven took a B.A. in mathematics at Washburn University. His first story was published in 1964, only a year after he began trying to write fiction professionally. His 1966 short story "Neutron Star" and 1970 novel *Ringworld* won the Hugo Award. *Ringworld* also won the Nebula Award. He has also received Hugos for the following short stories: "Inconstant Moon" (1971), "The Hole Man" (1974), and "The Borderland of Sol" (1975). At last count he has published eight novels (three in collaboration with Jerry Pournelle) and more than five dozen shorter works. He and his wife Marilyn reside in Tarzana, California where they are active in the Los Angeles Science Fiction Society and Georgette Heyer fandom.

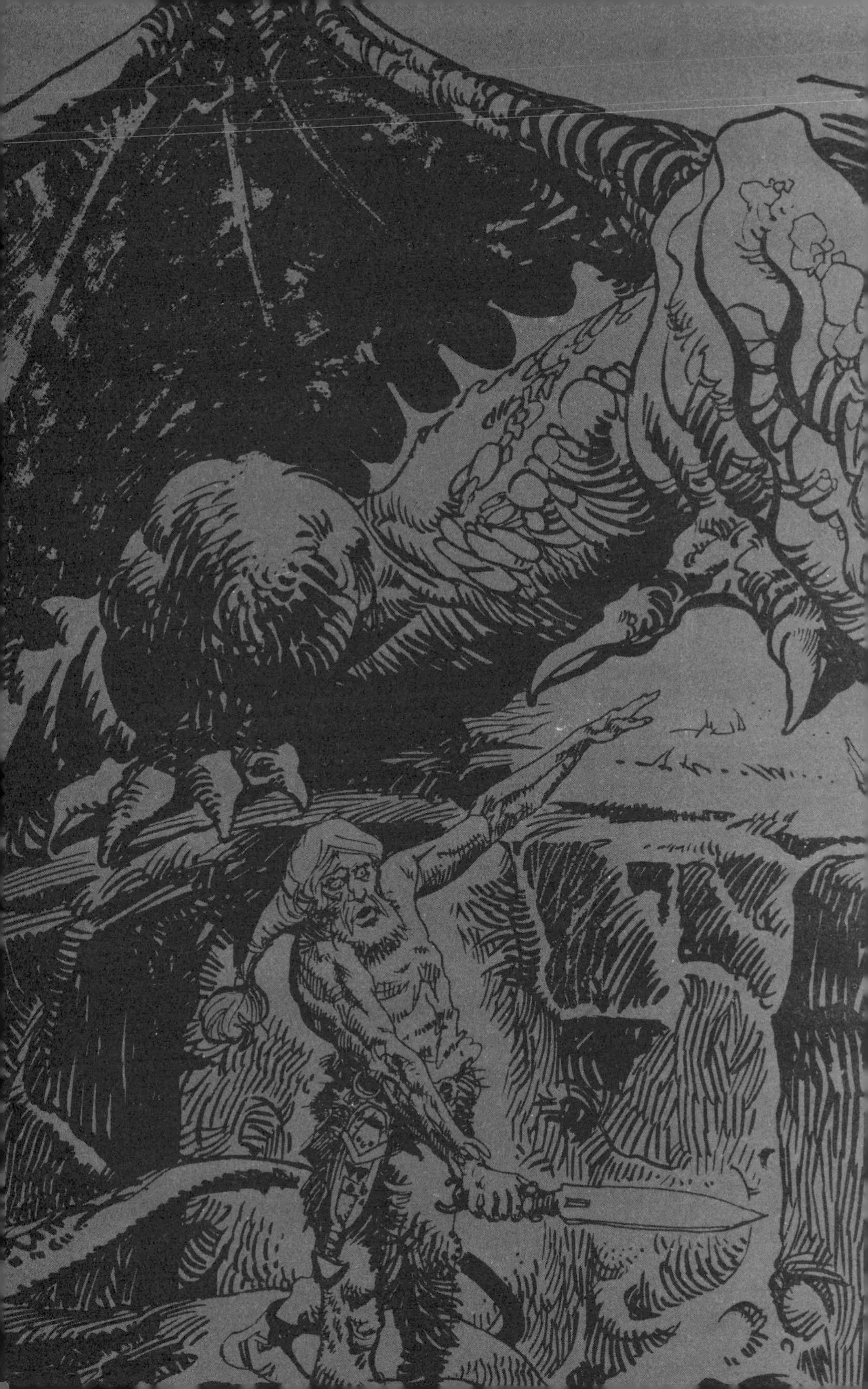

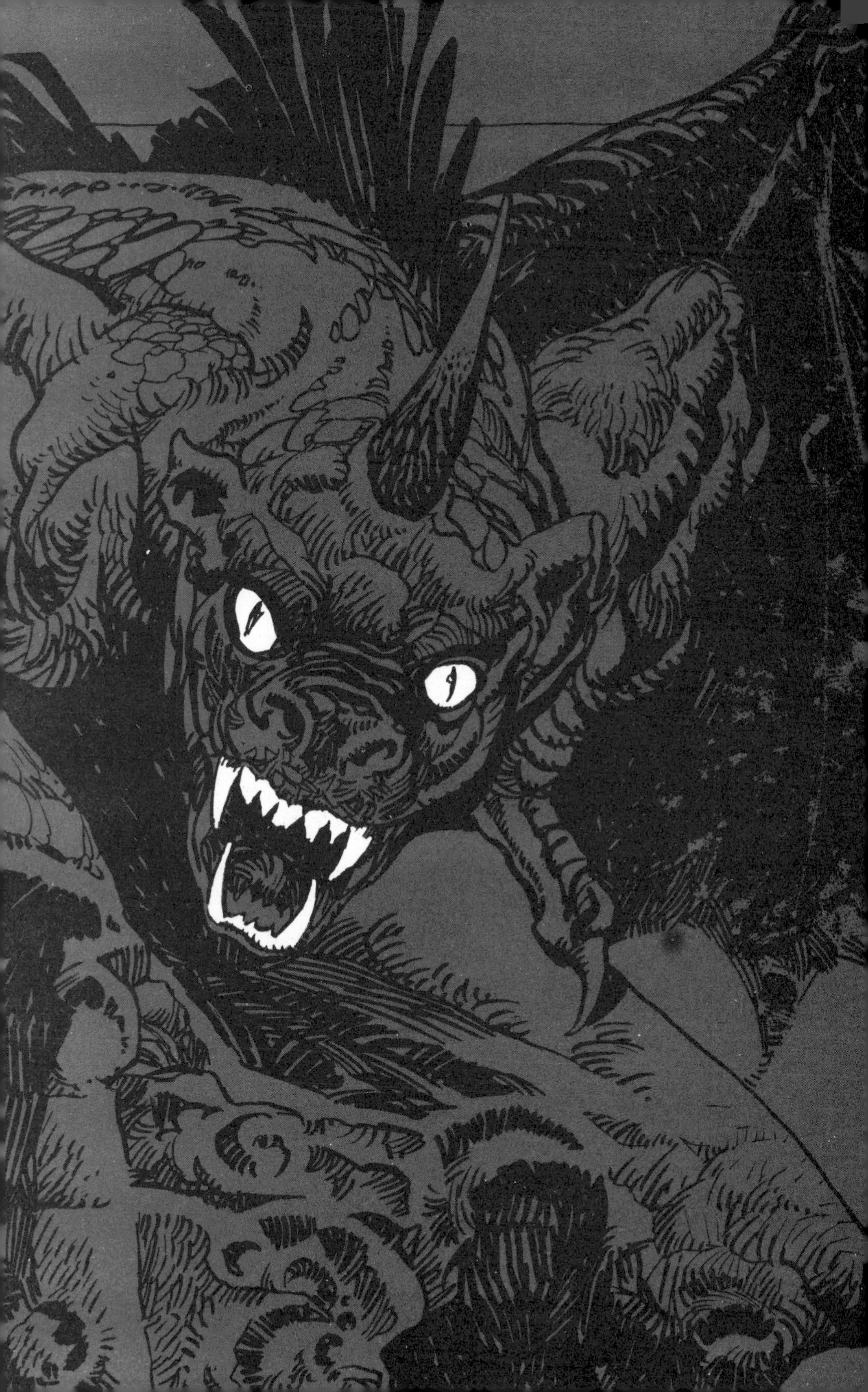

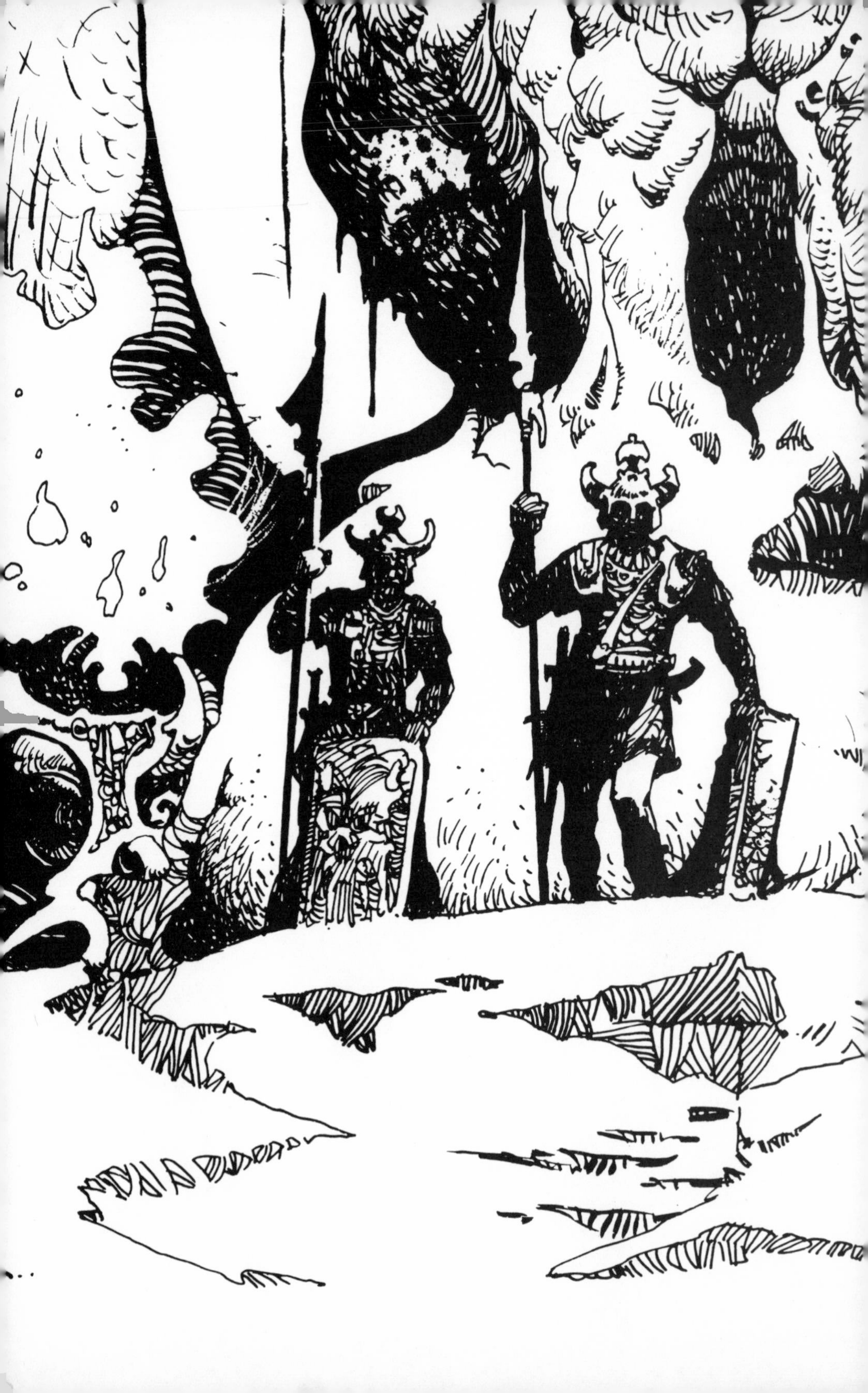

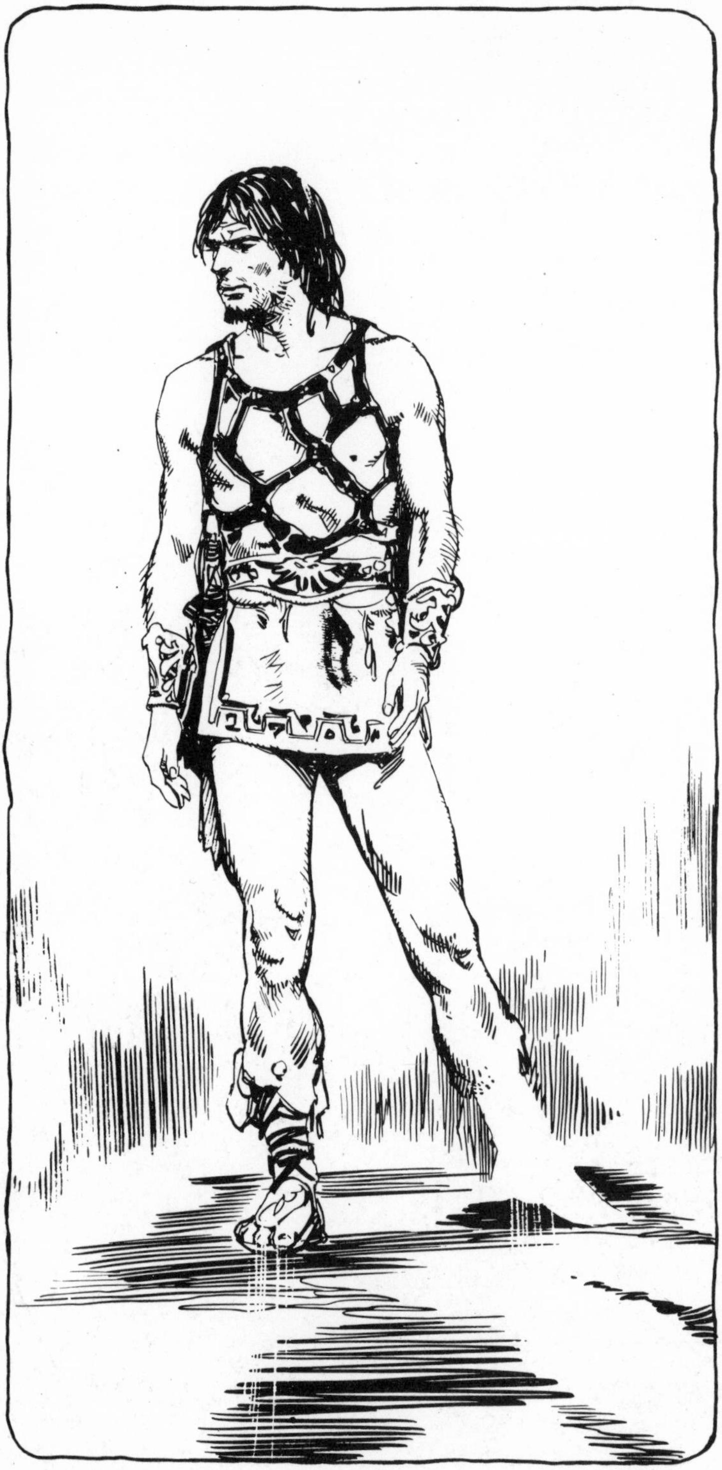